The **COMPLETE**

IDIOT'S
GUIDE TO

Downloading

by Aaron Weiss

A Division of Macmillan Computer Publishing
201 W. 103rd Street, Indianapolis, IN 46290

To all my creditors everywhere.

©1995 Que® Corporation

International Standard Book Number: 0-7897-0567-2

Library of Congress Catalog Card Number: 95-71422

97 96 95   8 7 6 5 4 3 2 1

Interpretation of the printing code: the rightmost double-digit number is the year of the book's first printing; the rightmost single-digit number is the number of the book's printing. For example, a printing code of 95-1 shows that this copy of the book was printed during the first printing of the book in 1995.

Screen reproductions in this book were created by means of the program Collage Plus from Inner Media, Inc., Hollis, NH.

Printed in the United States of America

Publisher
Roland Elgey

Vice President and Publisher
Marie Butler-Knight

Editorial Services Director
Elizabeth Keaffaber

Publishing Manager
Barry Pruett

Managing Editor
Michael Cunningham

Acquisitions Coordinator
Martha O'Sullivan

Development Editor
Melanie Palaisa

Technical Editor
Martin Wyatt

Production Editor
Audra Gable

Copy Editor
San Dee Phillips

Cover Designers
Dan Armstrong, Barbara Kordesh

Book Designer
Kim Scott

Cartoonist
Judd Winick

Indexers
Virginia Bess, Christopher Cleveland

Production Team
*Steve Adams, Brian Buschkill, Jason Carr, Terri Edwards, Bryan Flores,
DiMonique Ford, Trey Frank, Amy Gornik, John Hulse, Damon Jordan,
Daryl Kessler, Stephanie Layton, Michelle Lee, Julie Quinn,
Michael Thomas, Scott Tullis, Kelly Warner, Karen York*

Dear Reader:

Seldom will you use the Internet or any other online service and not encounter file transfers. Go ahead and try it, I dare you. You may have heard people bragging about such acts as *downloading*, *uploading*, or grabbing files off of UseNet. While none of these concepts are particularly complex in and of themselves, computers and computing have
a way of confusing everyone.

In this book, we'll explore some obvious sorts of file transfers—direct downloads and uploads—and everything attendant (such as modem configurations, terminal programs, and that sort of thing). We'll also look at moving files around with SLIP/PPP accounts using such fabulously named facilities as "FTP." In addition, users of commercial online services such as America Online and the new Microsoft Network will find some guidance. There's something for everyone, really, except those patrons over in the "Romance" section. Ptui.

Files are tucked away in various nooks and crannies in the online world, and you'll learn how to find 'em, grab 'em, and rustle 'em into a good meal (or at least a useful set of data). And a number of related issues swirl about the edges of file transfers: compression, archiving, and other file management matters, for example. Don't worry. I cover them all here. And none of it need be scary; everything in computing can make sense if you see it the right way, which is often sideways…

…and with humor. Because the topic of this book is admittedly only exciting to a handful of people (ever born), I've added humor to lift it over that wall and make it mildly interesting too. By the end of the final chapter, not only will you be downloading, uploading, compressing, and loving it, you'll also have a spectacular bright orange addition for your home library.

Aaron Weiss

aaron.weiss@pobox.com

Contents at a Glance

Contents

5 A Digital Warehouse: File Archives   35

6 The Evil Virus   45

Introduction: A Bit of Transfer

Congratulations on your purchase of the Tomato Weas—whoops! Wrong introduction! My apologies. One gets so easily confused these days…. Ah, yes, this is the book about file transfers. But that is such an awkward, non-buzzy term. To say that this is a book about *downloading* would sound more catchy, but it's somewhat inaccurate. After all, one can't ignore *uploading*—assuming that one has any idea what *either* means.

So let's start with the basics. I have a computer, and you have a computer. So far so good. I have a file containing data that you want. Or need. Or bribed me for. We need to get a copy of the file on my computer onto your computer. We have several options:

➤ Copy the file from my hard drive onto a floppy diskette, carry that disk to your computer, and copy the file from the disk onto your hard drive. This will work, but the process grows increasingly problematic as the file or files become larger and your computer becomes further and further away.

➤ Open up the case on my computer, remove my hard drive, carry it to your computer, open your case, install my hard drive, and copy the file to your hard drive. This could work, except that it's stupid. While it does overcome the file size problem, it is still subject to the geography constraint, and it's a major effort—and risk.

➤ Connect our two computers with a cable and send the file by that cable from my computer to yours. Ah, now we are getting somewhere! The size of the file is no longer a concern (assuming we have patience), and you don't have the huge effort, hassle, and risk of physically transporting a hard drive. Unfortunately, it is still difficult to string a cable 500 miles, as the case may be.

But wait. Even though it would be difficult for us to string such a cable, what if a cable already existed? Could we use someone else's cables to help? Like the phone company's? They're always willing to lend a hand. And so it is by way of modem (the details of which we'll explore later) that computers can be connected. No distance is too great if you have a modem and a phone line (and a dream).

Some of you may use computers that do not utilize phone lines (such as a LAN in the workplace), but no matter what the medium, something is connecting them. And it is via that "connecting stuff" that we can transfer files from one computer to another. Don't misinterpret the word *transfer* in this usage; the file is not being removed from the source computer. It is being copied. If the parties involved *want* to remove the file from the source, they can do it that way; however, such a case is unusual.

Which Way Is Up?

A file can move in either of two directions when being transferred: up and down. More commonly, though, people use the terms *upload* and *download* to distinguish data flow. The definition of either of these depends entirely on the speaker's position in the process.

The computer that is on the receiving end of a file transfer is *downloading*. The computer that is sending the file is *uploading*. Which computer you, the speaker, are sitting at determines whether you are uploading or downloading. (Many people seem to confuse these two concepts, which tends to confuse other people, who then confuse themselves and end up leaping out of a window hollering something about "can't take it anymore.") The great majority of readers will perform many more downloads than they will uploads. This is especially so when we're considering the usage of the Internet and commercial online services. And that is what we're considering. For that reason, this book may appear biased toward talking about downloading; it is not an ideological prejudice. I have many friends who are uploaders—really.

Breakdown

This book breaks down into three basic concepts (and two appendices!). First are the issues surrounding all files: from what they're made of (sugar and spice) to how they're packaged and handled. These matters affect how you must caress the files both before and after transfer. That's the first concept and, not coincidentally, it's covered in the first section of the book.

Once an understood fact, the method of transfer now varies depending on your type of online connection. There are two major types and, therefore, two notable methods of uploading and downloading—which are the basis of the next two sections of the book. Notice that I'm avoiding using technical terms to describe any of this. That's so I can roll them out and define them with appropriate fanfare in due time.

Because no model is so perfectly angular, a number of file and transfer-related issues hang around the edges of these concepts. They've all been chucked somewhere in the back of the book (known as Part 5). Thank whoever invented the closing chapters of books.

In addition, two appendices round out this square tome. The first is a brief menu of available and popular terminal program software for the PC and Macintosh. The second gives you a look at some of the popular TCP/IP clients for the above platforms (if that doesn't make sense now, it will by the time you reach Appendix B).

You Know Who You Are

One simply has to make certain assumptions about you, the reader. I presume you're not dead. I like to imagine that there is *some* computer use in your background; otherwise, the mere title of this book is not going to bring much enlightenment. Beyond that, the more experience you've had with any online communications the better—so long as you haven't outlearned this book and decided to pass it up for that other one there on the shelf.

Even if you have used some online services and transferred a few files, I'd like to think that there's enough detail in these pages to offer a more complete understanding of this whole crazy world. The world of file transfers, that is.

How to Read

The first letter of the alphabet is **A**, which is sometimes written **a**. There are 25 more where that came from, and this book is loaded with combinations thereof. Beyond the basics of English, there are some less-well-known conventions that this book relies upon.

```
When you see letters in this typeface…
```

…it represents text that you'd see on the screen. What's on-screen is exactly what you see in that typeface, with one exception:

```
I would like a hamburger with cheese and condiment
```

Note the bold and bold/italic words. A bold word shows what you type. When you see a bold italic word, it means that I don't necessarily know exactly what you need to type because it may be situation-dependent. In that case, you should type what's bold and replace the italic part with whatever is appropriate in that context. It's fun and easy!

This book contains a number of screen shots. I made them myself. (I know, thank you.) Screen shots represent specific programs on a specific computer (mine). What is pictured here may differ from what you see, depending on what programs you use, what computer you use, and even what version of a program you have. Nonetheless, they do attempt to represent important concepts fairly specifically, and most succeed in doing so.

In addition to regular ol' text, this book also has extra information scattered throughout the chapters. Technically, we in the biz call them sidebars; there are a couple of types you should know about:

These sidebars contain information, definitions, or tips that can provide additional help. Plus, they taste great!

The "Techno Talk" sidebar rambles on about related issues of a more advanced nature; they may be of interest to some readers but are not absolutely necessary information.

Thus ends my preparatory lecture. If you're as excited as I am, turn the page, and let's get to some file transfers! If you're not as excited as I am, run around the living room a few laps, and then return. That should do it. And, of course, intravenous doses of caffeine help, too.

Acknowledgments

This is where I'm supposed to get all warm and mushy and fuzzy. Well I'm not gonna do it. I'm my own Ayn Rand. No one to thank but myself. With the possible exception of the people at Que. Such as Melanie Palaisa and Audra Gable for their comprehensive editing. And Marty for his techie insights. And my stereo, for not completely self-destructing, even if it did decide to boycott the final tracks on all CDs. Oh, can't forget this wonderful air conditioner that I picked up in **tor.forsale**. Sure gets hot here in Canada—who would've thunk it? Lastly, everyone say hello to Dagney, who is a cat. A very sleepy cat.

Trademarks

All terms mentioned in this book that are known to be or are suspected of being trade-marks or service marks have been appropriately capitalized. That goes for all proper nouns, frankly. Que Corporation cannot attest to the accuracy of this information. Thus, use of a term in this book should not be regarded as affecting the validity of any trade-mark or service mark. In other words, nobody should be suing anyone.

Part 1
The Exciting World of Computer Files

or "A bunch of stuff you need to know"

Before you can happily transfer files, you need to give them attention and care. Caress, massage, compress. Archives and downloads will experience mirth and joy. This section weaves lazily through the garden path of file management issues that you need to understand before you begin to download.

## Chapter 1

Top of the Charts: What You Need to Know

At first one might think that *downloading*, or even *file transfers*, is a bit too narrow a topic for an entire book. One might be right. But here it is—an entire book anyway. And what's more, it comes with a "no-fluff" guarantee. However, just because everything in this book may be useful to someone, you certainly don't need to memorize every last word to learn the basics of mundane, everyday downloading. You might memorize *only* the last word, but that won't help much either.

So this chapter is a schoolboy's dream: I'm telling you what you really need to know so you don't even *have* to crack open the first chapter of content. But it's not only out of sheer kindness—Que forced me, too. On with it, though, shan't we....

1. Compression and Archival

The chance that you won't encounter compressed archives when downloading from the Internet or an online service is, as the statisticians jokingly say, "zip." So before you can make use of most files you download, you'll have to know the basics of compression and archival. Chapters 4 and 5 lead you through the steps of taking one useless but transportable file and unpacking it into several usable files.

2. La Modem

For most of the users most of the time, the modem is the means of data transport. Like a border guard checking for illicit fruit, the modem passes over all data that moves into or out of your computer. Fortunately, Chapter 7 explains the role of the little beast—and tells you how to configure and troubleshoot it when necessary.

3. Configurations Ad Nauseam

In a two-part investigative series by our award-winning muckrackers (mostly me, really), the seamy underbelly of terminal configuration is exposed. Many readers have to rely on what is defined as *dumb terminal emulation* to access the Internet, and doing so with success requires properly configured terminal program software—and a thorough read of Chapters 10 and 11.

4. Membership Has Its... Commercial Services

Alternatives to direct Internet access abound, in such forms as America Online, The Microsoft Network, CompuServe, and Prodigy. Members of these services don't necessarily follow the same rules and procedures as many other readers. Chapters 15, 17, and 18 contain useful know-how on squeezing file transfers out of these services.

5. How to Actually Download

If you want to download a file, you'll have to know how to download a file. Very Zen. In addition to the preparatory information throughout this book, Chapters 12 and 14 give up the goods, including specific instructions for terminal emulation users everywhere.

6. Top of the Charts

To properly transfer files, one may be helped by this book. In reading this book, one may be helped by a brief rundown of the most important topics within and where they can be found. Chapter 1 is just such a summary, which includes this paragraph because it's part of Chapter 1, which includes this paragraph because it's part of Chapter 1, which ....

7. FTP for You and Me

Everyone else—that is, those not using terminal emulation—will be slipping and sliding along with FTP to perform file transfers. That means you'll need to know about "clients," how to use them, how to love them, and so forth. Chapter 16 is a good start.

8. It's *Not* a Small World (Wide Web) After All

If you travel the filaments of the Web at all, you're likely to encounter files available for downloading. There's a chapter for that sort of thing, and its name is 17.

9. Technicalities 'R' Us

If you don't know the difference between ASCII and binary, well, that's just not hip. What's worse, you may fall prey to corrupted or useless file transfers. We don't want that—hence Chapter 3. Another source of corruptions is misunderstood linefeeds, which may not make sense now, but will by the end of Chapter 19.

10. Inoculate! Vaccinate! Repent!

Nobody likes a virus, except perhaps other viruses of the same strain. Even then, they get testy. And so should we all: computer viruses can cause anything from annoyance to destruction—and high blood pressure often follows them. So anytime one talks about transferring files between computers, one must not forget about viruses. In Chapter 6, you'll learn what you can and can't do to protect your data, how viruses infect and how they do not, and who to trust and who to avoid (besides that guy down the block with the perpetual lawn sprinkler).

## Chapter 2

Just What Is a File? Is Space Curved? Do Cats Paint?

In This Chapter

➤ File basics

➤ Some two files are alike, some are not

➤ No beam-me-up-jokes here—file transport

Logic dictates. At least, people say that quite often, as in, "Well, Harry, logic dictates that if you don't drink your morning coffee and you're a caffeine junkie, you will eat the wallpaper at the office today." Thus, logic dictates that if we're going to have a book-length discussion about transferring computer files, we should spend a little quality time understanding computer files in their own right.

Bursting with Data

Essentially, a computer file is the "package" in which you store data for future retrieval. Data, in this case, can be virtually anything: the contents of a word processing document, the information that makes up a photo of your dog, or that which makes up the sound of a guitar. *Future retrieval* may involve displaying the graphic, playing a sound, or manipulating statistical data.

Techno Talk

blah blah
blah bla
ah bl
b

It's a Fact!

You can think of data in several ways. In a graphic file such as a GIF file, the data represents where each pixel should be, what color it is, and so on. In a word processing file, the data may represent such characteristics of the document as the fonts used, the page margins, and so on, as well as the actual text within the document. To the computer's eyes, though, all data looks exactly the same (like the famous necklace of 1s and 0s) no matter what it represents. Because your computer can represent just about anything using sequences of 1s and 0s, every file is basically the same thing to your computer.

At its heart, it is the computer file that encapsulates one of the more remarkable, and remarkably versatile, capabilities of computers (unless you delete the file, of course). That is, with the right software, your computer can convert just about anything from the "real world" into a format suitable for storage within a file. Within the bounds of a single computer, this allows you to organize your data based on the fact that each file represents a different set of data. Then, using file management software of the sort which we won't discuss in this book, you can shuffle the files around on your hard drive to keep them in whatever order makes you happy. One of the keys to such organization is the *file name*. Like naming your cats, naming your files makes it much easier to identify them in the future. In fact, most computer manufacturers know this and, therefore, make you name the file if you want to keep it—no exceptions.

Let's imagine you typed up a letter of resignation in WordPerfect on your employer's PC and saved it with the file name RESIGNME.DOC. To release steam, you then scanned in a picture of your boss and saved it as the file MYBOSS.JPG. As far as the computer knows and cares, both of those sets of data are files. End of story. That means you can manage the files (just like little packages) in any way you like, no matter what data lies within them. You can move them to new places on your hard drive; you can rename them or delete them; or—as is the thrust of this whole oeuvre—you can move them from one computer to another. But just because the computer doesn't care what's in the files when you chuck them around, doesn't mean *you* shouldn't. There are definite reasons to understand what makes one type of file different from another, reasons which will appear several times throughout this book.

What Makes This File Different from Every Other File?

It is when you attempt to retrieve the data within a file that the question of *type* arises. What is type? Actually, that's a pretty vague term that can mean several things. At my most ambiguous, it means the category under which your computer groups data. For example, there are "graphic"-type files, which contain data that represents a picture. There are "word processing"-type files, which contain data representing the contents of a document created in a word processor. However, you can further narrow down the categorical definition of a type, which is why I said the term is vague. Within the *type* of word-processing files, for instance, there might be WordPerfect-type files, Microsoft Word-type files, and so on. Within graphic images, there are GIF-type files, JPG-type files, and many others.

Of course, file types become most important when you want to access the data within them. After all, a program designed to display graphic images may have no idea what to do with a set of data that represents a sound. And even within the narrower type classifications, word processor A may not know what to do with the data made by word processor B. In the olden days of computing, a program had no real way of recognizing what *type* a file was before it tried to use the data the file contained. So, for example, you could load a word processing document into a sound player. The sound player wouldn't object, but when it attempted to turn word processing data into audio, you'd hear a series of ungodly screeches that drove away friends and enemies alike.

Format vs. Type At this level of focus, many people use the term "format" instead of "type" as in, "This file isn't in MS Word 6.0 format like I asked for. You're fired." However, some people (like me) persist in using "type."

Eventually, the computing community established a way to distinguish one file from another. The idea was simple enough: slap a little bit of data into the beginning of a file to identify it. That's what they did, and they called it a *header* (and there was light, and it was good). A header, then, is what distinguishes one file from all others—or at least from all other types.

It's a little difficult to examine a file header yourself (although with the right software you could if you wanted to). In most cases, what the computers do to help us humans identify a file is add an appropriate type-extension to the file name. For example, the computer would add the .JPG extension to the file name of a JPG-type graphic file (as in BANANA.JPG). However, whereas the header must always be contained within a file to identify its type, the file name extension is an optional marking. A JPG file does not *have* to have the associated extension, but I strongly recommend that you get in the habit of using the extensions you encounter. After all, if you received a file called simply BANANA, you wouldn't know what type it was. You could try opening it into different software packages until one worked, but that would be a royal pain. The simple addition of a type-extension makes life easier (and it has been known to cure baldness).

Thanks to file types, you can, for example, load the picture of your boss that you scanned into PhotoShop and give him one big eyebrow. But you can't load your WordPerfect-type resignation letter into PhotoShop (unless PhotoShop has a special feature for *importing* WordPerfect-type files).

Remember when I said that when you move files around, the computer doesn't care what data they contain? That's because type is irrelevant at that level. Yes, it's true. However, sometimes understanding file types will be relevant to the tasks that I discuss in this book (such as file compression). That's why we looked at the issue of file types—that and because I like cheese rolls.

Files They May Roam: Why We Move Them Around

One of the most exciting characteristics of files, in my opinion, is that they are like little packages. (I know you probably never thought anyone would get excited about files, but that's between myself and Dr. Mintz.) You can easily transport a set of data from one computer to another, carried neatly in a little file with a cute little file name. In the dark years of computing when floppy disks were wider than drinking coasters, you had to put a file onto a disk and physically carry that disk to another computer. Now, with the whiz-bang technology of the Internet and networking in general, one has the power to move files between computers with relative ease. And this, mind you, is an extremely powerful capability with many great and divine implications—such as access to the entire Internet.

On the one-to-one level, file movement enables you to send a copy of a document to your boss without losing your own copy. That's an obvious usage. However, at the one-to-many level, you can essentially create a file such as a UseNet posting and distribute it to the entire world. (That is, in fact, how UseNet works, more or less.)

Before computers could "talk to each other" (networking), each machine was essentially an island. That meant limited resources and limited opportunity. Now that millions of computers can speak freely to each other and exchange information (files), we have a massive continent of computing power at our hands. But don't think for a moment that the Internet is the only such resource; online services such as America Online, CompuServe, and The Microsoft Network all take advantage of the same technology and work essentially the same way.

Most of the Internet's facilities (from FTP to the World Wide Web to UseNet) all rest on this premise: you can distribute one file to many. The different ways in which this distribution can take place define most of the differences among those facilities and account for why some (the Web) are better than others (Gopher, for instance).

Because the Internet is so heavily premised on transferring files, as an Internet user, you'll get the most out of it if you understand and, to some degree, master the issues involved in transferring files to and fro. Thankfully, that's what this book is about.

The Least You Need to Know

The computer file is the basis for moving data around, whether that movement is within a single computer, between two computers, or among many computers (as is common on the Internet). A little background about files will help you in the future when you want to transfer them from one machine to another, especially if problems arise.

➤ A computer file is a little package in which you can store a set of data. That set of data can represent virtually anything from a birthday card to the sound of a rooster.

➤ You can classify computer files into *types*, depending on what kind of data they contain. There are graphic images, word processing documents, and so on. Within each type, there are often several subtypes, such as GIF, JPG, and PCX for graphic images.

➤ The easiest way for humans to distinguish a file's type is by the *extension* at the end of its file name.

➤ Real power and versatility come with the ability to move files among computers, and that is essentially what the Internet is—on a massive scale.

➤ Some cats do paint, but mine mostly sleeps.

## Chapter 3

Binary and ASCII Illustrated (Subscribe Now!)

In This Chapter

➤ What does ASCII mean to you?

➤ When computers sing in the shower, they do it in binary

➤ Don't mix alphabets; keep away from flames

➤ The power of observation: distinguishing ASCII from binary

People will talk. After all, that's what people do. And some of the time (hopefully not too much), they will be talking about *binary* and *ASCII*. When they talk about the latter, they pronounce it "ask-key" unless they're from the South, in which case you're on your own.

Among people talking about files and the Internet, the distinction between binary files and ASCII files is rather important. They're not lying: if you don't understand the difference, you could spend your time downloading a humongous file, only to find it rendered completely useless after the transfer.

In this chapter, we will take scalpel and peroxide in hand (no, it doesn't burn) and dissect the binary vs. ASCII issue just as they do on those repulsive surgery shows with all the sutures and blood and that slimy clear plasma stuff that has no name.

What's So Special About ASCII?

Like humans, who have moved from using Egyptian hieroglyphics to using modern alphabets, computers need a standardized way of representing information. In human written language, we have a given set of characters that we can combine in sequences to provide greater meaning. Computers are the same way, which isn't too surprising considering we humans designed the computers in the first place (unga bunga). Several different computer "alphabets" were created to accomplish different goals. ASCII is one of the most popular and widely used of these computer alphabets.

Check This Out...

What Kind of Word Is ASCII?
As you may suspect already, ASCII is an acronym. Spelled out, it stands for American Standard Code for Information Interchange. (Now you see why we would rather say ASCII, silly as it may sound.)

Within the computer, the ASCII alphabet represents the "Latin" character set we use ourselves. What is the Latin character set? You use it every day. It includes all 26 upper- and lowercase letters A–Z, the digits 0–9, and punctuation marks such as periods, colons, commas, and so on. In addition, ASCII represents other symbols we commonly use, such as the pound sign (#), the "at" sign (@), and the rest of the symbols that are above the digits on your keyboard. Tallied up, the ASCII character set contains 128 characters that allow the computer to represent the same set of characters we commonly use in Western languages. (Not all of those 128 ASCII characters represent Western characters; some represent such things as linefeeds. However, all of the Western characters are within the set of 128.) Computers usually save files that contain only text in ASCII format.

So How 'Bout Binary?

Good of you to ask. One of the most publicized facts about computers is that they "think" in 1s and 0s. This is quite true, even if it seems to make little sense (like buttered croissants). Because an electrical circuit can only be "open" or "closed," the computer only understands things in those terms. To best understand what a binary file is, let's have a brief lesson on this 1s and 0s theme.

A number that seems normal to us, such as 65, makes no sense to the computer. So the computer has to represent 65 as a series of 1s and 0s. How it makes that representation isn't important right now; suffice it to say that the computer requires a certain number of 1s and/or 0s to represent the "normal" number. Each 1 or 0 is a *bit*, and a computer representation of any number or character is eight bits long. That means that the computer needs eight 1s or 0s in some combination to represent the "normal" number. That's called *binary*.

> **Check This Out...**
>
> **Binary** The computer alphabet that consists only of ones and zeros. Computers use combinations of these to represent numbers and characters as we commonly know them, and those numbers represent data that can be anything from the sound of a shrieking parrot to a community newsletter.

For example, consider again the number 65. In binary, 65 would be represented as

    1000001

Notice that this is seven bits long. Using seven bits, the smallest number we can represent is 0 (0000000 in binary). The largest number we can represent is 127 (1111111 in binary). This should ring a bell... remember that ASCII contains 128 characters? That's no coincidence. ASCII is what is known as a *7-bit alphabet*, and it spans the binary numbers 0000000 through 1111111.

The problem is that seven bits are not enough to convey all the information a computer might need to represent. Seven bits are enough to convey Western character sets, but they're not enough to convey very complex sets of data such as audio sounds, graphic images, or word processing documents filled with font and page layout information. For this reason, most digital information is represented by an 8-bit alphabet. Adding that 8th bit makes it possible to represent twice as many numbers.

It's easy to get confused with ASCII and binary! At the outset I said that ASCII and binary were two different things. Now I'm saying that ASCII *is* binary: 7-bit binary. Well, both are correct. Because it uses seven bits, ASCII is in fact a *subset* of 8-bit binary. The catch is, when computer people say that a file is binary, they mean that it uses the 8-bit binary alphabet. ASCII technically means the 7-bit binary alphabet. This is the difference people are referring to when they use the terms ASCII and binary in commonplace computer speech—however commonplace that is.

Therefore, binary (as in the 8-bit alphabet) actually includes the entire ASCII set plus much more. Straightforward? Not at all, which is why those involved in computers must consume enormous quantities of caffeine. Keeps the synapses limber.

The Boring Truth About Binary

So, you're curious as to how 1111111 represents the number 127? Okay, fine, but I warn you: imagine the Oscars, the Grammys, and the Tony awards combined. This is a less-interesting base. The base determines how many fundamental units make up the counting system before repetition and combination. For a salient example, we in the modern Western world use a base-10 numbering system called decimal. There are 10 fundamental units in the decimal system: 0 through 9. After that, every number is a combination of these. Other systems of numbering use different bases such as hexadecimal (base 16). Binary, then, is a base-2 system, composed only of the two fundamentals 0 and 1.

When you read a binary number, each place (or bit) represents the value of 2^bit. That is, 2 raised to the power of the number bit it is. The zero'th bit is the rightmost bit in the binary number. If a bit is "on" (1), the value of that bit ($2^{bit\#}$) is added to the total. Therefore, the binary number 1 equals decimal 1. Binary 11 equals decimal 3. Binary 111 equals decimal 7. Binary 10011 equals decimal 19. How is that last one calculated? The same as the rest. Let me show you by examining the binary 10011 from right to left:

Binary 10011

Bit #0 is on. $2^0=1$

Bit #1 is on. $2^1=2$

Bit #2 is off.

Bit #3 is off.

Bit #4 is on. $2^4=16$

Total=19

So, if you whip out a pencil and paper—or better yet a calculator that converts decimal to binary—you can see that binary 1111111 equals 127 decimal. Adding an eighth bit (binary 11111111) means that the highest number we can represent is now 255. Twice as many numbers as 7 bits. Twice as much information. Half the calories.

Two Great Tastes That Taste Bad Together

The reason it's so important to keep the ASCII/binary distinction straight is that ASCII cannot hold as much information as binary. Some circumstances will occur as you're using this book (and in your own computing experiences) in which you will need to instruct the computer whether to download or upload a file as ASCII or as binary. Mixing them up can cause problems.

The most serious error occurs when you transfer a file that is actually binary (8-bit) as if it were ASCII (7-bit). If you tell the computer to accept an 8-bit binary file as an ASCII file, the computer will happily make the transfer. In doing so, it will also happily shave off the eighth bit from the data, thus eliminating up to half the information in the file. You, in turn, will be less happy. Much less as a matter of fact because, in most cases, the resulting amputee file will have been destroyed, rendering the data that you do have useless. Of course, you can go back and retransfer the file correctly, but if the file was large, you may have wasted a lot of time and, if you're paying for online time, a lot of money.

Looking at things the other way, what happens if you transfer an ASCII file as an 8-bit binary? In some cases, the file turns out okay. In other cases, the file's linefeed markers may be corrupt and, as a result, the text formatting will be messed up. It's less likely that the file will be totally destroyed in this case because 7-bit ASCII is a subset of 8-bit binary. It's mainly the resulting linefeed mess that's annoying. Considering the ease with which you can transfer the file properly (by choosing an ASCII transfer), none of these problems need arise—even in our imperfect universe with cigarette butts all over the beach.

This isn't the last you'll hear about this topic. When you actually get your hands muddy and start downloading and uploading later in the book, this issue will pop up again, and we will handle it with great aplomb. For now, simply be forewarned about this little caveat.

And How Exactly Do I Tell Them Apart?

Considering I've made such a fuss about the distinction between ASCII and binary files, how are you supposed to know which is which? You could always use extra-sensory perception and clairvoyance, but those are difficult skills to attain, and the experts charge far too much per minute. First let's look at the easier, more intuitive method. If that fails, we'll get down and dirty.

The quickest way to tell if a file is ASCII or binary is to use some heuristic rules of thumb. Take into consideration the file's contents, its file name extension, and which of the two types the creator of the file claims it is.

Behind Door Number 1...

Content is your strongest predictor of whether a file is ASCII or binary.

➤ If the file contains any information other than plain English text, it's nearly guaranteed to be binary. Audio files, graphic images, video clips, word processing files, desktop publishing files, spreadsheet files, graphs, charts, and presentations all are going to be binary (8-bit) files. Needless to say, most computer files are binary and not ASCII.

➤ ASCII files *tend* to be limited to short English-language messages that contain no complicated formatting. E-mail messages are a good example. Users of Windows-based PCs might be familiar with INI files such as WIN.INI and SYSTEM.INI. Those are also ASCII files, and if you look at them it's obvious why: they're simply made up of lines of plain text. That is the essence of an ASCII file.

There is one important thing you need to know about using the contents to determine whether a file is ASCII or binary. The Internet has popularized a facility known as *uuencoding* that enables you to convert from one to the other.

A number of newsgroups on UseNet carry sounds and graphics. Remember, though, that such data must be binary (not ASCII). The problem was/is that UseNet can display only 7-bit ASCII data, which makes it difficult for people to post pictures or sounds to UseNet. The common solution has been uuencoding, a process by which an 8-bit binary file is converted into a 7-bit ASCII file. That ASCII file can then be posted to UseNet or e-mailed (e-mail can generally only handle 7-bit information as well). The recipient then *uudecodes* the file, turning it back into an 8-bit binary that she can deal with. You'll learn how to uuencode/decode in Chapter 9; right now you simply need to understand why it is done.

A uuencoded file is an exception to the rules above because, although it is technically an ASCII file in its uuencoded form, it contains no readable English text (as it does not represent human language). In essence, it is a binary file that is temporarily masquerading as an ASCII file. As far as the computer is concerned, a uuencoded file *is* an ASCII file and must be transferred as such, even if it doesn't look like one to human eyes.

An Extension's Worth a Thousand Words

One way to get a clue as to the contents of a file and whether it's likely to be ASCII or binary is to look at the file name extension. (I discussed these briefly in Chapter 2.) You can use file extensions sort of like you use those check boxes on pizza boxes that list the possible pizza toppings (pepperoni, mushroom, Fruit-Loops, and so on). If the pizza guy checked the appropriate boxes on the pizza box, you can tell the contents with one glance. Likewise, if someone used the correct file name extension, it clues you in on the file's contents. Unfortunately, in my pizza-purchasing experience, the toppings check boxes are rarely used.

Although Internet users are generally better behaved about using appropriate file extensions, there are exceptions:

➤ File extensions such as GIF and JPG are very common, and they represent certain types of graphic files. Thus, they are most definitely binary—that is, unless someone misnames a file, which does happen.

Check This Out...

Someone Is on Your Side Note that most applications save files with the conventional extensions so the user doesn't have to add them manually. Letting the computer handle it decreases the chance of confusion.

➤ The DOC extension is a tricky one. In many cases, this refers to a word processing document, which is most likely binary. However, some word processors allow the user the option of saving a document as ASCII text. The file name may still end in DOC.

There is something of a loose convention that says the names of binary word processing files should end with DOC, and ASCII file names should end with TXT. This is loose, though, and it's not followed very stringently. I've seen plenty of DOC files that were ASCII, and some people like to name ASCII files with ASC. Nothing is sure in this world (as Billy Idol sang back when hair spray was still being used by men), so take these conventions as just that: conventions.

In the Net community, people seem to stick to the guidelines for using some extensions more often than they do others. The following table lists some extensions you can be fairly confident about.

Extensions You Can Be Sure Of (Almost)

Extension	Description	Type
JPG	"Joint-Photographic Experts Group" format graphic file	Binary
GIF	"Graphics Interchange Format" graphic file	Binary
WAV	"Waveform" format audio file for PC	Binary
AU	Sun-audio format audio file	Binary
MOV	Quicktime-movie format video file	Binary
MPG	"Moving Picture Experts Group" format video file	Binary
ZIP	Compressed archive in ZIP format	Binary
SEA	Self-extracting archive for the Mac	Binary
EXE	Either an executable program or a self-extracting archive for the PC	Binary
HQX	BinHex-encoded Mac file	ASCII
UUE	Uuencoded binary file	ASCII
TXT	A plain text file	ASCII
ASC	Possibly an ASCII document, possibly an ASCII-format PGP file	ASCII

Still Can't Tell?

What's the solution to this mess? Well, if in doubt, resort to plan B: the dirty look.

UNIX vs. PC
Note that the results would be the same if you used a PC instead of the UNIX shell; you would simply use a different program to view the file.

When all else fails, you can display the contents of the file in question. To do so, use any ASCII viewer or ASCII text editor. For example, if you're using a UNIX shell, use **more** or **cat**. On a PC, you can use **type** or **edit**. Let's look at some brief examples using a UNIX shell.

Suppose you have a file called RESUME.DOC, and you don't know whether it is ASCII or binary. Before you download it from your UNIX account to your PC, you may need to know. So, at your UNIX command prompt, enter **%cat resume.doc**.

If the file is truly ASCII, the result might look something like this:

```
Harry Milkson
Rural Post #134
Objective: To work in the field of tumbleweed management
Education: A-Z, can count to 100 by memory
Experience: Kept tumbleweed out of Earl's cow patch with a pitchfork
Skills: Pitchforking, spotting tumbleweed from afar
References: Earl
```

There are two ways you can tell this file is ASCII. First, it's plain text. Second, you can often tell a file is ASCII by what it *doesn't* look like.

For example, let's say Harry didn't save the above document in ASCII format. Instead, he saved it in WordPerfect 6.1 format. Let's replay the scenario. You type **%cat resume.doc**, and you see the following:

```
^?WPCD^D^^^A
^B^A^^^^B^E^^^^?^F^^^^B^^;^s,^gcwU-5<l0Kp"^LuS\9^Fe;f^^^B20Z@^UMcXXm?4L^M2!"^TLu
j"y^P^[UaF^Wc¦s9^Q^FCb  B&t7^Zx+.:T[d mK4#^OB^K0"!aa^?r]m^P=&:ZNJkqTc6^YLB
~s2IXQ^?l#i1Q\^O^Mv      ^Br
```

As you can see, this is not very meaningful. Actually, it is quite meaningful to Word-Perfect 6.1, but not to a human reader. This is your sign that the file shown above is *not* ASCII; it is binary. While it sounds unscientific, this is probably the best way to tell when you're looking at a file if it is binary or ASCII. If it looks like a bunch of junk, it's binary.

The Least You Need to Know

If you do not understand the difference between ASCII files and binary files, you can lose valuable time and money transferring a file that will turn out corrupted or damaged. You don't need to understand the complex details of bits and bytes and 1s and 0s to transfer files properly, but it does impress people if you can talk about it at parties.

➤ ASCII is a computer alphabet used to represent the characters we commonly use in Western written languages (such as English).

➤ Binary is a computer alphabet that can represent twice as much information as ASCII. It is used to represent almost any data that is not plain English text, including word processing documents, graphic files, sound files, and so on.

➤ You must transfer ASCII files in ASCII mode and binary files in binary mode. You'll learn the specifics of how to do this later in the book.

➤ Transferring a binary file in ASCII mode will completely destroy it; you will have to retransfer the file, which can be a waste of time and (possibly) money. Transferring an ASCII file in binary mode will mess it up slightly but will not totally corrupt it.

➤ You can often identify a file as ASCII or binary simply by its contents. The contents are often indicated by the file extension.

➤ Files that represent any data other than plain English text (with no formatting) are almost always binary.

➤ As a last resort, you can always view a file in any text editor to see if it is binary or ASCII. If the result looks like a garbled mass of junk, the file is binary.

21

## Chapter 4

Skin Tight Data: File Compression

In This Chapter

➤ Squish goes the data! Making the most of your data

➤ Different schemes for different 'puters

➤ What's a ZIP? An ARJ?

➤ Experience decompression

It takes time for wounds to heal. It takes time for love to bloom. And it takes time for computers to transmit data across a network. Poetic, no? Whether or not your time is money, your time *is* time—and whenever possible, most of us like to save that up for later.

Ever impatient, we especially notice when data transfer (such as by way of modem—even the fastest ones) seems to be slow in relation to the amount of data being transferred. Because of the complexity of modern data (from photographic-quality graphic images, to CD-quality sound, to massive productivity), applications require faster and faster transfer speeds to be practical. But, until the pace of development speeds to the point where we flare out of existence like a power-surging monitor, there are some things we can do to improve the situation.

Increasing the speed of data transfer is the most obvious solution. Another is to reduce the amount of data that needs to be transferred to begin with. And that's the topic of this chapter. To do this, you can use the appropriately termed *compression* process to reduce the size of a file without losing any of its contents. So, in this chapter, you'll laugh, cry, heal, and learn a heck of a lot about file compression.

Data Packed in So Tight It Itches

The basic theory behind compression is a simple one: you can replace repeating character strings with one character to cut down the file's size. Imagine you have a set of data that looks like this:

12 23 34 34 34 45 65 84 84 84 254 254 32 32 32 87 78 54 10 10 10

In this example, we have 21 data points. As you can see, though, some of the data points are repetitive. There are two 254s in a row and three 10s in a row, for example. (They tested you on this sort of pattern recognition back in high school in an attempt to determine which hair-length students you should be grouped with.) In simple compression, you can reduce any length of repetitive numbers down to two data points: one that represents the repeating number, and one that represents how many times that number is repeated. If we did simple compression in the data series above, it would look like this:

12 23 2 34 45 65 156 3 84 2 254 3 32 87 78 54 3 10

Now the set contains only 18 data points, a 15% reduction. At first glance, 18 data points might not seem much better than 21. But imagine the more likely situation of a file that's one megabyte in size. That's 1,024 × 1,024 data points: 1,048,576! If you achieve a 15% compression rate on this file like you did in the preceding example, the resulting file is only 891,290 data points in size—a difference of 157,286, or 154 kilobytes.

Now imagine for a moment that you have a 14.4kbps modem that can download data at approximately 1.6 kilobytes per second. (Did I lose you there? Don't worry, we're just imagining. Transfer speed is discussed in detail in Chapter 7.) With that particular modem, it would take you 96 fewer seconds to download the example compressed file than it would to download the decompressed original.

If that still doesn't seem like much of a savings, remember that 15% is a very conservative compression rate here. In reality, many files will compress at much greater rates. The compression rate you can get on any file depends on several variables; let's briefly chat about the two biggies.

The "Big Two" Variables

A screamingly obvious variable in how much a compression program will squish a file is how much repetitive data the file contains. The more repetitive the data is, the better the compression rate will be. That makes sense, so humor me and play theorist for a moment: imagine the theoretically "most squishable" file. It contains only one data point that is repeated for the entire size of the file. No matter how big it is to begin with, this file can be maximally compressed to just two data points—even if it originally had a million! Now, swinging way over to the other end of the hypothetical spectrum, consider a file in which the data points are distributed completely randomly throughout (you analytical types might have a fit over the phrase "completely randomly," but that's for another book to deal with!). This file can barely be compressed at all because very few data points are repeated in sequence.

Having established our outer boundaries, then, where do most files fall? That depends largely on the type of data the file holds. For instance, text (ASCII) files are famous for excellent compression. Because there's such a limited set of data to draw from in an ASCII file, repetition is high. Plain text files usually have compression rates over 70%. These suckers just fly through the wires.

On the other hand, common graphic files such as GIF and JPEG don't tend to compress very well at all. This isn't entirely because the data that makes up a graphic image is less repetitive than the data in a text file; it's because the GIF and JPEG format for storing data already includes compression. Thus, a GIF file contains graphic data that is already compressed. Generally, trying to compress data that is already compressed will not yield much of a savings, but this serves as a nice segue into the second biggie variable…the algorithm. (Hang on, it's not as technical as it sounds.)

Each compression program uses an algorithm to analyze and compress files. There are many, many, many algorithms out there, so which program you use also factors into how squished a file can be. Several programs have become de facto standards, and you'll use some of them later in this chapter (not the algorithms themselves—this isn't a computer science book). Needless to say, "better" compression programs perform better squishing. But by the same token, they generally demand increased computing power.

In the world of compression, there is always a trade-off to be made: is the time it takes to compress the data cost-effective? One could conceivably design an algorithm that squishes almost all files by 90%. That would be amazing (better than any miracle thigh cream), but what if it took two hours to compress a 100k file? Thus, the state of compression technology is in constant flux with the state of the computing power sitting on our desktops.

Not surprisingly, as our desktop computers have gained more muscle, so have the compression programs. So I can confidently say that as I write this book, we can compress data on our home PCs with speed and efficiency like never before. And I can confidently add that when you read this book, you'll be compressing faster and better than I was when I wrote it. The glass is always half full in the happy world of compression.

If You Compress, You Must Decompress

Of course, when your computer compresses a file, it alters the data in that file. You cannot use the file for its intended purpose in its compressed state. Before you can use it, you will have to convert the file back into its original *decompressed* state. This is why compression is usually a temporary state used to expedite the transfer of the file from one computer to another.

Actually, compressing a file is a lot like packing for a journey. When you go on vacation, you shove all your clothes into a suitcase to facilitate moving them all from your home to your cottage/bungalow/love shack/motel. But the clothes are not usable in their packed state, so you allegedly unpack them upon arriving at your destination. I know, I know. You don't actually unpack them; you just flip open the suitcase and leave it that way for two weeks. But you get the idea. Computers don't live like pigs.

You will face the task of decompressing files far more often than you will face the task of compressing them. Why? Well if you look at the transfer statistics of any Internet or popular online service, far more files are downloaded than are uploaded. If you never upload at all, you will probably do some downloading. And if you do some uploading, you will probably do a lot of downloading.

When you download, you almost always receive compressed files. Almost all files available on the Internet are compressed, usually with a popular compression program. This only makes sense; the people who upload them know that it saves vast amounts of storage space on the machines that hold the files, and it saves time for people downloading them. You'll find a detailed discussion on how to compress files in Chapter 22. The remainder of this chapter focuses on the art of decompression.

All About Those Extensions: ZIP, LHA, SIT, and ARJ

You learned in Chapter 3 that certain extensions are often used to designate a file's type as audio, graphics, and so on. The same is true for compressed files: the extension indicates which program the file was compressed with. This is extremely helpful because you have to use a compatible program to decompress a compressed file.

In terms of choosing a decompression program (as in a democracy), the decision has already been made for you by everyone else. You just need to get the right program to decompress a given compression program or *format*. There tends to be something of an allegiance between certain compression schemes and certain computer platforms. That is, you will find that one compression format is the default and most popular on one type of computer, while an entirely different format is used on another type of computer. This is meant to make your life more (not less) complicated, as computing sometimes tends to do.

As a dedicated follower of fashion, we'll first consider the current head monkey in Paris as far as compression goes: it's known as *ZIP*. The ZIP format is by far the most widely used compression format on the PC platform under MS-DOS and Windows. Such files are ubiquitous on the prairies of the Internet and are easy to spot with their telltale .ZIP extensions (sometimes in lowercase letters, but it doesn't matter). Other computer platforms prefer other compression formats. On the Macintosh, you'll most often see *StuffIt* format compression, which uses the extension .SIT. On the Amiga, the most common compression is known as *LHA*, and—shock of all shocks—files compressed with LHA usually end in .LHA.

Having said all that, I must mention that there is no technical reason why any of these computers cannot use any of the above compression schemes. The reasons why each platform has its own favorite are largely based in history and convention. With the right program, you can certainly decompress ZIP files on a Mac, LHA files on a PC, and so on.

The following table lists a bunch of extensions you may see on files in your Internet wanderings. It also includes some information about each extension that you can refer to in the future. Note that this table does not replace a good compass and a canteen for outdoor adventures.

What's ARJ, You Ask? Just another compression program that once was commonly used for the PC but is not anymore. Many older files on the Net are still in this format.

Be Careful! Just because you can use the ZIP format on any type of computer doesn't mean that you can use the decompressed files on any computer. ZIP is usually used to compress PC program files. Although you can "unzip" those program files on a Mac, the program will not run on the Mac. However, some files (such as sound files and graphic files) contain data that can be used on any computer with the proper software.

A Big Table of Common Compression Formats

Extension	Compression Program
.arc	Old format used on PCs.
.arj	Another older PC format; sometimes still used.
.cpt	Compact Pro format for the Macintosh.
.gz	Gnu Zip format commonly used in UNIX (sometimes uses the extension .z).
.lha	Commonly used on the Amiga these days.
.lzh	Older form of .lha. LHA decompressors can usually handle .lzh.
.sit	StuffIt for Macintosh. Very popular.
.zip	The widely popular ZIP format used predominantly on the PC.
.Z	UNIX compression format that's different from .gz/.z (note the lowercase vs. uppercase distinction).
.zoo	Quite old format used on PC and Amiga. Not much new stuff is in this format.

Finding the Right Silly Format for Your Machine

Time to get practical. What does this all boil down to? In general, it means that you should equip your computer with a decent stable of decompression software that can handle most of what you'll encounter on the Net. Primarily, that means getting the decompression program that will most often be used on your platform. Secondarily, it means that you should get software that can decompress some of the other popular compression formats, just in case you run into them in your Net travels.

Which decompression program should you have? Most people probably just acquire them on an as-needed basis, and after awhile, they have a whole bunch. I'd recommend the ZIP decompression program for any computer, as so many files are in ZIP format. Mac users most definitely want StuffIt, although PC users can probably get by without it unless they deal with lots of Mac-created files. At the less-common level, it would be a good idea to have the .Z decompression program (for the PC or Mac). In addition, if you work in graphics or sound, you may encounter many Amiga-generated files that are likely to be compressed in .LHA format, so an appropriate decompression program would be in order.

Here We Go

As an author, I face a sticky problem here. In the remainder of this chapter, I want to run through a few examples of how to decompress a file. The problem is, you don't have a decompression program yet. And if I told you how to get one, the usefulness of that advice would be limited because we've yet to discuss how to download!

Therefore, we're going to have to be a little strange right now. In our examples, we're going to decompress three common types of files: ZIP, SIT, and Z. For the purpose of the discussion, let's assume that you already have the given decompression program installed on your machine. (Don't worry, all this will come later. First you'll learn how to download, and then you can download the decompression programs you need from the Internet. Appendix A gives you a rundown of where on the Internet you can find the programs for your computer.)

Walk-Throughs: Decompressing with ZIP, SIT, and Z

There is a very good reason that we're going to look at these three formats for our walk-through: ZIP is the popular format on the PC, SIT on the Mac, and Z in UNIX. The majority of you readers are going to be ZIP-heads, because more people own PCs than anything else combined (that includes socks!).

Down with the ZIPper!

Suppose your brother wants you to print out the résumé that he meticulously constructed in PageMaker, which took more than five hours before he passed out. Even though he's the computer geek, you have the good fortune of owning a laser printer. And because his chances of employment are directly proportional to pixels-per-inch on a résumé, he has conscripted you for the task. Via means that we'll discuss later in the book, you have sitting on your hard drive a compressed version of his résumé in the file RESUME.ZIP.

There are two popular ZIP decompression programs for the PC. If you are an MS-DOS user, you'll most likely want PKUNZIP (see Appendix A). Windows 3.1 or 95 users, however, might prefer the graphical interface of WinZip. First, we'll manipulate RESUME.ZIP with PKUNZIP.

It's sensible to get an overview of the commands that PKUNZIP supports. We won't use nearly all of them in this book, but just to serve as a departure point, let's ask for a list of those commands by typing **pkunzip** on the MS-DOS command line. When you press **Enter**, you see something like this:

```
PKUNZIP Reg. U.S. Pat. and Tm. Off.
Usage:   PKUNZIP [options] zipfile [@list] [files...]
-c[m]              extract files to Console [with More]
-d                 restore/create Directory structure stored in .ZIP file
-e[c¦d¦e¦n¦p¦r¦s]  Extract files.  Sort by [CRC ¦ Date ¦ Extension ¦ Name
                           ¦ Percentage ¦ Reverse ¦ Size]
-f                 Freshen files in destination directory
-j¦J<h,r,s>        mask¦don't mask <Hidden/System/Readonly> files (def.=jhrs)
-n                 extract only Newer files
-o                 Overwrite previously existing files
-p[a/b][c][#]      extract to Printer [Asc mode,Bin mode,Com port] [port #]
-q                 Enable ANSI comments
-s[pwd]            Decrypt with password [If no pwd is given, prompt for pwd]
-t                 Test .ZIP file integrity
-v[b][r][m][t]     View .ZIP [Brief][Reverse][More][Technical] sort by [CRC¦
  [c,d,e,n,o,p,s]  Date¦Extension¦Name¦natural Order(default)¦Percentage¦Size]
-x<filespec>       eXclude file(s)from extraction
-$                 Restore volume label on destination drive
-@listfile         Generate list file
Press 2 for advanced/trouble shooting options.
Press any other key to quit help.
```

I know it looks like a complicated mess, but it's basically just a menu of options that you can refer to.

First, you're going to use the **-v** option, which shows you the contents of a ZIP file before you decompress it. If you do this with RESUME.ZIP, you might see something like this:

```
C:\>pkunzip -v resume.zip
PKUNZIP (R)    FAST!    Extract Utility    Version 2.04g  02-01-93
Copr. 1989-1993 PKWARE Inc. All Rights Reserved. Shareware Version
PKUNZIP Reg. U.S. Pat. and Tm. Off.
_ 80486 CPU detected.
_ EMS version 4.00 detected.
_ XMS version 3.00 detected.
_ DPMI version 0.90 detected.
Searching ZIP: RESUME.ZIP
 Length  Method    Size  Ratio   Date     Time    CRC-32  Attr  Name
 ------  ------    ----  -----   ----     ----    ------  ----  ----
  22327  DeflatN   9704   57%  07-06-95  22:07  1fb50b4a  --w-  RESUME.DOC
 ------,           ----   ---                                   -------
  22327            9704   57%                                         1
```

First PKUNZIP identifies some components of your machine. Then it shows you the contents of the ZIP file. As you can see, the file RESUME.ZIP contains the file RESUME.DOC, which has been compressed from its original size of 22,327 bytes to 9,704 bytes (that's 57% compression).

Decompressing RESUME.ZIP and ending up with RESUME.DOC so that it is ready for use in PageMaker is simple. Just run PKUNZIP with the ZIP file name, and the rest is magic. It goes a-something like this:

```
C:\DOCS\transfer>pkunzip resume.zip
PKUNZIP (R)   FAST!   Extract Utility    Version 2.04g  02-01-93
Copr. 1989-1993 PKWARE Inc. All Rights Reserved. Shareware Version
PKUNZIP Reg. U.S. Pat. and Tm. Off.
_ 80486 CPU detected.
_ EMS version 4.00 detected.
_ XMS version 3.00 detected.
_ DPMI version 0.90 detected.
Searching ZIP: RESUME.ZIP
  Inflating: RESUME.DOC
```

And there you have RESUME.DOC. Simple, no?

If you're a Windows user, you can save some typing and stick to comfy point-and-click interfaces by using WinZip. When you run WinZip, you see a happy little interface that looks like the following figure.

WinZip makes decompression a point-and-click breeze.

To view the contents and then decompress RESUME.ZIP, you first open the file. To do so, open the **File** menu and choose the **Open Archive** command (as shown in the following figure), or just click the **Open Folder** icon from the icon bar. In the dialog box that appears, select your file (RESUME.ZIP), and you see the same information that PKUNZIP reported.

Opening a ZIP file to decompress with WinZip.

To decompress the file, first click on the file to highlight it, and then click on the **Extract** icon. The Extract dialog box appears. You see a dialog box like the one shown below.

Choose a destination for the file you're decompressing.

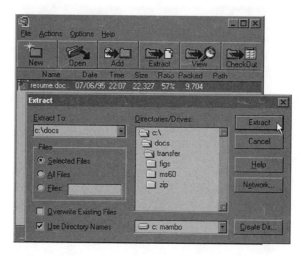

Once you select a destination directory and file name for the file, WinZip decompresses the file, and you're all done. It's quite easy, really, once you get through it the first time.

Why Don't You Just Stuff It?

More accurately, one should say, "Why don't you just un-stuff it!" On the Mac, the popular file compression format is known as "StuffIt," and its files often end with the extension .SIT. The concept behind unzipping a file and un-stuffing a file is the same, but the interfaces are a bit different. Unsurprisingly, the Mac interface is fairly easy to use.

Here you'll launch the program "StuffIt Expander" (widely available on the Internet and other online services). When the **File** menu appears in the Mac menu-bar, choose **Expand**. You'll see a dialog box like the one shown in the following figure.

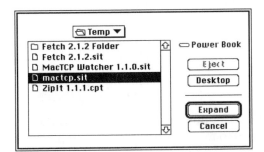

Decompressing a StuffIt-type file is as easy as pie.

Using the contols in this dialog box, navigate around the hard drive to find the file you want to decompress. In this figure, I've chosen MACTCP.SIT from the Temp subdirectory. Double-click on the file to un-stuff it, and the magic begins. A small status window keeps you updated on the progress. That's it! Less effort than a Flow-Bee haircut.

When in UNIX...

Some files on the Internet (often text files of instructions or documentation) are stored in UNIX-compressed format, which has the telltale .Z extension (note the capital Z; in this case it is significant). If you run into any of these files, don't worry. They are very easy to decompress. And you thought nothing in UNIX was easy!

In this section, let's assume that you are using a UNIX shell account and you have retrieved a file (perhaps by FTP or Gopher) that is in .Z format. Unlike in the ZIP and SIT situations, you probably don't need to get the decompression program this time. Every UNIX account I've ever seen has the decompress program already installed.

So let's say you retrieved a file called TOMATOES.TXT.Z with instructions on how to grow better garden tomatoes. Decompressing this is very simple. Just type **%decompress tomatoes.txt.Z**.

That's it! You end up with a file named TOMATOES.TXT, and there is no longer a file with the .Z extension. (Remember, that this is from within a UNIX account.)

The Least You Need to Know

Decompressing files isn't too difficult. You just need to know which decompression program to use for which file type, and you need to have that program installed.

➤ Your computer compresses data by looking for repeating sequences and essentially eliminating them. This creates much smaller files, which in turn saves storage space and cuts down transfer time. In the long run, this can save money.

➤ Data must be in decompressed form for your computer to use it. You need to use a specific program designed to decompress the data after you transfer it.

➤ Different decompression programs are popular on different computer platforms, but there are programs that can decompress any form of compression for every platform.

➤ PC users usually encounter ZIP format files with the extension .ZIP. PKUNZIP for MS-DOS and WinZip for Windows are the two programs that decompress these files.

➤ Mac users will often encounter StuffIt format files with the extension .SIT.

➤ The most common compression format in UNIX adds a .Z extension. The decompression program for this is installed with the UNIX account.

A Digital Warehouse: File Archives

As a little child with skinned knees, you might have spent your days collecting pennies from those household crevices where only roaches normally tread. After a good day or a string of good days, you could take your prized pile of copper and sit proudly at the kitchen table rolling them into little paper tubes. Banks prefer those rolls to 1,000 loose pennies.

And so it is with computer files as well. A computer program may be split up into many parts, each consisting of a file. But if you wanted to distribute that program to other people and you had to transfer each file separately, what are the chances everyone would get the whole package of files intact? And what a pain it would be if you had to transfer all kinds of files just for one program.

The solution: this chapter!

Compression's Other Half: Archiving

A file *archive* provides you with a way of storing multiple files within one larger file (just like those penny rolls you used to use).

As opposed to compression, archiving doesn't necessarily save transfer time in and of itself. Instead, it just combines a bunch of files into one big file—a "file of files." However, this does mean you have the convenience of only having to download one big file. When the downloaded file is on your computer, you can break the archive back up into its original component parts, (just like breaking open the penny roll). This is called *dearchiving*.

As it happens, compression and archiving go quite well together. By combining the two concepts, you can take one big "file of files" and squeeze it all into one smaller file. Pretty neat, eh? Because the combination of the two results in the most efficient way to transport files between computers, they almost always occur together. That is, you won't usually encounter single compressed files on the Internet or other online services, as I implied in Chapter 4. What you will run into are compressed archives: an archive of several files, each of which is compressed.

The good news doesn't end. Because compression and archiving are so wedded, just about every decompression program we discussed in Chapter 4 is also an archiving program! Two for the price of none, and they even throw in this handy cheese grater! What this means in "real life" is that the process you use to decompress is often the same one you would use to dearchive. That is, when you tell a program like PKUNZIP to decompress a file, if that file is actually an archive with several compressed files in it, PKUNZIP can tell that. So it automatically *extracts* each file from the archive and then decompresses them all. Life is good.

Yet More Silly Extensions: TAR and Friends

There is only one example in which a popular archiving format does not handle compression, and vice versa. That is in UNIX. In Chapter 4, we looked briefly at .Z files that were UNIX compressed. Unlike ZIP and most other modern programs of this sort, UNIX compression *does* only compress. Therefore, it can only work on a single file; you cannot have a .Z file that contains several other files within.

In UNIX, the archiving program is known as *TAR* (for no particular reason that I'm aware of; it probably does mean something, but only eight people know). In UNIX, then, the archiving task is a two-step process that usually includes TAR-ing together all the files for the archive and then compressing the one big TAR file using UNIX compress. Unwrapping the package must then be done in reverse. (You'll find a specific example of this toward the end of this chapter; it's not as loopy as it sounds.)

Except when working in UNIX with TAR, you will encounter the same extensions when looking at archives that you did when working with compressed files (the oft-seen ZIP and SIT as well as LHA, ARJ, and so forth). All of these are also archiving programs. So when you see a file that ends in one of these extensions, you can't assume that it is only one file compressed. It could be 100 files. But it doesn't really matter to you; the procedure for unwrapping the package is the same in all cases.

Doing the Right Thing (with the Right Archive)

Because all these programs perform both functions, the extension table in Chapter 4 also applies to archives. Knowing what to do, then, is quite easy: the same thing you did in Chapter 4. For the sake of clarity, here are a few examples of archives (first for the PC, then the Mac, then UNIX—order not based on personal bias) so you can see what they're like. But first, a word about location.

Don't Just Put Them Anywhere—There Is a RIGHT Place

If you want to extract and decompress the archive, you first need to consider *where* you want all these files to end up. I didn't address this issue when decompressing single files because you can easily move a file if you want to. But with a whole bunch of files, you really would like them to be extracted to the correct place on your hard drive initially.

Note that "correct place" usually means wherever *you* want. First, consider what types of files are in this archive. If they are pictures or sounds or other sorts of data files, you might have an appropriate folder on your drive for such things. However, if you're downloading an archive of a program, keep in mind that these often like to install themselves from a set of uninstalled files. That means you

Be Sure to Vaccinate
When you dearchive and decompress files, consider the possibility of nasty viruses. (You'll learn more proper treatment in Chapter 6.) If you dearchive and decompress in a separate subdirectory, you can use it as a sort of quarantined "holding tank" that you can scan for viruses before you use any of the files.

must dearchive/decompress the original archive and then run the setup program that results. Because of this, you probably want to create some sort of "temp" folder for dearchiving these types of packages. Once you install the program (usually after running "setup" or something similarly named) and you're sure it works properly, you can delete the stuff from the temp directory.

ZIP

Remember how your brother wanted you to print his résumé in Chapter 4? Suppose his last job application was rejected and he's decided to go all out this time. He wants you to create a "pamphlet" for him that advertises his questionable skills. He has created all the artwork for the pamphlet (he digitized his photo, drew lots of poofy clouds, added fancy curly fonts, and so on), and he wants you to put it all together in PageMaker. He's a very dependent brother. So he ZIPs up all the files and sends them to you in one archive, again called RESUME.ZIP. Your mission: dearchive and decompress RESUME.ZIP. This is gonna be easy—trust me.

When dealing with file archives, the **-v** option ("verbose") of PKUNZIP becomes a bit more useful than it was in Chapter 4. It allows you to see which files are in the archive before you actually go ahead and extract and decompress them. Take a look:

```
C:\DOWNLOAD>pkunzip -v resume.zip
PKUNZIP (R)    FAST!    Extract Utility    Version 2.04g  02-01-93
Copr. 1989-1993 PKWARE Inc. All Rights Reserved. Shareware Version
PKUNZIP Reg. U.S. Pat. and Tm. Off.
_ 80486 CPU detected.
_ EMS version 4.00 detected.
_ XMS version 3.00 detected.
_ DPMI version 0.90 detected.
Searching ZIP: RESUME.ZIP
 Length  Method   Size  Ratio   Date     Time    CRC-32   Attr  Name
 ------  ------   -----  -----   ----     ----    ------   ----  ----
 176128  DeflatN  68515   62%  11-03-94  01:06  3f9fe916  ---   resume.doc
  56384  DeflatN  27246   52%  11-22-94  21:07  0b0c0e6d  ---   doggy.gif
   4088  DeflatN   1816   56%  02-06-95  08:33  23ffbd0b  ---   clouds.gif
  49359  DeflatN  34955   30%  02-22-95  12:01  33651a56  ---   greatme.txt
 200762  DeflatN  49058   76%  02-06-95  09:36  851c5e4a  ---   hireme.txt
  43659  DeflatN  16030   64%  02-06-95  09:39  711957b5  ---   kisschild.jpg
 ------           ------  ---                                   -------
 530380          197620   63%                                         6
```

Again, you see that PKUNZIP first recognizes some aspects of your computer. After that, it shows the inventory of the archive. You may find some of the reports (such as ratio of compression) interesting, but others (such as time and CRC-32) are not of major concern. Notice that on the right-hand side of the output you can see the names of all the files in the archive RESUME.ZIP. On the bottom line, you see such totals as the total decompressed size of all the files in sum (left-hand side) and the total size of all files compressed (to the right of that).

Sometimes it's useful to look into an archive this way before you extract it just to see what's in it. That way, you have some idea what to expect, and you aren't surprised when the archive starts writing 1,000 files to your hard drive.

In this case, you're going to dearchive the file RESUME.ZIP into a directory that you've created specifically for it beforehand. Notice the syntax of the PKUNZIP command in this example:

```
C:\>pkunzip resume.zip c:\docs\resume
PKUNZIP (R)    FAST!    Extract Utility     Version 2.04g  02-01-93
Copr. 1989-1993 PKWARE Inc. All Rights Reserved. Shareware Version
PKUNZIP Reg. U.S. Pat. and Tm. Off.
_ 80486 CPU detected.
_ EMS version 4.00 detected.
_ XMS version 3.00 detected.
_ DPMI version 0.90 detected.
Searching ZIP: RESUME.ZIP
  Inflating: c:/docs/resume/resume.doc
  Inflating: c:/docs/resume/doggy.gif
  Inflating: c:/docs/resume/clouds.gif
  Inflating: c:/docs/resume/greatme.txt
  Inflating: c:/docs/resume/hireme.txt
  Inflating: c:/docs/resume/kisschild.jpg
```

As you can see in the first line above, you include the intended destination directory after the file name you wanted to dearchive. If you don't do that, the files wind up wherever you were on the hard drive when you ran PKUNZIP.

Life isn't too difficult for Windows users using WinZip. The following figure shows the WinZip screen (from Chapter 4) with the archive RESUME.ZIP open. The contents of the RESUME.ZIP file appear in the window.

WinZip displays the contents of the archived file, along with appropriate and semi-interesting related information.

If you want to extract only some, but not all, of the files in the archive, select them with the mouse by holding down the **Ctrl** key and clicking on each one. If you want to extract all of them, don't worry about selecting anything. Either way, hit the **Extract** button, and you'll see the Extract dialog box (shown here).

Extract the contents of a file archive to the selected destination directory.

Take My Advice When you dearchive files, do not delete the original archive. You probably should keep it around for a little while in case you damage one of the files; then you won't have to download it from the Net again. If you amass a collection of file archives after a while, you might want to purge from time to time (depending how often you wash your socks).

Be sure to check **All files** if you want all the files in the archive extracted. Usually this is the default, but sometimes it is not. Enter the destination directory in the **Extract To** text box, or select the destination from the **Directories/Drives** list. Then click **Extract** and that's it. WinZip does the rest for you automatically.

There is a variant of ZIP files that's worth mentioning: .EXE files. Some developers choose to make life easier by creating compressed archives that can extract themselves. This eliminates the need for you, the user, to handle the task manually as I just explained. Often these files end with the extension .EXE, which means they can be executed (by using the File, Run command from the Windows 3.x Program Manager or the Start menu in Windows 95, for example). When you run them, they'll take care of extracting themselves. You can still manually unzip an .EXE file if you want by opening it with PKUNZIP or WinZip. But there's no need to.

StuffIt

Almost everything I said above for ZIP archives applies equally to StuffIt archives: the concepts are exactly the same. And just as ZIP has a self-extracting variant (.EXE files) for the PC, so does the Mac. However, on the Mac, the practice of distributing self-extracting archives is even more widespread. You may often encounter files that don't have .SIT extensions, but have .SEA extensions instead. You can simply launch these files by double-clicking them in the Finder. They'll do the rest automatically.

For those unfortunate times when you do not have a self-extracting archive, though, you can fall back on StuffIt to do the dirty work. The procedure is identical to the one you used to decompress a file in Chapter 4.

Again, launch the StuffIt Expander, choose **Expand** from the **File** menu, and choose the file (archive, technically) that you want to expand. StuffIt automatically recognizes that multiple files are archived into one, and the status window reflects this. It lists each file it has extracted and expanded, and the progress bar moves towards the right. Once this process is complete, that's the whole ball of wax (such a pretty image).

Having said all that, let me add this one potential caveat: many times Mac archives are in "BinHex" format in addition to being stuffed. BinHex is much like uuencoding, in that it is a way of storing 8-bit binary data in 7-bit ASCII format. You can recognize this format by the extension .HQX. Therefore, many Mac files on the Net or other services will have file names such as GREATPROGRAM.SIT.HQX.

In these cases, you need to un-BinHex the file before you un-stuff it! I know—this is getting crazy. Depending on the un-stuffing application you use, it may automatically take care of the BinHex. That would be nice. If not, you can use a program such as, "BinHex 5.0," which I'll explain right now.

Assuming you've got a .HQX format file on your hands, you first launch BixHex 5.0. Open the **File** menu, select **Download**, and select **Application**. A friendly ol' dialog box comes to the fore, in which you can choose the .HQX file to process. Double-click on the file you want, or highlight it and click on **Open**.

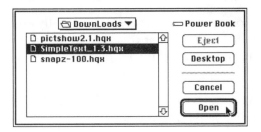

Select the .HQX file for processing. Wash hands after use.

BinHex prompts you to choose a destination location and file name (even though it gives you a default file name that is usually correct).

*Choose your
destination.*

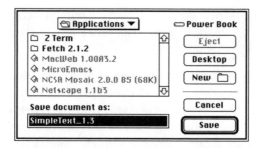

BinHex plops the resulting file wherever your mouse pointer desires. At the end, you get the satisfying flush of the message shown in the following figure. It signals the completion of the task. The resulting file may be in any number of formats: it may be a ready application that you can launch immediately, or it may be another archive (such as a .SIT file) that needs to be un-stuffed.

You did it!

```
File conversion successfully completed!
```

That UNIX Magic: .tar.Z

This is the form of archival/compression that you will least likely encounter (unless you need to compile source code on UNIX accounts). Nonetheless, you may still run into the odd .tar.Z file somewhere, perhaps as a pack of documentation or something.

Handling this is a two-step process because it is actually an archive (one large compressed file that contains several others). First you need to decompress the archive file, and then you need to dearchive it. It takes a tiny bit more work than the PC and Mac examples did, but it's not *too* hideous considering this is UNIX.

This time, let's say you retrieved a file called GARDENING.TAR.Z that contains several documents on home gardening. First you decompress the TAR file with this command:

%uncompress gardening.tar.Z

You're left with a file called GARDENING.TAR in place of the .tar.Z file. The **tar** command has many possible options, but to avoid confusion, you can use the most straightforward form for dearchiving. To do so, type **%tar xfv gardening.tar**. You may see output similar to this:

```
gardens/tomatoes.txt
gardens/peppers.txt
gardens/beets.txt
gardens/carrots.txt
gardens/rodents.txt
tar: ustar vol 1, 32 files, 337920 bytes read, 0 bytes written
```

This is a list of the files that were extracted (note that they were put into a GARDENS directory, which **tar** created for you) and some totals. That's it; you've finished the tar.Z. two-step. Not too bad, really. Unlike the .Z file that replaced itself, the .TAR file sticks around even after you've dearchived it, just like ZIP and the others. So you may want to delete it at some point.

Techno Talk

TARred and Feathered

The UNIX **tar** command can accept a number of options, some of which are more commonly used than others. They can also be combined on the command line if necessary. Here are a couple of useful ones.

c Creates a new .TAR file (for creating an archive)

t Shows the names of files archived within a .TAR file

v Offers verbose output during the process for the user's benefit

f Indicates that you're going to specify the file name to process (you need to include this in most cases)

If you want to learn more, you can read about it in graphic detail by typing **man tar** in your UNIX account.

The Least You Need to Know

A file archive is essentially a big filing box that you can throw a bunch of files into for easy transportation. Virtually all sets of files belonging to one application or program suite on the Internet or any other online service are in archived form.

➤ In the interest of maximizing file transfer efficiency, archived files are usually compressed as well. This can turn many large files into one smaller file.

➤ To be useful to the computer, archives needs to be disassembled before use. The process is called dearchiving.

➤ ZIP, SIT, LHA, and ARJ are all forms of archival as well as compression. Thus, whichever program you use to decompress a file will also dearchive it.

➤ The only common exception to the above is UNIX TAR, which is a form of archival but not compression. Therefore, to combine effects, many UNIX programs are stored in .tar.Z format, which means they are first archived and then compressed. You have to reverse the two steps to regain the original files.

## Chapter 6

The Evil Virus

In This Chapter

➤ How to speak proper English

➤ What viruses can do for you

➤ Where viruses come from—and where they don't

➤ Happy hunting

➤ Seek and ye shall disinfect

Apparently unsated by the naturally occurring varieties, humans have gone and created infections in the digital realm. Computer viruses have always been a problem, but the Internet has the potential to spread disease like a Roman aqueduct. All those wonderful files that you'll learn how to download from the Internet and other online services to your system can be infected—which can cause all sorts of horrible problems. So if you're going to be downloading files, *viruses* are definitely something you need to know about. In addition, if you know what you're looking for, you might be able to spot viruses in programs before you upload them to the Internet to infect everyone else.

But It's "Octopi," Isn't It?

We may as well get it over with. You've read the chapter title, you've read the intro paragraph, and you're thinking, "Hey, I thought the plural of *virus* was *virii*! Were the editors at Que passed out at their desks when this chapter went in for review or what?"

In the "everything-you-learned-in-school-was-wrong" department, let it be known that the plural of *virus* is *viruses*. The reason, so they say, is that *virus* in Latin is a mass noun (like the word air, for which there is no correct Latin plural). So there. If someone insists on saying virii around you with the airs of educated dignity, kill his cat.

Is My Computer Going to Die?

There are some things that a few viruses do, some things that many viruses do, and some things that no viruses can do. First, it's worth looking at the matter of computer platforms again.

Different computer platforms are more or less vulnerable to viruses. The reason for this is a combination of the design of the computer and the size of the user base (and, therefore, how many potential virus writers there might be). The heavyweight champions by far are PC clones, which most often run MS-DOS/Windows. These machines are the biggest breeding ground for viruses. There are at least 1,500 known viruses that can infect a PC; however, it's important to note that only a fraction of them have gained widespread dissemination.

You Can't Hide Behind Windows 95

Newer operating systems such as Windows 95 are not automatically protected against many of these viruses, so all PC users should take the same precautions covered in this chapter.

The runner-up, although quite a bit behind, is the Macintosh, which can be infected by maybe a few dozen potential viruses. Dead-last, at the back of the pack, is UNIX, where viruses (other than experimental ones written for specific research purposes) are basically nonexistent. The other less-common computer platforms such as the Amiga, Atari ST, and Archimedes fall somewhere in the middle to low part of the risk spectrum. Because a virus is a piece of software, it can only infect the computer platform that it was written for. So if you are a Mac user, a PC virus is not going to be able to harm you (unless you run a PC emulator, in which case, it could infect that portion of your system).

There are several reasons for the differing levels of risk. One is the sheer number of computers of a particular type. The fact that there are so many more PCs around than just about every other computer platform combined is obviously a great factor in these statistics. Other risk factors are more technical and have to do with the way that the different platforms manage files, memory, and so forth.

Viruses work in several different ways, which experts have broken down into classes. I'm not going to go into any of that here, however, because it's boring and it's not relevant to the topic of protecting your computer when downloading files. Ultimately, though, a virus can affect your computer in a number of ways. It can infect files and spread to other files without ever causing any damage. It could infect every file that you open on your computer, or it could just hang out and infect a file every so often. A virus can even lie in wait until a certain condition is met (like a certain date and year) and then leap out and wreak havoc.

While a lot of viruses are more of a nuisance than they are a serious threat to your entire system, some can really destroy everything—especially if you're too lazy to keep backups of important programs or data. And even those programs that are not programmed to cause explicit damage are likely to cause problems just by spreading around your system. For example, they can corrupt files or boot records beyond repair, which can be especially devastating if you don't have backups to restore from.

The Internet as Communal Water Fountain

In elementary school, hundreds of little kids stay together for hours on end, day after day, eating dirt and drinking from the same water fountain. Is it any surprise that they're always sick? Not at all. Well, in some ways, the Internet is like that water fountain (save for the piece of green gum stuck to the drain).

Some illnesses are communicable by the water fountain, and some are not. Because a virus is a software program, it has to be *executed* or *run* to be able to infect anything. For this reason, viruses

This Is Important
Let me stress that point: the mere existence of a virus within a program on your computer cannot spread the infection. Not until the program (and therefore the virus hidden within it) is executed can the infection take place.

tend to try to infect other executable programs. Sometimes, however, whether on purpose or not, a virus may infect a data file such as a word processor document or a graphic file that is not an executable program. Although the virus generally can't further propagate itself from that file because it needs to be executed, it can damage the file, possibly beyond repair.

To Run or Not to Run

When you *execute* or *run* a program, you tell the computer to begin reading and following the instructions that the program is composed of. Some types of computer files are programs and can be executed. Other sorts of files are not instructions, but are some other form of data. For example, a graphic file that contains a picture of a house is not a set of instructions to the computer, it is a set of data representing the picture. Such a file cannot be executed, but it can be read or manipulated by another program that can be executed (such as an image processing application, in this case).

Just because a virus can infect only the specific computer platform for which it was designed doesn't mean that it cannot be carried by a different platform. It can. For example, suppose you use FTP to get a program from the Internet, and you retrieve the file into your UNIX shell account. From there, you might normally download the file from your UNIX account to your PC (in ways that we'll discuss in Part 3). But suppose the program you retrieved contains a PC virus. That virus couldn't infect the UNIX system on which you're temporarily storing the program, but it does remain in the program. So when you transfer the program to the computer it was meant for and execute that program, you also transfer the virus, which can then infect.

Fact, Myth, and the Teenager

The implications of the aforementioned concept are the source of a lot of rumors and myths, especially on the Internet. Many people have made announcements about "new" forms of virus that are transmitted over the Internet by unusual means, and many of the people who hear those announcements just aren't sure what to believe.

To repeat the main principle you need to know:

> *A file that is not going to be executed by the computer for which the virus was programmed cannot spawn viral infection.* (Say it again with me, friends!)

E-mail messages, picture files, and UseNet postings, for example, are all data files that you use some other program (a mail reader, a picture viewer, a newsreader) to manipulate. Yet, these are all types of files that have been rumored to carry viruses on the Internet. They don't; it is not possible.

To clarify, if someone sends you a GIF image file and claims there is a virus in it, and if you run a virus scanner when you download the file, it is possible that the scanner will detect a virus. So technically, yes, there is a virus infecting that GIF file. However, a GIF file is not executable; it is a graphic image. Therefore, the virus has no way of spreading out of that file. So even if the GIF file itself were damaged by the viral infection, it could not spread the virus any further.

Now if you download an executable program or an archive that contains executable programs, that's another story. A GIF viewer, for example, is an executable file; were that infected by a virus, it could spread the infection. But remember that the mere act of downloading an infected executable program will not spread the virus throughout your computer. Remember also that archives can't be executed in and of themselves; you have to extract the executable program first. But if you ever execute that program or if another program on your computer executes it, the virus can infect your system and begin spreading.

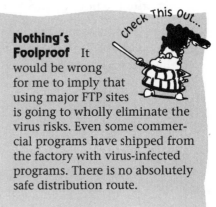

BBS (Bulletin Board System) Usually a local computer run by one person or organization that you call with a modem. Although some BBSs offer connections to the Internet, BBSs on the whole are not part of the global network of computers that compose the Internet.

So how many programs on the Internet carry viruses? 45,843. Okay, okay, don't panic! I'm just kidding. No one really knows, and it would be impossible to know considering how many new programs are transferred across the Internet and stored on Internet-based sites every day. Traditionally, BBSs have been a more troublesome source of viruses than the Internet, but I wouldn't suggest that you find a false sense of security in that. The massive explosion of people who are starting to use the Internet is bound to bring a fair amount of trouble—and troubling and troubled people with it.

Albeit far from ideal, a mediocre rule of thumb to follow when finding programs on the Internet is to stick with major distribution channels. For example, the major computer platforms all have a few FTP sites, which are the dominant storehouses of software for those computers. Often there are a number of "mirrors" of those sites that carry the same inventory. Because these sites are the major troughs for users, they tend to have more vigilant administration than do smaller FTP sites. Therefore, the administrators of these sites usually scan the uploaded files more closely for viruses, and implement quicker removal and/or notice of any files on the site that are found to be infected.

Nothing's Foolproof It would be wrong for me to imply that using major FTP sites is going to wholly eliminate the virus risks. Even some commercial programs have shipped from the factory with virus-infected programs. There is no absolutely safe distribution route.

The Prudent Hacker

With all these digital infections floating about, you need to protect yourself. There are some practices and behaviors that you can undertake to reduce your risk. I think we both know that the obvious joke here is just too easy, so I'll let it rest.

➤ As I mentioned previously, you should take note of the source of the computer files you're downloading. Although not 100% secure, major FTP sites are far less risky sources than some guy on the Internet chat channels who types in all capitals.

➤ If, after following the techniques in this chapter, you feel your system is virus-free (clean), BACK IT UP! (If there was ever a mantra in computing, it's "BACK IT UP!") But remember that you don't want to back up a virus itself or an infected system, so make sure it's clean first.

➤ And from now on, in combination with the vigilant techniques in the remainder of this chapter, back up important programs or data as quickly as possible. You can back up your data on floppy disks or jumbo tape drives.

If you have a floppy disk that contains a backup of a $150 ant farm design program and the ant farm data file that took you two years to perfect, you really don't want to stick that floppy into an infected system. Or rather, you don't want the virus spreading to your floppy, which can not only destroy the files on it, but spread to another computer in which you later use the disk.

Fortunately, that's what *write-protect notches* are for, and no virus can overcome the little plastic window. Keep track of the write-protect status of your floppy disks (see the following figure), and in general, keep them write-protected. Only close the write-protect window when you specifically need to save some data to that floppy disk. It's also a good idea to use only a virus-free computer to save data to the disk; otherwise, the virus could get onto the floppy. Once you save to the floppy, write-protect it again.

Using floppies given to you by other people—especially others that you don't trust to be virus-vigilant—can be dangerous. If you must do this, the best course of action is to scan the disk for viruses before you do a single thing with the floppy. Even before you type **dir** to see what it contains, scan it for viruses!

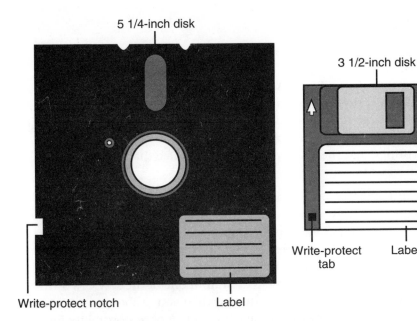

5 1/4-inch disk

3 1/2-inch disk

The anatomical details of your floppy disks.

Write-protect notch   Label

Write-protect tab   Label

Floppy Basics

Although it's considered basic knowledge by many, let's make sure we're on the same terms here. On both 3 1/2-inch and 5 1/4-inch disks, the relevant hole or notch is in the upper-right corner when you hold the disk with the label at the top and facing you. To write protect a 3 1/2-inch disk, you flip the little notch up so that the hole is open and you can see through it. Closing the hole write-enables the disk, allowing you to save data to it—and allowing for possible viral infection. On a 5 1/4-inch floppy (if you still have any of those fossils), the situation is reversed. Cover the notch in the 5 1/4-inch floppy to write-protect the disk; leaving it open write-enables the disk.

Above all, remember that there is no single, perfect virus prevention method. Any program or application that you get that mentions the capability to prevent viruses is only an additional tool and/or weapon; it is not the be-all and end-all of what should be your virus vigilance. Believing otherwise can only lead to a false sense of security, which can make you even more vulnerable.

Online Service Safety

While all of what you've learned applies to all files and file archives you may find any-where, the Internet is probably the least-regulated of services other than local BBSs. Users of private online services, such as CompuServe, America Online, and The Microsoft Network benefit from a little more protection. These services have "forums" or "libraries" where they keep software repositories maintained by specific persons. Those persons check the archives for soundness before approving them for public download. Nonethe-less, viruses can be sneaky things, and there's never a 100% guarantee that just because someone screened a file it is virus-free.

One potential point of confusion is the distinction between files from the Internet and files from the online services. All of these services now offer "access" to the Internet, which includes Internet resources such as FTP. But it's important to remember that the services can have no control over what is out there on the Net. So even if you retrieve all your archives from an online service, consider whether they are ultimately coming from the Internet via the online service (and are unregulated) or from one of the service's own private file library areas. Some of the services will warn you when you're about to initiate an action that involves the Internet, so they can absolve themselves of responsibility for what you find.

Turn Your RAM When You Cough

As is true when you come down with the flu, there are a series of ways in which you may come to notice the malady. When you start to feel achy and a little fuzzy in the head, you suspect something might be up.

Don't Panic! Some drives do access them-selves from time to time, so unnecessary hard disk access alone is not a 100% predictor. But pay attention to whether it's accessing at different times than it has in the past.

On your computer, you may also notice some opera-tional oddities. Inappropriate hard drive access may be a tip-off. For example, if you see or hear your hard drive accessing at times when you didn't tell it to (such as loading or saving a file), that may be a tip. Another sign is decreased free space on the hard drive. Some viruses may act in such a way that they reduce your free space; if your hard drive space is decreasing at a rate different from what you think it should be, that may also be a clue.

Similarly, you shouldn't overlook any other strange happenings with your computer. Unusually sluggish operation or apparent hardware problems can sometimes be traced back to viruses. For example, there is a virus for the PC that messes with high-density floppy access and makes it appear as if the floppy drive is malfunctioning. Some viruses aren't nearly so subtle, though. Some will proudly announce their presence with an animation or musical indulgence. Needless to say, if you see a strange message fly across your screen when you boot up the computer, be afraid—be very afraid.

Some viruses may make other changes to your system that aren't so easily detectable by the human senses (unless you have a sixth sense, which can be very useful in a variety of situations). For example, some viruses change the contents of files and their file sizes. Likewise, some alter certain memory locations in your computer to create a "home" for the virus to live in and attack from (note that memory changes only remain in place while the computer is powered on). These aren't changes that the user is likely to notice, however, which is why virus detection utilities exist.

One Form of Protection...

Virus scanners, appropriately enough, scan your computer's hard disk and RAM memory for known viruses. But note the word *known* in that sentence. As is true of biological viruses, every computer virus has its own characteristics; a virus scanner can only detect the viruses that it has been programmed to recognize. Therefore, you should always be sure to use the newest, most up-to-date version of a particular virus scanner program (which is updated frequently for this very reason). If, for some reason, the manufacturer of the virus detection program you are using stops updating it, stop using it and find another.

Even if you don't think you have any viruses right now, it's a good idea to stop and pick up a virus scanner and check your system. Remember, though, that most virus scanners cannot find viruses hidden inside file archives or compressed files. You'll need to check files that are dearchived and decompressed. And be warned that no virus utility can work 100% of the time; the world of computer viruses is just too complicated and too dynamic.

The best defense is a combination of being a vigilant user who practices "safe computing," keeps an eye out for weirdness on the system, and uses virus detection utilities to scan and prevent viruses.

Scanning for Problems

I've talked about keeping your eyes open and practicing safe computing. Now let's look at using various virus scanning programs. Then we'll top it all off with a beer-n-toga party at your house.

Once again, I face the awkward problem of having to talk about downloading a particular program before I've told you how to download. So, once again, read through this section now to understand the concepts, and then read it again after completing the book (when you can retrieve and install the files explained here).

PC? Try Using F-PROT

On the PC side of things, one popular and high-quality virus scanner is called *F-PROT*. You can find F-PROT on any major FTP site that stores PC software (see Appendix A for a resource listing). One such FTP archive is **ftp.cdrom.com**, which contains a mirror of the popular Simtel PC archive. To get F-PROT, fire up your FTP application and open the connection to **ftp.cdrom.com**. When you get in, change to the **/pub/simtel/msdos/ virus** directory. There you should find a file called fp-*xxx*, where *xxx* is the current version of F-PROT. Retrieve that file to your PC.

Let's take a quick tour of F-PROT. (No flash cameras, please; it scares the monkeys.) When you get the F-PROT archive, unzip the fp-*xxx* file. You can launch the program by typing **f-prot** at the C:\> prompt. Immediately, F-PROT scans your computer's memory (RAM) for any viruses that may be hiding in there. Then it displays the main menu, which should look like this picture.

The main menu of F-PROT.

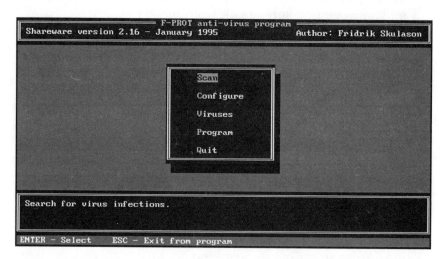

On the main menu, the option of choice is Scan. Select **Scan**, and you see five configurable options: Method, Search, Action, Targets, and Files.

Check This Out...

For More Information
Read the documentation included with F-PROT to learn more about the program's other features.

➤ **Method** is set to **Secure Scan** by default; leave it that way.

➤ **Search** tells F-PROT where you want to scan. Your three basic options are your entire hard disk, a floppy disk, or a selected directory of your hard disk. If you want to scan your entire system, which you do for our example, leave it on **Hard disk**. (You can choose Floppy to scan floppy disks later.)

Stop It Before It Starts

When you retrieve a new program from the Net in the future, after you unzip it (before you try it out), you should run F-PROT, change the **Search** option to **User-Specified**, and enter the path of the unzipped files. F-PROT will run a scan on the new files just to be sure they're clean. This is a peremptory defense that can find a potential virus before it has the chance to spread.

➤ **Action** determines what F-PROT will do if it finds a nasty little booger. Leave it on **Report Only** for now, so that it will just tell you about the possible problem. You can decide what to do about it after you see the full report.

➤ **Targets** tells F-PROT where on your system it will scan. By default, the boot sector, files, and packed files options are all marked **Yes**. Leave it that way.

➤ **Files** determines which files on the system F-PROT will scan. Leave the default option, **Standard Executables**, selected for your first scan. If you find out that your system has been infected, rerun F-PROT and select **All Files**. F-PROT will hunt down the virus in nontraditional virus hangouts, in case it has really gotten out of hand.

After setting up all of the above, select **Begin Scan**, and the hoe-down begins. When it's done, you get a report of the results. For now, if F-PROT reports anything funky, just hold tight. I'll go over your options in the final section of this chapter.

Macintosh? Try Using Disinfectant

For the Macintosh, let's look briefly at the very popular virus scanner/prevention utility called *Disinfectant*. You can find Disinfectant at major Mac FTP sites or at its "home" site, where updates will appear first: **ftp.acns.nwu.edu** in the **/pub/disinfectant** directory. Retrieve the file and install it on your Mac. Double-click on the **Disinfectant** icon to launch the program, and you see the screen shown in the following figure.

Fortunately, this program is very easy to use. It basically has two modes of operation: Scan and Disinfect. Right now, let's consider the Scan feature. Like F-PROT for the PC, Disinfectant scans your system for known viruses. The Scan menu contains several choices: File, Folder, Floppies, All disks, Some disks, System file, System folder, and Desktop files. Simply choose whichever elements you want to scan. If you've never scanned your current system before, choose **All disks**. Once you've chosen the portion of your system to scan, Disinfectant begins the search and reports whatever it finds in the output window. If it turns up something untoward, see the final section in this chapter, "Cleaning the Tubes," for advice.

Disinfectant for the
Macintosh: its two
basic modes of
operation are Scan
and Disinfect.

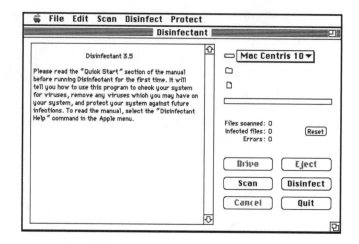

Nip It in the Bud

In the future, when you get new program archives from the Internet,
use Disinfectant's **Scan, Folder** option to check out the new folder
before you execute the program for the first time.

Using the Facilities—I Mean Utilities

**Which Is
Which?** If
you're not sure
which file is
the program
you're looking
for, many FTP sites have a file
called something like
00_index.txt or index.txt
within each directory path.
Retrieve this file and view it
with an ASCII viewer, and it
gives a brief description of each
file within that directory. It's
quite helpful.

Similar to the U.S. health care system, virus scanners
don't practice preventive medicine. Instead, they tend
to try to find and diagnose existing problems. However,
attempting to prevent a viral infection in the first place
is a good idea and can save time and heartburn. What a
virus prevention utility does is sit in the background of
your computer and watch the goings-on. It watches
memory access, file access, file changes, and so on. If it
thinks something funky is going down, it pops out of
the woodwork and gives you a holler.

One such virus prevention tool for the PC is VSHIELD.
As with F-PROT, VSHIELD can also be found at major
PC FTP repositories, such as the aforementioned
ftp.cdrom.com site in the same directory path as
F-PROT. Its file name should resemble something like
vsh-*xxx*, where ***xxx*** is the current version number.

Installing and running VSHIELD is easy. Just type **vshield** at the C:\> prompt, and it installs itself into memory. Then it lurks there watching for evil. You may want to include VSHIELD in your AUTOEXEC.BAT file so that it automatically executes at startup. If you execute a program that contains a virus VSHIELD recognizes, the execution is halted, and VSHIELD pops up to talk to you about the problem.

Check This Out...

To Learn More...

F-PROT and VSHIELD aren't the only virus scanners and prevention utilities for the PC, and both types of programs have more detailed modes of operation. Read each program's documentation for a much more comprehensive lesson. If you have questions concerning viruses, which scanners and prevention utilities to use, or how to operate them, try asking the folks in the UseNet newsgroup **comp.virus**. They'll be happy to help you out with the latest detailed information about viruses and virus utilities.

Macintosh users are in luck. Disinfectant, the virus scanner program you just read about, also has the capability to work as a prevention utility. You can install Disinfectant as a startup INIT by choosing the **Protect/Install Protection INIT** menu item. For further information on this matter and more details on all of Disinfectant's features, don't forget to read the documentation, which you can easily find by selecting **Disinfectant Help** from the Apple menu in the upper-left corner of the screen. Once it's installed for startup, Disinfectant runs upon startup and sits in the background leering for the little boogery viruses. It alerts you if it sniffs one out.

Again, it's important to remain up-to-date with these sorts of programs to keep up with the ever-changing world of viruses. So try to retrieve new versions of the programs from their respective FTP sites on a periodic basis. Check every couple of months to be safe.

Cleaning the Tubes

Suppose the worst is true: Bob Hope is funny. Oops, I meant, suppose your virus scanner or virus prevention program reports that you have a *nasty*. (It's amazing—and convenient—how well the medical model analogy works for this topic!) What do you do? Get a second opinion!

As it happens, some virus detection programs can actually confuse other such programs. For example, if you are running a virus prevention program that sits in the background (such as VSHIELD), a virus scanner might see that little program wedged into memory and think that it is a virus. So if you run a virus scan and find a hit, try another virus scanner and see what it says. It may agree; it may not find it at all; or it may conflict. If you're using new, up-to-date scanners and you get reasonably congruent analyses of your system, you can be more assured that you do, in fact, have a virus before you actually perform surgery.

In most cases, *surgery* is too severe a word. You probably won't have to reformat your entire hard disk and wipe your system clean to remove the viral infection. Of course, that is *probably*. If you've been receiving infected software for months and taking no precautions, and you have corrupted everything on your hard drive, you may have to wipe it all clean. However, if that's you, you would have noticed something was awry by now, and you'd be in too much of a panic to have gotten this far in the book. (Unless you're standing in the bookstore flipping through this book, hoping that the clerks don't figure out that you're trying to read the entire thing in small portions on each trip back. But they know. I know. We all know.)

If your virus scanner reports that only a small number of files are infected, and if you have properly backed up those files previously, run a virus scan on the backups. Hopefully, you managed to back them up before they became infected. If so, you simply insert the backup floppy (write-protected!) and restore the files on your hard drive from that. Then rescan the system to be sure.

When Your Backup Doesn't Back You Up

If you don't have backups, or there are too many files to backup, or you just don't want to use backups, the next most popular step is to use a *disinfectant* program. Generally, good scanners and prevention utilities (such as those I mentioned earlier) offer disinfectant capabilities that you can use if you spot a virus.

For example, let's look again at the F-PROT program. When you choose **Scan** from the main menu in F-PROT, you see the Action option. This defaults to **Report only**. However, if you click on the **Action** option, six options appear in addition to **Report only** (see the following figure).

Choose **Disinfect/Query** to have F-PROT ask you about disinfecting each individual file that is found to have a virus. On the other hand, choose **Automatic disinfection** to have F-PROT bypass asking you for confirmation. (I prefer being queried because it prevents the computer from just going off and doing whatever it wants unsupervised.) There may be a file that you'd like to leave alone for the time being; querying lets you have some say in the matter.

Below these two options is another pair of query/automatic choices, in this case, for deleting the file. If you don't need the file, it's best to delete it. However, if you haven't got a backup and you need the file, stick with disinfection. Lastly, there's a pair of choices for renaming the file in case you want to "hold" the supposedly infected file (perhaps for further examination later) but don't want it to have the same file name it did before.

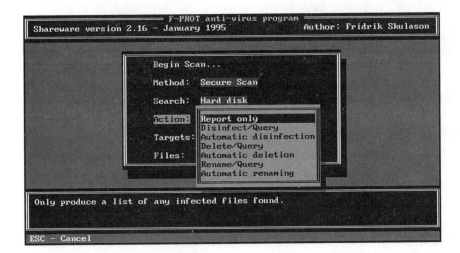

The possible actions F-PROT can take if it finds a virus on your system.

Macintosh people will once again rely on Disinfectant. In fact, Disinfectant's menu options under Disinfect are exactly the same as those under Scan. The only difference in this process is that after you select the portion of your system to work on and the program scans it, the program goes ahead to disinfect any problems. Simple enough? So, if when you scanned your system previously, Disinfectant reported problems, select the same portion of the system (such as **All disks**) from the **Disinfect** menu, and the program holds your hand through the clean-up process. The Mac sure is an easy computer.

In the worst-case scenario, where so many files and programs on your computer are infected and/or corrupted that disinfecting is not feasible, you may have to wipe the system clean. Hopefully, you have a clean, virus-free backup of your system—or at least the vital parts— that you can restore from. If not, well, there's not a whole lot one can say or do in such a situation, except that Hallmark has a new possible market in our digital age: "Deepest Sympathies on the Loss of Your File System." In any case, if this fate does befall you, it's best to consult an expert on your particular computer platform to find out how to go about completely wiping it clean and rebuilding.

What Does It Mean?

Disinfect, in the case of computer viruses, means that the program will try to remove the virus from the infected file but otherwise leave the file intact. If you have a clean backup of the file, it's probably safer to delete the infected file and copy the clean one from the backup. But if you have no other way out, disinfecting is your only option.

The Least You Need to Know

Computer viruses are, to put it frankly, a pain in the butt—and sometimes much worse. Unlike biological viruses, there's not even an arguable reason for them to exist; all of this education, prevention, protection, and disinfection is necessary because a frighteningly large number of humans have serious problems. Oh well, cynical reflections on human nature are better left to cab drivers. We have viruses to defend ourselves against.

➤ It's *viruses* not *virii*! Yes it is! Is so.

➤ Not every computer platform is at equal risk of being infected by viruses. PC clones are the highest risk machines; Macs face risk of a much lesser degree; UNIX systems face virtually no virus threat at this point in time.

➤ Viruses are computer programs, and as such, they must be executed to infect a computer and that computer's files. This means that a viable virus can only be carried by an executable program, not a data file.

➤ Viruses can work in a variety of ways, but ultimately their mission is to spread to as many portions of your system as possible. Whether or not they are programmed to be malicious, the mere act of spreading can probably result in damage to your data.

➤ As the human operator, you are the first line of defense against viral invasion. Don't take programs from little-known sources; watch for unusual system activity such as hard drive access or hard drive free space reduction; and be disciplined about backing up important programs and data on floppies. Always keep floppies write-protected except during the minimum amount of time necessary to copy files to them.

➤ Your next defenses are virus scanners, detectors, and disinfectants. Find the latest of each (in some cases, one program does it all) for your computer platform, and get updates every couple of months.

Part 2
Stepping Up and Online

or "So what does any of this have to do with the Net?"

Not merely a delay tactic, this section offers an overview of methods for connecting to the Net, which is important in ways other than the obvious (not being connected would be a serious hindrance to file transfers). Because much of the remainder of the book rests upon what sort of connection you have, this section sets out to make clear which is which, what is what, A is A, and so on.

This section ends with a chapter that surveys the landscape of files online. Still-interested readers will be salivating on the edge of preparedness.

Your Modem and You

There's more than one way to move files from one computer to another. If you're like most people, you have a dog, an improper-fraction-number of children, a mortgage, and a *modem*. That small, cute, cheap modem is the most popular technology used to connect one computer to other computers. All interaction between you and the Internet or any online service is mediated by your modem, which is why it makes a teeny bit of sense for you to know a thing or two about it—including how to regulate its operation and how to read cryptic diagnostic messages. This chapter sets the lofty goal of trying to explain all that—and provide spiritual enlightenment as a bonus.

Meet Your Modem

Modems (like most modern technology, grandmothers, and muscles) have shrunk over time. Despite all that, its function has remained the same. Modems exist because of

Alexander Graham Bell's lack of superhuman foresight. While computers love to chat with one another, they talk *digital talk*, and when Bell created the telephone, he didn't accommodate digital talk.

As you learned in Chapter 2, the computer has a limited language that consists of series of only two magic numbers: 0s and 1s. The problem is that phone lines don't talk the binary language. In fact, they don't talk any language; they just transmit the sounds that vibrate through the microphone in your telephone receiver. Enter our hero: the modem. The modem takes the computer's binary language and translates it into sounds that can be played over the phone line. On the receiving end, another modem listens to these sounds and turns them back into binary digital data. Not a very elegant solution, but you do what you gotta do.

The most important—and the most advertised—feature of any modem is how fast it performs these transformations and, therefore, how fast it sends and receives data. Many, many variables affect the speed with which the modem transfers data over a phone line. You have control over only some of these variables. The main one to consider is written in huge numbers all over the packaging: *baud rate*.

You usually see these particular numbers when shopping for baud rates: 2,400, 9,600, 14,400, and 28,800. What these numbers actually stand for is the nonobvious term: *kilobits per second*. The short explanation is that the more kilobits per second the modem can handle, the faster it'll transfer data. And that's a good thing—it saves time and money.

The Long Explanation...

The long explanation for kilobits per second goes a little something like this (kick out the jams, please).

There are 8 bits in a byte. A 14.4kbps modem can transfer data at a maximum speed of 14,400 bits/8 bits in a byte seconds. Do the dirty math, and you get 1,800 bytes per second (about 1.75K/sec). Now, the 8-bit calculation is a bit erroneous, as there some extra bits tacked on for control purposes. Some people advise to divide the kbps rate by 10 instead of 8, in which case you wind up with 1,440 bits per second. The reality is somewhere in-between: most files transfer at about 1,600–1,650 bits per second on a 14.4kbps modem connection. Therefore, a 28.8kbps modem can transfer data at twice that speed and cut transfer times by 50%. However, 28.8kbps connections are difficult to achieve over less-than-perfect phone lines. Nonetheless, 28.8 modems can usually fly faster than 14.4 modems, even on imperfect phone lines.

There are, however, a few limiting factors. These numbers represent the *maximum* speed at which the modem can transmit data. How close to the maximum you can actually reach in practice is limited by two main variables:

➤ **The speed of the modem on the other end of the connection.** You can't transmit data any faster than the slower of the two modems. So even if you have a blazing 28.8kbps modem, if the modem you're connecting to is 2,400kbps, that slows down the transfer speed to a crawl. The solution to this one is to make sure you connect to places (usually Internet service providers) whose modems are as fast or faster (in case you upgrade) than yours.

➤ **The quality of the phone line in your quarters, and elsewhere.** The faster you ask the modem to go (up to its limit), the more difficult its task is. The world's phone lines just weren't meant for this sort of thing, and the more data you try to push through at a faster rate, the more data you're likely to lose. When you lose data, the modem has to resend it, which adds inefficiency into the transfer, slowing it down even more.

If there is interference anywhere on the phone line between you and the destination, problems can prevent you from reaching maximum speeds—especially when you're asking for 14.4kbps and 28.8kbps connections. Most often, this interference is in the lines between you and your local phone company and stems from the wiring in your quarters (house, office, whatever). Older buildings with older wiring are more subject to problems when trying to achieve maximum *throughput*. Additionally, there isn't just one cable connecting your modem to the destination modem. The phone company routes your call through a whole pachinko game of switches and intersections. This is far from ideal.

In addition to their throughput, most modems have other features such as *error-correction* and *data compression*. These are useful features that help keep the throughput level up. Compression tells the modem to attempt to compress the data as it transfers. This helps with files that were not compressed previous to transfer. Although both error-correction and data compression are important features, I can't recall any name-brand modem that works at any of the higher speeds (14.4 and 28.8) that doesn't have these features. However, that doesn't mean all modems are created equal.

If reliability is important to you, it's probably a good idea to buy one of the bigger name-brand modems. Peruse the UseNet newsgroup

Throughput
A macho computer term that refers to how much data you can push through the lines in a given time period. It's usually measured in kilobits per second. Somewhat like the maximum speed of a car, people talk about it with nearly as much bravado. They're true geeks. Admire them.

comp.dcom.modems for up-to-date discussion and debate about the latest and greatest modems (and prices) before you buy! No matter what, there's not much reason to spend money on a low-end modem that's slower than 9,600kbps. The cost of a 14.4kbps modem has dropped dramatically, and it's well worth it compared to the cost of a much slower modem. Even 28.8kbps modems will be affordable for most people soon—probably by the time you read this book.

Whither the Poor Modem?

Just how much faster are modems going to get? Are you going to have to upgrade constantly? Most computer users are used to this love/hate treadmill by now. But in the field of modems, there's good news on the horizon—for us users, not the modems. The truth is that the current phone lines are basically maxed out. They have enough trouble handling 28.8kbps connections; there's little chance that modems can possibly achieve rates higher than that on any consistent, reasonable basis.

Does this mean we've reached the end of throughput increases? Ah, not at all. Actually, the possibilities really open up now. Up till now, phone lines have been the biggest burden. But maxing out their capacity will be a great thing for the computing world: now, we have to develop alternatives to using traditional phone lines. And in fact, that's already been done. Alternatives already exist that finally let the computer speak its own language (without awkward conversion to sounds) and, therefore, boost throughput rates enormously.

Two technologies on the horizon are already in use by some lucky people:

➤ **ISDN** Called an "Integrated Services Digital Network" by people who wear photo IDs, this is something you'll hear about more and more in the near future. Because the phone line between you and your local phone company is often the weakest link, the phone companies have begun to replace these "local loops" with digital lines. Most of the lines that crisscross the country are already digital; it's these pesky lines coming out of your houses that have been a real problem. Once they replace those lines, you can ditch the modem, get a newfangled (and currently expensive) device to hook your computer into the wall, and expect transfer rates at least five times faster than those of the fastest current modems—64kbps and sometimes 128kbps.

➤ **Cable** Cable companies have a gold mine at their feet, and they're beginning to see it shine. Those lines that carry Flow-Bee infomercials into your home can also carry data—at massive speeds, in fact. How does 500kbps sound? What about 4mbps (that's 4 *million* bits per second). The speeds will vary depending on cable companies' technology and competence (!), but the turtle-like modems we have now can't even compete with these numbers.

Wedded Bliss for Your PC and Modem

Fortunately, connecting a modem to your computer is usually pretty easy. I'm going to assume that if you own a modem it's already connected physically (that topic is beyond the scope of this book, and the modem manual probably explains it adequately). The real problem lies in the complexity of the situation.

The modem is essentially a minicomputer of its own. As such, it accepts commands that alter aspects of its behavior. The intimidating thing is that there are about nine million commands. The less intimidating thing is that you *probably* won't need to use more than a couple of them under normal circumstances.

Most modems are instructed by a set of commands known as *AT commands*. (Coincidentally, all modem commands begin with the letters AT. That means "Attention" and lets the modem know you're speaking to it.) You enter these commands using a *terminal program* (which I discuss in Chapters 10 and 11). While terminal programs vary in their capabilities to achieve the things you'll achieve as you work through this book, they all let you send the modem some commands. Both Windows 3.x and Windows 95 come with a terminal program (Terminal in Windows 3.x and HyperTerminal in Windows 95); Mac users can find the very popular Zterm program relatively easily.

The simplest command you can send the modem, just to see if it's alive and well, is **at**. Fire up your terminal program, type **at** and hit **Enter**. You'll see this:

```
at
OK
```

That's the modem saying "OK" to let you know it's alive and well. The following figure shows the terminal program PROCOMM PLUS for Windows 95. Notice the AT command and the modem's response. It's that simple.

AT commands vary slightly for different modems; your modem's manual will include a list of all the AT commands it understands. Hopefully, there is also an accompanying manual that explains the function of each command. Many of the functions are going to seem extremely esoteric and nonsensical (except to modem geeks). That's okay. You won't need to use many of them for normal use.

Most modems have factory default settings that work on most computer configurations. You can sometimes invoke these configurations by using the **AT &F***x* command (where *x* is a number); that is a detail your manual will explain. The computer will return to the settings saved in "memory bank 0" when you power it on or reset it using the **AT Z** command. To save your current modem settings and make them the defaults, use the **AT &W** command.

You communicate with the modem using a terminal program and AT commands.

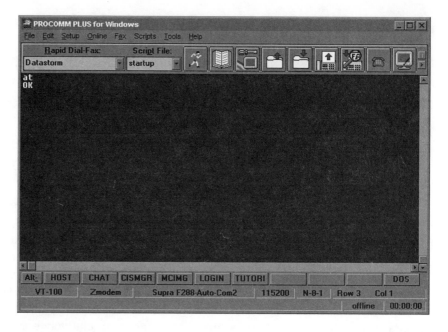

Output? Yes, But Not Much I'm not including the output of these commands because (as usual) the modem only says "OK" to each one. Not very telling, but it doesn't much like talking to people.

Some Internet service providers require that your modem use certain *init strings*, which means you need a special configuration for that provider. An init string is a series of modem commands sent to the modem before it can dial and connect to anywhere. An init string might look something like this:

AT &w0 &q0 &m1 &n

Most terminal programs allow you to define the init string for your modem. If your service provider requires a certain init string, you can insert it into the terminal program you use. Your service provider will tell you what command to use if necessary (I can't predict it because there are too many possibilities).

Who's to Blame? The PC Factor

On the other end of the modem/computer connection, your computer controls some variables that can affect proper modem operation. The computer doesn't actually affect the modem, as such, but it does have jurisdiction over the port your modem is hooked into. This port, sometimes called a *COM port* on a PC or a *serial port* on other computers, handles the transfer of data between the computer and the modem. The computer controls certain characteristics of this port, such as what speed it works at.

Most terminal programs allow you to set options to control this port. The following list explains those options and provides guidelines on how you should set them:

Baud Rate   Defines the maximum rate at which your modem can transfer data. This can be tricky. Normally, you would think that an owner of a 14.4kbps modem would choose a baud rate of 14,400. However, don't forget about file compression. The modem will attempt to compress data coming through it and will be most successful (as all compression schemes are) with plain text files. Given perfect compression circumstances, the modem can actually increase its throughput by four times (not by increasing the speed at which it transfers data, but by decreasing the amount of data it has to transfer). For this reason, you should normally set the baud rate to four times the speed of your modem. Thus, 14.4kbps modem users should choose 57,600, and 28.8kbps users should choose 115,200.

However, some computers—and more often some serial ports—have trouble transferring data at these maximum speeds even if the modem is capable. If you notice that you are losing characters in your connection (letters are missing, for example), try lowering the baud rate one notch (i.e. lower it to 38,400 or 57,600). Note that you shouldn't change this value while connected; you must change it before you dial.

Parity   I have seen few modern connections that require a parity other than **None**, so choose that. If your provider requires something different, they'll tell you what to set it to.

Data bits   Again, I rarely see this vary. The common selection is **8**, so use 8 unless a specific provider tells you differently (I wouldn't bet on it, though).

Stop bits   Another option with an easy choice. Choose **1** (again, unless you are specifically told otherwise). It's what everyone's doing these days.

Duplex   This determines whether your modem can communicate in a two-way or one-way manner with the other modem. If this isn't getting too monotonous, I haven't seen a modem that required Half duplex in ages. Choose **Full**.

Software Flow Control Xon/Xoff   To perform the "traffic cop" function of regulating the flow of data, the modem uses certain signals. The traffic cop role can be performed in either of two ways: in the software brain of the computer (Xon/Xoff) or in the hardware cabling inside your modem cable (called *hardware handshaking* or *RTS/CTS*). The latter is much preferred and is more likely to maintain maximum transfer speeds. Therefore, try to get a modem cable that supports hardware handshaking. If your modem came with a cable, you can be pretty confident that it does. If your modem did not come with a cable, ask a knowledgeable salesperson in any computer store to help you find one that supports handshaking.

69

If you have a cable that supports hardware handshaking, you do *not* want Xon/Xoff enabled, so make sure it is off (unchecked). You *do* want RTS/CTS enabled; however, this option may be under a different settings menu in your terminal program. Either refer to the terminal program's manual or just poke around. When you find the RTS/CTS setting, make sure it is enabled. If you fail to find an appropriate cable or you are in a pinch, enable Xon/Xoff and disable RTS/CTS.

What to Expect—and What Not to—from Your Baudfriend 2,000

A modem isn't a perfect device. Sometimes a problem is the modem's fault, and sometimes it is the fault of the world around it. There are just so many variables that go into maintaining smooth communications that it's like choosing wallpaper. The basic formula to use when working with modems is this: the more you expect from it, the more likely it will fail. Pessimistic? To a degree, but that's the way it works.

What does that mean? If you expect to transfer a 90 megabyte file over a 14.4kbps modem—a transfer that would take many, many hours *without* problems—well, expect again. Line quality often fluctuates during a connection. The faster the connection is and the longer the duration is, the more likely it is that line quality will hit an unsustainable level. The modem may slow down, or it may just hang up (disconnect). Many modems have trouble maintaining connections for extremely long periods of time. In general, higher-end modems (such as those that BBSs and service providers use) are more able to maintain very long, even 24-hour connections. Lower-end modems, which are more common for home use, are going to be more spotty in maintaining long-duration connections. Some will, some won't.

While 28.8kbps is considered "blazing" by today's modem standards, programs and data files are growing larger and larger. Consider one of the largest types of data files, the MPEG video stream. These can often reach several megs in size for a rather brief duration of video. And even on a 28.8kbps modem, they are going to take more than a few minutes to download. At the maximum, you can expect to download such files at a rate of about 1.4 megs every 8 minutes at 28.8kbps. If you're one of those people who enjoy "surfing the Web," keep in mind that even at 28.8kbps, many graphics-heavy Web sites will take several minutes to download fully. Fortunately, as alternative communications technologies such as ISDN and cable begin to replace our modems, these problems will lessen.

Certainly, if you own a slow modem (such as a 2,400 baud), don't expect to be incredibly productive. It will suffice for very simple operations such as transmitting small amounts of text to a file or your screen, but that is about it. Modern applications just require too much data for 2,400 baud modems to be of any practical use.

Checking the Oil: Diagnostics

Your modem probably has a bunch of little lights on it. Yeah, they flash, and they're neat. But they also provide you with some information. This information can be, at least, a crude way for you to see what's going on in the mind of the modem. At best, it might help you solve some problems.

Different modems have different forms of information displays, depending on the manufacturer's design. Many modems only have a short series of lights along the front panel or on top. Each light has a cryptic label, and some stay on, some stay off, and some flash. Let's consider what some of these lights tell you.

On-Hook   This may be displayed as **OH** on your modem. Generally, if this light is on, the modem is on the phone line. Surprisingly, if it's off, the modem is off the phone line. Keep in mind that you cannot use another hand-held phone on the same line when the modem is using the line. If you pick up another phone while the modem is online, you will destroy the modem connection and, therefore, interrupt any data transfer that is taking place.

Receive Data/RD/Rx   Different modems label this light differently, but all of these indicate that the modem is receiving incoming data. This light is usually on or flashing rapidly when the modem is downloading. It's a very good way to tell if data is coming into the modem. If this light goes off for any length of time during a download, something in the universe has gone awry. Then you yell and break stuff—or maybe that's just me. (Some modems may have combined this light and the Send Data light; if so, the light flashes in either condition, which makes it much more difficult to tell what's actually going on.)

Send Data/SD/Tx   This light indicates that your modem is sending data upstream to the remote modem. In normal use, this light flashes much less frequently than the Receive Data light does because you usually receive more data than you transmit. Again, some modems may have combined this light and the Receive Data light.

DTR/TR   This is a strange light. It tells the status of the DTR signal, which is used to help determine whether the modem should be On-hook or Off-hook. Many terminal programs have an option such as "Drop DTR on quit." If you do drop the DTR, the modem usually hangs up—that is, unless you tell the modem to ignore the status of the DTR, which is what the **at &q0** modem command does. (I mentioned this earlier when we talked about how to prevent the modem from disconnecting when you quit your terminal program.)

Carrier Detect/CD   This signals when your modem receives a "hello" from the intended connection modem. It usually lights up when the connection has been made and lets you know the two modems are in communications with one another. Needless to say, if this light is not on, or if it goes off, you've lost all contact.

Some modems, such as the current Supra series, also include an LED display that gives more detailed information about the inner goings-on. These can be very useful. For example, this display enables the modem to tell you what speed it is connected at, if it has received any transmission errors, what form of compression it is using, and so on. The accompanying manuals for your specific modem are a better source of enlightenment on that particular topic.

The Least You Need to Know

Because the modem is your link between your computer and the world—or at least, other computers—it's nice to know a thing or three about it. A modem is not a perfect device, but that's more Alexander Graham Bell's fault than the modem manufacturer's fault. The manufacturers are just trying to work around Bell's unforgivable lack of foresight.

➤ You need a modem to convert digital information into sounds suitable for the phone lines and to convert the sounds back into digital information. If you've ever picked up the phone when a modem was calling you, you know what this sounds like. It's not pretty, but it works most of the time.

➤ The modem's speed is probably its most important feature. Speed is commonly measured in kilobits per second; the higher the number, the faster the modem. For almost all uses, you should consider only 14.4kbps and 28.8kbps modems—the latter being the fastest on the market today.

➤ The proper function of your modem depends on two players: the modem's internal configuration and the configuration of the computer's port where the modem is plugged in (usually the serial port). Defaults on both sides of most modern systems usually work fine, but this chapter details some of the things to look out for on both sides.

➤ You use a terminal program to instruct the modem; it is the interface between the modem and yourself. You can often adjust the computer's port settings using the terminal program, too.

➤ Understand the diagnostic lights on your modem so you can tell that everything is working properly and you can have a peaceful state of mind. If you don't under-stand the lights, things may be going wrong. (And although you might not want to know, you really should.)

## Chapter 8

Plugged In, Turned On, Too Cool: Your Internet Connection

In This Chapter

➤ Playing dumb, or emulating it anyway

➤ TCP/IP fluency

➤ The Ying and Yang of preference

➤ Parting ways

Any self-respecting Internet writer avoids vehicular metaphors, having seen them co-opted into so many headlines of cool. But in the case of this chapter, one just can't resist.

There's more than one way to get to the airport. Drive your own car, call a taxi, rent a limo, or sucker a friend—each has its pros and cons. When you drive your own car, you control your trip, but you're restricted by your car's limitations (depending on what you were able to afford). When you rent a vehicle or ask someone else to take you, you can make use of better equipped hardware (air conditioning, leather seats, and dry bar maybe), but you may lose control of the trip. Regardless of which you choose, you will probably get to the airport—or at least to the filled-up parking lot.

And so it is with the Internet: you can use a number of different vehicles to reach the same destination, but which you choose will affect many of the operations you undertake. In this chapter, we'll look at the most common ways you can connect to the Internet (with respect to downloading) so you can understand which is best for you. Then we'll do the dance of joy.

The Easy Way: Dumb Terminals

Back in olden times when horses ruled the streets and people ate oatmeal regularly, powerful computers were too large and expensive to plop onto every desk. I'm talking about 1980, of course. Nonetheless, even back then people needed to use computers (mostly to write FORTRAN programs in concrete university buildings). What was common then was to have one "machine room" filled with large, noisy, powerful computers that could perform about as well as your 386—but they were impressive at the time.

Sprinkled around the local area of the machine room (in adjacent offices, around campus, and so on) were *dumb terminals*. In essence, these were keyboards and monitors at which you could sit and access the *mainframe* computer in the machine room. The dumb terminal would simply pass along whatever you typed to the mainframe. The mainframe would interpret your commands, produce results, and send those back to the monitor at your dumb terminal. The dumb terminal had no real computing skills of its own other than displaying and formatting text on a screen and accepting keystrokes.

While one might think that dumb terminals might as well be in a landfill today, the Internet has actually given rise to a new, good reason for their existence. Internet *service providers* have sprung up who can afford the hardware and connections necessary to maintain high-speed, highly reliable Internet access. Most people don't have such resources, so they pay for a share of the service provider's. In essence, because the service provider's computer can "talk" on the Internet and yours cannot, you use his. That's one of the resources you pay for. Thus, this picture begins to look increasingly like the mainframe era.

For example, let's say you want to connect to an FTP site to retrieve some dandy new screen saver program. Your service provider's computer has access to the Internet and, therefore, FTP sites. So you need to tell it to connect to the site for you, to retrieve the file, and to send the file to your own computer. The way you instruct the service provider to do all these things is with—you guessed it—a dumb terminal. Well, sort of....

Technically, you don't own a dumb terminal; you probably own a PC or a Mac. But you can get software known as *terminal emulation* or *terminal program* software that makes your computer act dumb. Examples of terminal emulation programs

> **Check This Out...**
>
> **Remote**
> Whenever two computers talk to one another, one of them is the *local machine* and one is the *remote*. Which is which depends on where you're standing. The one you are at is local, and the one it connects to is remote. So when you dial up your service provider, your computer is local, and his is the remote. It does make sense actually.

for the PC include Terminal, a program included with Windows 3.1; HyperTerminal, a program included with Windows 95; and ProComm, which is a commercial product. Mac users might find such products as Zterm and ProTerm. These programs enable you to communicate via your modem with a remote computer, simulating the classic dumb terminal scenario. So while your entire computer is not actually a dumb terminal, when we use that term in this book, we're referring to *dumb terminal emulation*, the process of using a terminal program to access the Internet.

Candid Camera

The typical dumb terminal connection to the Internet goes a little something like this:

1. You fire up your terminal program. This does not involve fire, but probably requires a double-click on the proper desktop icon.

2. You dial up your Internet service provider. You may have created a script or phone book entry to do this (many terminal programs support such automation); if not, you just dial manually using the **atdt** command.

3. You get a busy signal. You're right, this *is* a bad and annoying thing, but it does happen. If it does, hang up and try again. If it does not, you're successfully connected, and you probably see a prompt to log in with a user name and password.

4. After you log in, you are connected to your service provider through whatever interface they offer. Most often, you see either a menu system or a plain UNIX shell. Assuming you've connected to this service provider before, you know what to do from here to take care of your Internet needs.

The following figure is an Idiot's Guide exclusive photo of this process in action; the photo was shot secretly somewhere north of the border. If this whole section describes the way you access the Internet, or more specifically your Internet account, you use dumb terminal emulation already.

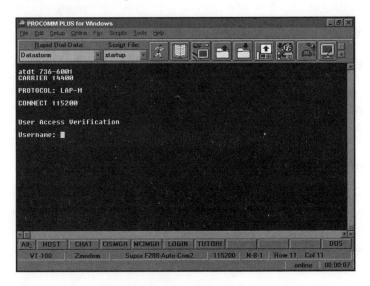

You connect to a service provider using dumb terminal emulation.

Squawkin' the TCP/IP Talk

The central theme in the dumb terminal scenario is that of a tangible middleman: one computer merely routes keystrokes to another, which interprets and processes them and the final results. In recent years, there has been a rise in the number of people who can avoid the middleman. Leapfrogging the middleman requires two elements: software that allows your computer to "speak" TCP/IP and a connection capable of communicating the necessary data. *TCP/IP* is the current form of communication that computers use to talk to one another on the Internet. Because numerous software packages handle TCP/IP, the software part has been the easier hurdle to overcome. The bigger problem has been the hardware connection.

Ethernet

In the past, the most popular form of TCP/IP connection has been via something known as *Ethernet*. Commonly used on college campuses and in networked businesses, Ethernet is essentially a cable used to connect one computer to another. Not only does it offer flexible communications capabilities (TCP/IP is just one of many forms of networking communications that can be used on Ethernet), but Ethernet is also very fast.

The problem is that it requires that computers be physically connected by the Ethernet cable. This, as you can imagine, is something of a problem for home users buying service from a provider. Stringing a cable directly from your provider's office to your living room is a very problematic solution: for one, people will trip over it, and more importantly, the Ethernet technology cannot support such lengths. So Ethernet is out as far as most people's Internet usage goes.

But the Cable's Cable...

You may be thinking, "But, the cable company has already strung a cable directly into my living room! Can't we make use of that?" And the answer may well be yes; I describe those *future possibilities* in a sidebar in Chapter 7. But right now, as I write this, the answer is still no for most people.

SLIP/PPP and Friends

Those computer hackers never stop thinking and tinkering. Fortunately, what they lose in personal hygiene, we gain in technology. So, instead of sleeping one night, they devised some software that allows TCP/IP communication over a modem. And it was good, and they named the baby *SLIP*, which obviously stands for *Serial Line IP*. If a service provider installs SLIP software, a user with a modem and the right TCP/IP software can dial up and "talk" on the Internet the same way that a user with an Ethernet-connected computer can. Very popular among users who no longer had to use their 486s as dumb terminals, SLIP became fruitful and multiplied.

Soon a contemporary known as *PPP (Point-to-Point Protocol)* came along. Although internally PPP works very differently from SLIP, it offers essentially the same functionality. Thus, today we often lob around the phrase "SLIP/PPP," which usually refers to using TCP/IP communications over a modem.

Most service providers offer both UNIX shell accounts (dumb terminal emulation) and SLIP/PPP accounts. The latter often tend to be more expensive and have greater time restrictions. To use a SLIP/PPP account, you don't use a terminal program like those I discussed earlier in the chapter. Instead, you use some form of TCP/IP software with a *dialer* that controls the modem and connects it to the provider. Users of Windows 3.1 will most likely use the popular shareware package Trumpet Winsock for this task, while Windows 95 users may take advantage of its built-in Dial-Up Networking

Check This Out...

For Clarity
SLIP, PPP, and Ethernet use different technologies and hardware to accomplish the same thing: TCP/IP communications on the Internet. So no matter which you use, you can follow the discussions on downloading using TCP/IP.

support. Mac users are likely to use MacTCP. Here are some shots of Trumpet Winsock and Windows 95's Dial-Up Networking, which you can compare with the terminal programs revealed earlier.

The Trumpet window displays any messages that Trumpet has for you. However, because most of its work is done behind the scenes, there isn't much to see really.

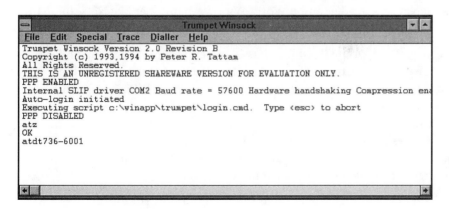

Trumpet Winsock TCP/IP software for Windows 3.x.

Dial-Up Networking is the feature in Windows 95 that gives modem users TCP/IP capabilities. Again, the action takes place inside the computer. The following figure shows some of the relevant windows that you use to launch Dial-Up Networking. You get to Dial-Up Networking via the My Computer icon.

Components of Dial-Up Networking, the TCP/IP software that's included with Windows 95.

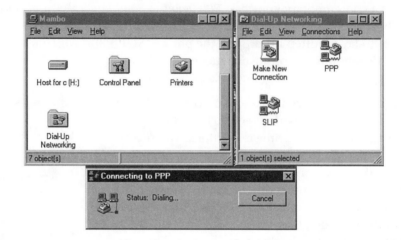

Which Is Better, Huh?

The TCP/IP connection (SLIP/PPP, for example) is certainly more flexible. Because you don't have to rely on a middleman to communicate for you, you have the freedom to use any software you'd like that's available for your computer. In addition, this software can take better advantage of your computer's own features, such as graphical interfaces and audio feedback. (On a dumb terminal, you must rely on text only.) Furthermore, using TCP/IP, you can often engage in multiple Internet tasks at the same time, such as opening a Telnet session, a UseNet newsreader, and a World Wide Web browser like Netscape. This is not nearly so easy using dumb terminal emulation.

On the other hand, you may face configuration hassles when getting TCP/IP up and running with a SLIP or PPP connection that you just don't run into when using dumb terminal emulation. In addition, more things can go wrong with TCP/IP. And decent TCP/IP places higher demands on your machine, whereas a dumb terminal emulation requires very little computing resources. So if you're chugging along on a 286 or a cheap portable, dumb terminal emulation may be your only feasible option. But, more room for problems and more demands on your system are basically par for the course when you talk about a technology that provides more capability.

Ultimately, which is best depends on what you use the Internet for. For example, if you enjoy browsing the World Wide Web in full-color graphics, a dumb terminal is not going to cut it. You need a SLIP/PPP account with the fastest connection speed you can get—probably a 28.8kbps modem (Ethernet would be even better, if that's available to you). On the other hand, if all you do is use e-mail and perhaps read some UseNet news every now and then, a dumb terminal will do the job just fine, even with a modem as slow as 9600 or 2400 baud.

In the end, whether you choose to use dumb terminal emulation (with a menu-based or UNIX account) or full-blown TCP/IP access depends on what you can afford, what you use the Internet for, and what type of hardware you have. Neither one is better than the other in all circumstances for all people. No matter which course you take, though, it is important to understand the distinctions between the two. The following lists help you do just that.

Dumb Terminal Emulation	TCP/IP Connection (SLIP/PPP)
Very simple to connect and log on to	Potential configuration pitfalls
Reasonably useful on slower modems	Truly benefits from 14.4 and 28.8kbps modems
File transfers monopolize entire connection	Can perform several simultaneous tasks
No graphical Web browsing	Potential for full-color Web browsing
Must use 2-step download process	Can download directly from Net
Must use menus or UNIX shells	Easy-to-use graphical interfaces
Overall, good for simple tasks	Overall, overkill for simple tasks such as plain e-mail; great for "serious" Net use

A Fork in the Road

After all, there is a reason why all this matters—and it's not just for the pure sake of knowledge. As advertised, this book is allegedly about downloading, even though we haven't discussed actual "downloading" yet. It's a slow build. At the heart of it, the concept and practice behind downloading is completely different depending on whether you are using a dumb terminal or a TCP/IP connection. Therefore, this chapter marks a major fork in the road: the subsequent sections, Parts 3 and 4, focus on each type of connection individually and how to transfer files using that connection. The aforementioned middleman is responsible for many of these differences, but that doesn't mean you should read only the section that's immediately useful to you.

The Least You Need to Know

Because the procedures for transferring files differ, you need to understand the distinction between the major types of Internet connections. The majority of you will use modems for either dumb terminal emulation or SLIP/PPP TCP/IP emulation. Know thyself.

➤ The dumb terminal relies on a middleman to communicate with the Internet; this middleman is your service provider. Using dumb terminal emulation, you send keystrokes to your provider's computer, which then interprets them, processes them, and sends you back the text-based results.

➤ TCP/IP is the form of communication that computers on the Internet use to talk to one another. With the right software, your computer can speak TCP/IP, and with a provider who can provide the right connection, you can skip the middleman and communicate directly over the Internet.

➤ The "right connection" could mean specific hardware such as Ethernet or, more commonly, a modem and a service provider who can provide TCP/IP emulation (known as SLIP or PPP).

➤ Neither dumb terminal emulation nor SLIP/PPP is wholly better than the other; they are suited for different purposes.

UH... GO
ASK YOUR
FATHER.

## Chapter 9

"Mommy, Where Do Computer Files on the Internet Come From?"

In This Chapter

➤ Where the files are

➤ Where the files were

➤ Like a file in a datastack, the search goes on

If we're going to talk about transferring files, and I promise that we will, it would be nice to know where to find files in the first place. There certainly will be times when you already have the file you want to transfer, but many times, you'll want to draw from the vast warehouse of data that is the Internet. To develop another absurd analogy, imagine one of those ever-popular "depot" stores. You know, the ones where the distributors got so lazy they just left everything in boxes, stacked the boxes on shelves that reach from floor to ceiling, and opened the doors to the public so you could trek down the highway and purchase 20-gallon tubs of mustard and pickled beets. Similarly, on the Internet, some items are difficult to find or hard to reach, and there isn't a hired staff to help you. Good thing for the publishing market....

They Come by FTP, Gopher, and Even the Web

Line of Sites The word *site* pops up a lot in Internet discourse, but it really just means a computer. So an FTP site is just a remote computer containing files that are available for retrieval, and space in which files can be placed. A site address looks the same as any computer user's address on the Internet (such as ftp.bob.com).

By its nature, the Internet is something of a scattered potpourri of information and data. It reminds me of those children's arcade games in which they pluck a toy from a heap with a crane-arm; all the information is there, but you need to use the "right" crane to pluck certain sorts of data. Some of the tools you can use to get this data include Gopher, UseNet, WAIS, the Web, and FTP. Each can draw certain sorts of data from the Internet, although there is also plenty of overlap in their uses. One of the most commonly used and most capable retrieval resources is FTP.

By design, FTP is perhaps the "purest" of the file-based resources on the Internet. (Its acronym stands for File Transfer Protocol, so you see that its mission is clear: it tells the computer how to get a file from one place to another.) An *FTP site* is basically a computer that stores a whole bunch of files. More often than not, the files in a given site are related in one way or another. For example, one FTP site might contain images of space, or (more likely) a site will contain several categories of images, such as space and farm animals. Moving up one level, a particular FTP site might contain a set of sounds and a set of images. Basically, what the site holds depends on how much storage space the site has and what its owners want to carry.

Client A paying customer. Seriously, in computer-ese, a client is a program that requests and receives information from another program (called a server). Think of it this way: the client is like the patron in a restaurant who requests food from the waiter (the server). Unfortunately, computer programs don't tip so well.

FTP sites are the most popular form of file storage on the Internet, and you will encounter many of them. Of course, the files will almost always be stored in archived and compressed formats. You access FTP sites using an *FTP client* (you'll learn more about FTP clients in Chapter 16). An FTP client enables you to transfer files from or to an FTP site.

Whereas FTP is a file-retrieval system, Gopher is more appropriately an *information retrieval system*. Because it has recently lost popularity to the World Wide Web, you may not have used Gopher before. Essentially, it is a text-based hierarchical information system in which you move your way up and down through menus (see the following figure). You connect to a Gopher site, weave your way through the information it provides, and retrieve whatever information you're looking for. (Sometimes that "information" is in fact a file, which does make Gopher a sort of file-retrieval system.) As with FTP, you access a Gopher site with a Gopher client—another topic discussed a bit more in-depth when the time is right. No clients before their time, as they say.

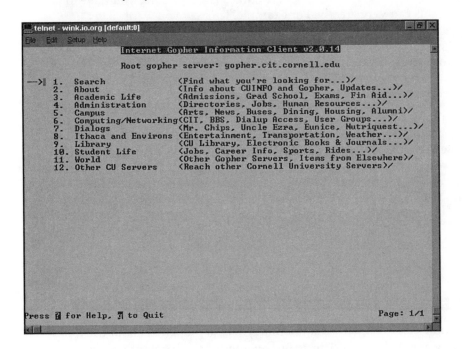

A Gopher menu. That's all.

Similar to an information retrieval system is the massively popular World Wide Web. Somewhat like Gopher on steroids, the Web also allows you to weave through information, but in a much more flexible way than does Gopher's rigid hierarchical system. Not surprisingly, you access the Web with a Web client (or *browser*). You may have used the Web already with a popular Web client such as Mosaic or Netscape.

One of the powerful features of a Web browser is its capability to retrieve information that is a superset of Gopher or FTP. By that, I mean that a Web browser can actually access FTP sites and Gopher sites in addition to standard Web (HTTP) sites. The major advantage of this is that you can use a Web browser to retrieve files from virtually any other aisle on the Net. However, that doesn't render programs such as FTP clients completely obsolete; the Web browser may be less flexible than the FTP client.

Flexible Shmexible

While any FTP client can retrieve a file from an FTP site, and any Web browser can also retrieve a file from an FTP site, that doesn't mean the FTP client and the Web browser are equal. The flexibility you have in doing this can vary greatly. For example, let's say you want to get multiple files from a particular site. With a graphical FTP client (such as WS_FTP, which I cover later in the book), you can select each file you want to download. Web browsers, on the other hand, usually download a selected file immediately, which means you have to download one at a time. That makes it difficult to automate a large transfer so you can go to the can (john/lou/latrine).

But wait, there's more! What if you want to download all the files that begin with the letters d-o-g? Some FTP clients (especially in UNIX) allow you to request all files matching specified criteria, which can be very convenient. Even many graphical FTP clients don't let you do this, and Web browsers certainly do not. Lastly, consider uploading. With an FTP client, you can send a file from your computer to the remote site; with a Web browser, you cannot.

The moral of this story is that although several applications can handle the same sorts of protocols, they are not necessarily equally adept at it.

They Even Come by UseNet, If You Know the Secret

Way, way back in some early chapter (Chapter 3 maybe?), we laughed about the differences between binary and ASCII data. This issue becomes very important on UseNet, which was set up for the purpose of discussion groups instead of file transfer. However, over time, people wanted to trade files as well as ideas, and the binary vs. ASCII problem arose. As you may remember, most data files such as pictures and sounds are in binary 8-bit format. But UseNet is designed to handle 7-bit ASCII data. So some genius came up with a way to turn binary data into ASCII and then convert it back to binary, at least for the purpose of file transfer.

The conversion process is known as *uuencoding*. You don't really need to know how this works to use it. The idea is to use extra 7-bit characters to represent non-ASCII 8-bit characters; then, after the file is transferred, it is converted back to its original 7-bit format by a process called *uudecoding*. Because it takes more than one ASCII character to represent an 8-bit character, a uuencoded file will be approximately 30% larger than its binary original. What people do, then, is uuencode a binary file that they want to post to UseNet and post the resulting ASCII file. When a UseNet reader decides he wants the file, he saves the post and then uudecodes it. That's the theory. You'll see the practical execution of this process in Chapter 18, which just happens to be about this very topic.

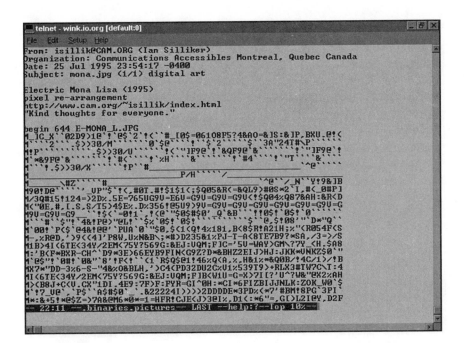

A UseNet posting of a uuencoded binary file. The ASCII representation of 8-bit data is not so easy on the eyes.

The universe being what it is, nothing is quite so simple as it's intended to be (especially those child-proof aspirin caps). Many people cannot receive posts that are extremely large. It's all well and good if you have a lovely 950k GIF of a Ferrari that you want to share with the world (in the appropriate newsgroup!). But when you uuencode that file, you're looking at a ball of data more than 1 megabyte in size. Many people do not have the capability to receive such files. Therefore, another convention was born: *multipart posting*.

Often when a person wants to upload a large file, she splits up the uuencoded file into multiple smaller parts and posts each part to the newsgroup. That way, anyone can download each part, tie the parts back together, and then uudecode them. The following figure shows a multipart uuencoded file.

Yeah, I know this seems like a lot of work. And the truth is, it once was. But hey, this is the age of computers! What better application than to have computers save you time while computing? (DISCLAIMER: The above was a highly recursive concept. Que is not responsible for exploding heads.) Actually, the tasks of uuencoding, multipart splitting, and their opposites can all be automated by contemporary newsreaders. The details vary from newsreader to newsreader. We'll look at some examples of actual downloading from UseNet in later chapters.

This JPG graphic file is split into five parts; part 0 is simply a small description file.

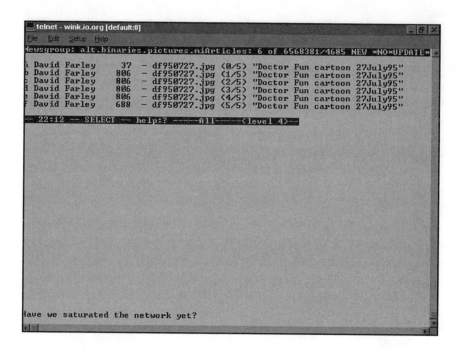

But You Don't Know Where They've Been

In light of Chapter 6 and computer viruses, it's worth paying some attention to where you scavenge files from. This is far from a scientific process, but rather one of practiced caution. If you go shopping for a Mickey Mouse sweater in the city, you're more likely to get the genuine thing at the Disney Store than from Carlos on the corner.

Assuming you don't want to catch any computer viruses, you can lessen the risk by sticking to high-profile, well-maintained sites. No one can guarantee that you won't get an infected file from any source. Even the online services (such as America Online) who scan their files beforehand, cannot positively guarantee safety. However, some of the major software distribution sites have maintainers who may scan for viruses; at least if they find one, they will be quick about notifying users and removing the culpable file.

Granted, many sites don't really fit into the category of "major," but they are the only places to get particular files. That's one reason why this is a guideline and not an empirical law. But, I do want to contrast the above with the other extreme.

Let's say you're skimming through the UseNet newsgroup **alt.binaries.utilities**, and someone posts a multipart binary of some claimed fantastic kaleidoscope demo. Grabbing this file is essentially the equivalent of buying your Mickey Mouse sweater from Carlos on the street corner. Not one to incite rampant paranoia, I'm not advising that you avoid all binaries posted to UseNet. You should be aware, though, that any individual person could have posted that file, which he may have infected or which may have been infected without his knowledge. This calls for more caution, such as remembering to scan the file before you execute it.

The ultimate moral here is that, within the spectrum of paranoia, UseNet posts should be considered most vulnerable to infection, and files available in online service libraries are least vulnerable. Nonetheless, all remain vulnerable to some degree.

It is definitely good practice to scan the files you get, regardless of how you got them. But we all know that none of us are perfect goodie-goodies. Heck, sometimes I wear the same socks twice before I wash them—but don't you tell anyone. When possible, download files only from the safer sources, and don't be lulled into a false sense of security. If a program is offered by a software company and it is available on their site, that's probably the safest place to get it (although it's not guaranteed).

The Great File Search

Oh, the catch, gentle reader. You've heard about the thousands upon thousands of files; you've heard about sites; you've heard about cryogenic preservation. But where are they? The very brief answer: all over the place!

Keeping the Internet in order is subject to the powerful forces of punctuated organization. Like the bedroom of a child, the Internet undergoes, at best, brief snapshots of nonchaos. If you're looking for a particular file but don't know at which site or sites to find it, you could have a problem. While not optimal, there are a couple of methods you can use to search for a file. Neither is perfect, but they'll *usually* get you somewhere, and they *often* get you exactly what you want.

Archie (Hey, I Don't Name These Things!)

While there is no official "catalog" of every file available on the Internet, Archie is about as close as it gets. What the heck is an Archie? *Archie* is a facility for searching the contents of thousands of FTP sites all over our little green planet. Archie's advantage is that it provides very wide coverage of sites, which should increase your chances of a find. Of course, there are potential disadvantages (or at the least, caveats) to using Archie.

The first is that the contents of every FTP site that Archie catalogs are not always updated at the same time. You may find that files are reported to be at sites that no longer have them—or at sites that don't even exist anymore. Luckily, the Archie output report does say when the database for a particular site was last updated (as you'll see in a moment), so you're not totally in the dark.

Second, you can't search for file descriptions, just file names. This is mainly a problem when you don't know what file you want, but you know you are looking for a file that meets some criteria. For example, if you want to search for a file called MACKENZIE.ZIP, Archie will likely be of great help. But if you're looking for all Windows screen savers, Archie isn't going to be a very helpful resource.

You can access Archie in either of two ways: via the Web using ArchiePlex or by telnetting to an Archie server. In the spirit of order, we'll talk about the first of those first and the second, well, second.

ArchiePlex

The Web generally makes life nice and simple. Once they get it to pay my bills, it will be perfect. For now, we'll just use ArchiePlex and be happy. Remember that even though you're using the Web to access Archie, the files found are located on FTP sites.

First and foremost (is there any difference between the two?), launch your Web browser and connect to an ArchiePlex server near you. To get a list of servers, open a URL to **http://web.nexor.co.uk/archie.html**. There you will see a bunch of links to other servers. Choose one (preferably one that's geographically near you to save time and Net traffic). The following figure shows a Web browser connected to the ArchiePlex server at Cybersmith Canada.

The ArchiePlex form, in all its glory.

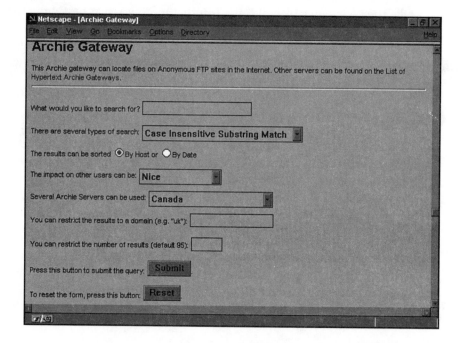

What we have here is a series of entries that you fill in to create your search request. The first entry (what you would like to search for) depends on your selection for the second entry (search type). So we'll consider the search types first. There are four:

➤ **Case Insensitive Substring Match** This is probably the most popular choice. If you select this, Archie looks for any file name that contains your search entry anywhere in the full name, ignoring uppercase and lowercase. For example, if you search for "bob," Archie will find a file named JoeBobBriggs.tar.Z as a match. If you don't know the exact file name you need, this is a good option to use, but it may return a lot of irrelevant finds.

➤ **Exact Match** As you can guess, this option tells Archie to find only the files that match exactly what you type, and even the use of upper- and lowercase letters must match. So if you search for "tom.zip," only tom.zip counts as a match (not Tom.zip or any other variation thereof). This is useful only if you know the exact file name you're looking for.

➤ **Case Sensitive Substring Match** A variation on the first search type, this tells Archie to find files that contain your search entry anywhere in the file name, but the case must match. So "bob" will match with JoebobBriggs.tar.Z but not with JoeBobBriggs.tar.Z.

➤ **Regular Expression Match** This is the most complex and, therefore, the most flexible search type. It's also beyond the scope of this book. *Regular expressions* in computing are something of a minilanguage that allows you to define search wild cards. They can get very elaborate in terms of which characters to include and which to exclude in the search. If you are interested in very detailed searches using regular expressions, pick up Que's *The Complete Idiot's Guide to UNIX* to learn about them in detail.

Now that you know how this search works, you can enter a phrase to search for in the first entry. In this example, enter the word **dog** and select **Case Insensitive Substring Match** for the search type. The third selection entry asks whether to sort by host or by date. If you care about finding the newest matches, choose **by date**; otherwise, **by host** is fine. (This isn't the most important selection. You get the same results either way, but the order in which they are presented differs.)

Next you get to choose how polite you'd like to be. Essentially, this affects how Archie prioritizes search jobs if others are trying to search at the same time. The default is **nice**, and that's a reasonable position. In the next entry, you can choose which Archie server to use. Normally, you'll want to select one closest to you (that will probably already be selected by default). Sometimes, however, servers go down. So if that one fails to work, you can select a different one.

The next option is about restricting the results to a particular domain. For example, perhaps you only want to know about files at FTP sites located in one country. I can't say I've ever used this feature, though. Unless you know you need to, just leave the entry blank. After that, you select how many matches to report. By default, Archie restricts the output to 95 matches (see the following figure). Perhaps you'd like more, or less. It's good to have some restriction; otherwise, you might end up with a mountain of hits.

Having filled out all the options, your form looks something like the one shown here.

Fill out the ArchiePlex form.

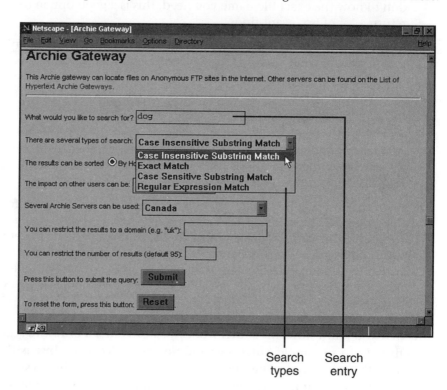

Search types
Search entry

When you are ready to search, click on the **Submit** button, and the magic starts to happen. The following figure shows the candid results of your little search with ArchiePlex.

One advantage of using ArchiePlex over using the Web is that in ArchiePlex, the resulting matches are all hyperlinked to the actual FTP sites. So you can just click on one of the matches to retrieve the file. When you do, you're prompted to enter a download path. You'll learn more about downloading this way in Chapter 17.

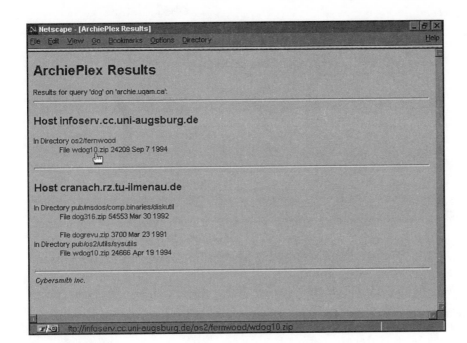

*The results of your
Archie search.*

The Telnet Way

If you don't have a Web browser available, you can use the somewhat more clunky method of connecting to an Archie server by *Telnet*. Again, you want to choose a server somewhat close to you geographically. You'll have to connect to one server before you can get a list of the rest, so for our example, let's use **archie.internic.net**. Note that Archie is a heavily used resource on the Internet, and servers may be very busy, especially during the daytime. Therefore, if you try this at a bad time, you may get very slow responses from the server.

To begin, let's open a Telnet session to the server. If you're using a SLIP/PPP account, you probably have a Telnet program. There are several of these available, such as WinQVT/ Net and Trumpet Telnet for Windows, and NCSA Telnet and Comet for the Mac. In any flavor, when you run one of them, it opens a window on your desktop and offers you the opportunity to enter a site to telnet to. For example, the following figure shows how to connect to a Telnet site using WinQVT/Net for Windows.

Connect to a Telnet site with a typical SLIP/PPP Telnet client.

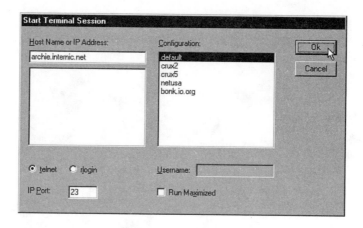

If you're using UNIX, you can just use the **telnet** command. In this example, you'll use a UNIX shell account. Other than initiating the Telnet connection, everything is the same and should look the same no matter which system you use. So, first open the connection:

```
wink:~--> telnet archie.internic.net
Trying 192.20.239.132...
Connected to archie.ds.internic.net.
Escape character is '^]'.
             InterNIC Directory and Database Services
Welcome to InterNIC Directory and Database Services provided by AT&T.
These services are partially supported through a cooperative agreement with
the National Science Foundation.
First time users may login as guest with no password to receive help.
Your comments and suggestions for improvement are welcome, and can be mailed
to admin@ds.internic.net.
AT&T MAKES NO WARRANTY OR GUARANTEE, OR PROMISE, EXPRESS OR IMPLIED, CONCERN-
ING THE  CONTENT OR  ACCURACY OF THE  DIRECTORY  ENTRIES AND DATABASE  FILES
STORED  AND  MAINTAINED  BY  AT&T.  AT&T EXPRESSLY DISCLAIMS AND EXCLUDES ALL
EXPRESS WARRANTIES AND IMPLIED WARRANTIES OF MERCHANTABILITY AND FITNESS FOR
A PARTICULAR PURPOSE.
SunOS UNIX (ds2)
login:
```

At the login prompt, type **archie**. Easy enough. Then, if the moon is in the proper phase, you'll see this:

```
******************************************************************************
            Welcome to the InterNIC Directory and Database Server.
******************************************************************************

# Bunyip Information Systems, 1993, 1994
# Terminal type set to 'vt100 24 80'.
# 'erase' character is '^?'.
# 'search' (type string)has the value 'sub'.
archie>
```

Ultimately, you can do the same things here that you did using ArchiePlex on the Web. However, there is no simple point-and-smile interface—you have to use commands. Note the line just above the **archie>** prompt; it tells us that the default search type is **sub**. That's short for "substring case insensitive," which you can determine by entering the **help set search** command to get an explanation of the abbreviations for the search types. For example, if you want to use an "exact" search type, you enter the **set search exact** command at the **archie>** prompt.

First, you really want to get a list of servers so that you can find one or more near you. To do this, type **servers** and hit **Enter**, and you'll get a nice big list. Find a couple you like and write them down so you can quit using the one at Internic (unless it's one of the ones near you). Quit by typing **quit** at the prompt.

Once you find a server, open a Telnet connection to it and log in again with the name **archie**. (This will be very similar to what you just used at Internic.) Repeat the search you did in ArchiePlex: search for the word **dog**. The default search type is **sub**, which is what you want. To begin the search, enter the **find** command with the search phrase in quotes, like this:

```
archie> find "dog"
# Search type: sub.
# Your queue position: 2
# Estimated time for completion: 13 seconds.
working...
```

The server kindly lets you know your position in line and how long it might take to complete the search. If Archie finds some matches, you'll get a list like this:

```
Host ftp.germany.eu.net    (192.76.144.75)
Last updated 20:11  9 Feb 1995
# Your queue position: 2
    Location: /pub/newsarchive/news.answers.
      DIRECTORY    drwxr-xr-x    1024 bytes  01:13 31 Jan 1995  dogs-faq
    Location: /pub/newsarchive/comp.sources.amiga/volume91/utilities
      DIRECTORY    drwxr-xr-x     512 bytes  15:20 14 Jan 1995  dog
Host ftp.isri.unlv.edu   (131.216.20.4)
Last updated 23:58 12 Jan 1995
    Location: /pub/isri
      FILE     -rw-r-----       15 bytes  16:33  6 Jan 1995  dog
```

This is just an excerpt. It reports first on the FTP site **ftp.germany.eu.net** and says that the database for that site was last updated on February 9, 1995. Because that was so long ago, it's possible that the file is not there anymore. Note also that the matches found for this site are actually directories, not files. That may or may not be of use to you, depending on what you were searching for. In the second report, on the **ftp.isri.unlv.edu** FTP site, you see that Archie found a file named **dog**. Yay!

When using the Telnet method, you have to write down the sites and locations of the file and then use an FTP client to go get them because there's no capability to link directly (as there was with ArchiePlex).

By Way of Index

While Archie lets you search a wide surface area of the Net, it's difficult to find a file to meet a certain need if you don't have any clue what its name might be. For example, imagine you want some screen savers for Windows. How would you search for that in Archie?

When you have a taste for depth over breadth, try to take advantage of a site index. Some FTP sites carry an index file containing a list of all the files available plus a brief blurb about what they are. For example, take a look at a bit of the Windows software directory of the popular FTP site **ftp.winsite.com**.

```
dr-xr-xr-x  27 0        1        1024 Jul 27 09:15 .
dr-xr-xr-x   7 0        0        1024 Jul 19 22:11 ..
dr-xr-xr-x   4 0        0        1024 Jul 21 11:52 .admin
-r--r--r--   1 0        1        2667 Jun 26 09:57 .cache
-r--r--r--   1 0        0          46 Jul  5 09:08 .message
-r--r--r--   1 0        1        2107 Feb  2 10:08 CDROMS.TXT
-rw-r--r--   1 0        0      340925 Jul 26 18:42 INDEX
-rw-r--r--   1 0        0      144671 Jul 26 18:43 INDEX.ZIP
-rw-r--r--   1 0        0       98744 Jul 26 18:43 LS-LTR.ZIP
-r--r--r--   1 0        0       22713 Jul 27 09:15 README
-r--r--r--   1 0        0        9257 Jul 21 22:43 SYSTEM.TXT
dr-xr-xr-x   2 0        0        2048 Jul 26 18:39 access
dr-xr-xr-x   2 0        0        5120 Jul 26 18:40 demo
dr-xr-xr-x   2 0        0       16384 Jul 26 18:40 desktop
-r--r--r--   1 0        0         496 Dec  6  1993 dirtree
dr-xr-xr-x   4 0        0        1024 Jul 12 01:22 drivers
dr-xr-xr-x   2 0        0        1024 Jul 26 18:40 excel
dr-xr-xr-x   4 0        0        3072 Jul 26 18:40 fonts
dr-xr-xr-x   2 0        0        9216 Jul 26 18:40 games
dr-xr-xr-x   2 0        0        2048 Jul 26 18:40 icons
```

As you can see, there are two files called INDEX. One of them is a ZIP file, which means it is compressed. You can get the decompressed file, or you get the compressed one and decompress it yourself. Both contain the information in the following form:

```
** Index of:
**    Windows Desktop Apps, Screen, Image, and BitMap Files
**
** In Directory: ~ftp/pub/pc/win3/desktop
**    On Archive: ftp.winsite.com [129.79.26.27]
** Last Updated: Wed Jul 05 1995 at 08:23:22 PM EST
**
```

```
1mbill.zip      950123  One Million Dollar Bill (640x480x84 bmp)
3dem.zip        95041-  Produce ray traced landscape scenes from USGS DEM Files
3dmania2.zip    940114  Displays rotating box frames as a screen saver (.scr)
3dvcp21.zip     941128  Visual Calendar Planner 2.1 for Windows
acdc124.zip     950421  ACDSee: Fast Image (jpg;gif)Viewer
aclnch.zip      950116  AceLaunch 1.05: task switch, app launcher, doc mgr
aclock.zip      940917  Astronomy Clock for Win 3.1, v. 1.14
```

At the top, you see which directory these files reside in. Then the index lists each file with a brief annotation. This is useful because you can search the index file for key phrases that might help you locate files to meet your needs. You can search the file using any text editor or other search tool; it's simply a plain ASCII file.

In UNIX, you can use the **grep** command to search. So search the index file for anything that might relate to a screen saver. Screen savers are also known as screen blankers in many circles, so use the keyword **blank** to search on (note that the **-i** option used with the **grep** command below makes the search case insensitive).

> **Limited Scope** Of course, the index lists only the files on the FTP site that the index comes from. So the index doesn't give you a view of the entire Net as Archie does.

```
wink:~--> grep -i blank INDEX
blank20.zip     940216  Blanker Screen saver with password
blanker.zip     940622  Fade to black screen saver (.scr)
explosiv.zip    920222  DOS/Windows Screen Blanker
ms20b.zip       910820  Monitor Saver 2.0b Windows 3 screen blanker Util
noblank.zip     940822  A non-screen blanker module w/password prot (w/src)
savscrns.zip    920907  Collection of Windows Screen Blank Modules (.SCR)
scrnac12.zip    920927  Activate Windows Screen Blanker with Hot Spots
scrutl91.zip    910823  {S,V,E}GA Screen Blanker Util Ver 9.1 (was egautil)
uzblk111.zip    941201  Uzblank Laptop Screen Blanker v1.11
winblank.zip    920413  Win3.x Screen Saver for Toshiba Laptops
windim12.zip    920723  Windows SVGA Screen Dimmer (Blanker)
winsave.zip     950427  Add hot corners to Windows screen saver
staffs1.zip     930807  Staff Sargeant 1.0: Print Blank Music Sheets
```

And there you have it: a list of files whose description contains the word **blank**, and some of them are actually screen savers.

One word of caution, though: not every site calls its index file INDEX. Some other common file names are 00_index or some variation thereof. And a more serious word of caution: not all sites even have an annotated index. No one forces them to. But it is something worth checking for.

Check This Out...

Your Inner Rockefeller: Net Philanthropy

While a lot of this book emphasizes downloading files from sources such as the Internet, the community activist in me has to make this point. The Net is a shared resource and, as such, thrives on the contributions of all its users.

So part of the answer to the question, "Where do files on the Net come from?" is "you." Oh, and only you can stop forest fires. As we'll see in Chapters 12 and 13, you can upload files to FTP sites just as easily as you can download files from them. And many modern newsreaders make it simple to post binary files to UseNet, assuming it is a newsgroup that can handle binary files (the name usually contains the word "binaries").

The Least You Need to Know

There are files all over the Internet. In some sense, they are organized by how you must retrieve them. In a greater sense, they simply lack organization, at best.

➤ Like a giant warehouse, the Net is filled with files stacked high and deep. You can use just about every Internet facility, including FTP, Gopher, the World Wide Web, and UseNet news to retrieve files. However, the files available through each may not be the same.

➤ You can attain the majority of files by way of FTP. You connect to FTP sites, which contain file libraries for your pillaging.

➤ On UseNet, files are posted in a *uuencoded* format, which allows 8-bit data to reside in 7-bit ASCII form for the sake of transport. The files must be converted back into 8-bit binary format (a process called *uudecoding*) before use.

➤ Computer viruses may infect files from any source, but some sources are safer than others. Major FTP distribution sites for software, either for a particular platform or for a particular company, are safer bets than individuals posting programs to UseNet. But these are just guidelines. Most posts to UseNet are virus free, and some files from major sites may be infected. So caution is always in order, which means you should scan all files for viruses before you use the files.

➤ You can search for files all over the Internet using Archie. Archie locates FTP sites with files whose name matches your search criteria. For more detailed searches, look for "index" files on given FTP sites, which may contain annotated descriptions of the files within.

Part 3
Using Your Terminal for Fun, Profit, and File Transfers

or "Actually doing something useful instead of all this talking"

We weren't lying; this book really is about transferring files. This section begins at the last leg of your preparation and then dives into some actual downloads and uploads. There's even a special twist for UNIX users. Coverage of the commercial online services rounds out the section, capped with some sparkling distilled water.

## Chapter 10

BAD COMPUTER PUNS

I'M SORRY, THERE'S JUST NO HOPE.

(TERMINAL PROGRAMS, GET IT?)

Terminal Programs: Part I

In This Chapter

➤ Modem commander

➤ Terminal mimicry

➤ Configuration merriment

➤ HyperTerminal

➤ Words of wisdom

Here we travel down a prong in the fork. Terminal programs, or *terminal emulations*, enable your dumb-terminal-like computer to access a remote computer. In this case, your remote account is likely to be either a UNIX shell or a menu system. (It will not be one of the online services, such as America Online or CompuServe, because those services do not use dumb terminal interfaces or normal SLIP connections. Therefore, they get their own chapter in this book: Chapter 15.)

The main functions your terminal program will undertake include managing the appearance of incoming text on the screen and transferring files to and/or from your remote account. Coincidentally, we'll discuss those functions in the next two chapters (and if there's time, we'll play a little Parcheesi or Boggle).

Talking to Your Modem

Terminal programs and modems get along very well; one could almost say they were made for each other. Actually, they were, so it's not really much of a joke. The terminal program enables you to send commands to the modem. These commands always begin with the letters **at**, which may stand for "Attention Modem! Listen up!" Although we blabbed about this somewhat in Chapter 7, one can never talk too much about modems.

You enter modem commands simply by typing them in to the command mode of your terminal program. By default, most terminal programs start up in command mode so you can just begin typing. Sometimes you have to choose command mode or some other menu option in order to send a command, but that is not the norm and should be considered a freak of nature. Another exception is Windows 95's HyperTerminal program, which is unusual in its own right. We'll look at it up-close and personal later in this chapter.

The simplest modem command is just plain **at**, which basically says "Hello, anyone home?" to your modem. If you enter that in command mode, you see this:

```
at
OK
```

That means your modem is ready and waiting for your orders. If you find that you can't type **at** or anything at all, the modem is not responding. This could be due to an improper physical connection or incorrect configuration settings. In our quick tour of a prototypical terminal program (coming up!), we'll make a stop at configuration settings.

All of that is usually the easy stuff. But because we haven't even touched configurations yet, running the terminal program and issuing the **at** command may or may not work for you, depending on the state of your setup. So let's look at the things you need to consider before you connect to a service provider.

Terminal Emulation (It's Not As Much Fun As It Sounds)

Remember the dumb terminal? One of its few capabilities is to display text on the screen. Sound easy? Well, it isn't necessarily as simple as it sounds. Think of what it has to account for when displaying text: at the least, margins and spacing; in some cases, justification (such as centering); in more advanced settings, character formatting (such as bold and text colors). Furthermore, the terminal needs to know how to interpret keystrokes for sending back to the remote host. Most keystrokes, such as letters and numbers, are simple; but some, such as the cursor keys, are problematic. Both the dumb terminal and the host have to agree on which cursor arrow is which for them to operate properly.

A terminal emulation is a set of specifications that defines all these things. Actually, there are several sets of specifications, some of which are more comprehensive than others. The important thing is that your terminal program and the remote host use the same terminal emulation. Terminal emulations have strange names because they were named by strange people. Perhaps the most common you will encounter is known as *VT-100*. Because it's a widely recognized standard, most terminal programs support VT-100 (or VT-102, which is similar enough to be the same thing). Other terminal emulations include VT-220, Heath 19, ANSI, and IBM 3270. Most UNIX machines can support multiple terminal emulations and can detect which one you're using. However, the safest bet in the majority of cases is to stick to VT-100 or 102. You'll learn how to set this in the quick tour (no flash cameras, please).

Unfortunately, not all programs and programmers are created equal. For example, some terminal programs that claim to emulate a VT-100 don't necessarily do a good job. If you're getting messy text formatting on the screen, you may be using the wrong emulation. But if you are connecting to a UNIX system, VT-100 is a very safe bet. So if the mess continues, it may mean that your terminal program is half-baked. Find a fully-baked one, such as one I've mentioned in this book.

Quick Tour: The Prototypical Terminal Program

Fortunately for us, most terminal programs are very similar. Even if you compare programs for the PC and Mac, they mostly do the same things in much the same way. One important exception, as I mentioned earlier, is Windows 95's HyperTerminal. Because 95 is the "Hot New Thing," we'll look at HyperTerminal on its own after this tour.

In this tour, I'll use the prototypical terminal program ProComm Plus 2.1 for Windows by Datastorm Technologies for my examples. This particular program has a number of bells and whistles and all sorts of shortcut buttons and icons, but those are icing. Even if your terminal program looks a lot simpler on-screen, it will support the same configurations I show you in ProComm. Of course, your program may have slightly different menu names and other minor variations, but on the whole, ProComm is quite typical.

Terminal Program Settings

You will find most of the vital configurations for a terminal program in a Settings area. On ProComm, the Setup menu contains a number of submenus. You can click on **Setup** and **Extended Menu** to see the menus shown in the following figure.

ProComm's Settings menu. Other terminal programs will have something similar.

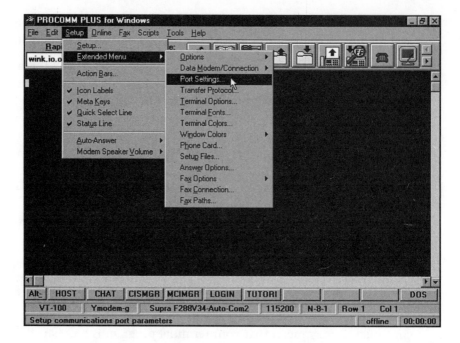

The first important settings are the Port Settings. These control variables related to the port on your computer to which the modem is connected (via the nice long, gray modem cable). When you click on **Port Settings**, ProComm displays the array of options shown in the next figure.

The topmost option is *baud rate*. Normally, your choices range from approximately 300 to 115,200. Which setting you choose depends largely on your modem's speed. If you remember, modems come in speeds of 14.4kbps and 28.8kbps, for example. You want to select the baud rate that gets the most speed out of your modem. Remember, though, that many modems (basically all modems of the 14.4 and 28.8 variety) have built-in compression, so theoretically they can transfer data faster than their reported speed by reducing the amount of data being sent.

The maximum compression is four times the modem's normal speed, so I recommend that you choose a baud rate according to that formula. However, some computers— especially older ones—have difficulty keeping up with such speeds. If you get a lot of errors or missing characters using those maximum baud rates, try reducing your baud rate by one step, from 57,600 to 38,400 or from 115,200 to 57,600. You won't often achieve optimum 4× compression unless you transfer a lot of plain ASCII files, so reducing the baud rate in this way shouldn't affect the transfer speed of most operations.

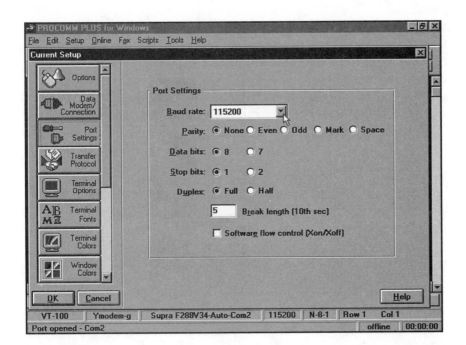

*ProComm's Port
Settings window.*

Following the baud rate selection are settings for parity, data bits, stop bits, and so on. As I explained in Chapter 7, the rule of thumb for these is "8N1," which means 8 data bits, No parity, and 1 stop bit. For Duplex, you generally use Full. It is unlikely that you'll need to vary from these settings; if you have a mutant provider, they will inform you.

Some terminal programs offer "break length" settings. A *break* is a signal that, if sent, is handled by the remote computer. How it's handled exactly depends on how the remote computer is set to handle a break. (For example, it might be used to get out of a hung Telnet session.) Anyway, this setting enables you to control how long the break needs to be for it to "count." This is not an important option, and the default should be fine. In the ProComm window shown in the figure, it is set to half a second (five-tenths of a second, actually, but I reduced).

Figure It Out To save you the challenging math, four times the normal speed for a 14.4kbps modem means a baud rate of 57,600; for a 28.8kbps, use a baud rate of 115,200.

The last setting in this window is the Xon/Xoff software flow control option. *Flow control* is a method by which each computer can regulate the moving data without losing track of it. If there is no flow control or incorrect flow control, you're likely to experience overruns and interrupted communications (as I discuss in Chapter 11). Software flow control relies on special characters to perform the regulation; hardware flow control utilizes a special wire in the modem cable. As I mentioned in Chapter 7, you should not have software flow control enabled in most cases. Only use it if your modem cable does not support hardware flow control, also known as handshaking or RTS/CTS. It is best to use RTS/CTS. (For some strange reason, RTS/CTS is rarely on the same settings menu as Xon/Xoff, but it will appear soon.)

Modem Settings

Next we'll look at the settings that control the modem setup. On ProComm, this is known as Data/Modem Connection, but on other programs it might be called Modem Settings or something akin (good use of the word "akin," eh?). Most modem settings windows look similar to the ProComm window shown here, which you can access by selecting **Setup, Extended Menu, Data-Modem Connection, Connection Setup**.

ProComm's modem configuration window.

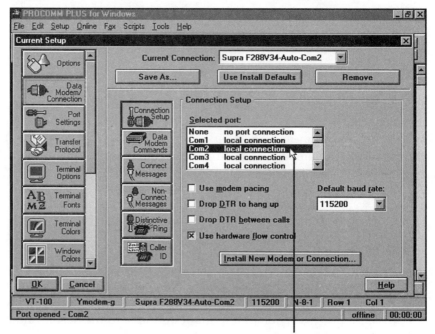

Choose the correct Com
port or nothing will work.

What's Current Connection For?

At the top of ProComm's modem settings window is a box labeled Current Connection. This is a ProComm-specific feature that allows you to define which particular modem you are using. Most terminal programs don't have this, and for the most part, it's of no great advantage.

In the Connection Setup area is the Selected port drop-down list. This is a very important setting: you use it to tell the terminal program which computer port the modem is connected to. On the PC, this will usually be what's known as a "Com" port. You may have multiple Com ports on your PC, and your modem might be on Com1, Com2, or even Com3. I can't tell you which.

Some programs try to automatically detect the port for you. If yours doesn't, you have to figure it out for yourself. If the components on the back side of your computer are labeled, you can just follow the modem cable to the port to which it's attached to find out. If you have a cheap computer and the ports are not labeled, you can always resort to trial-and-error. (It works for monkeys.) Experiment by choosing each one and then typing the **at** command. When you get an **OK** response, you've got the right one. Your modem is most likely on either Com1 or Com2, but some setups are freaky.

The first option below the drop-down list is called Use modem pacing. When ProComm starts up, it initializes your modem. In doing so, it may send the initialization commands as quickly as it can, or it may send them very slowly. By default, this option is disabled, and it should usually remain that way. In most cases, the quick pacing doesn't pose any problems. However, if your modem fails to initialize properly (if it returns an error message because the init string was received incompletely, for example), enable this option.

The next two options concern handling the *DTR*, otherwise known as *Data Terminal Ready*. The modem can react in a number of ways when the DTR signal is dropped, and you may or may not find them desirable. Under most conditions, the modem hangs up the line when it loses the DTR signal. If your modem is configured to do this (which it probably is; check the manual), these options concerning what to do with the DTR are important.

In ProComm, you can specify if you want the modem to drop the DTR signal when you choose Hang up and between phone calls. If you enable these options and your modem is configured to hang up on loss of DTR, that is what will happen. However, if you prefer, you can configure your modem not to hang up when the DTR signal is dropped (in many programs, you use the **at &d0** command to do this). If you configure your modem that way, it doesn't care if you drop the DTR signal, so these options are irrelevant.

The next option is extremely important, and it's the one I've harped about more times than you probably care to count. Because we did not enable Xon/Xoff flow control when we changed the port settings, we must (and want to) enable hardware flow control. This is normally called *RTS/CTS*; however, as you can see in the figure, the ProComm people decided to just label it *hardware flow control*. It's the same exact thing. Make sure it is checked if you have an appropriate cable (which you probably do, especially if it is new and/or came with the modem).

Yes, I'm Going to Say It Again You should never have both Xon/ Xoff and hardware flow control enabled—only one or the other. Unless you just don't have the proper cable, you should always use hardware flow control.

You can tell if you have a flow control problem with your connection because there will be serious, horrible problems. Most likely, incoming text or incoming files will just freeze up. In addition, if you experience long delays between bursts of data, you may have a flow control problem.

Two insignificant options remain in ProComm's modem settings window. The Install New Modem or Connection button is that ProComm-specific feature that identifies your modem. The Default baud rate setting is not of much consequence as we set the baud rate in the Port settings window.

Terminal Settings

Okay, we've ripped through two settings screens so far, and no one appears hurt. Now it's on to terminal settings. And if you think this chapter has been exciting thus far, well, there are more than enough therapists to go around. Save me a good one.

Moving along to the next figure, you see a late 20th century replica of the Terminal Options window of ProComm. The most important option is the terminal emulation type. Of course, ProComm puts it right at the top and calls it Current Terminal, but it's the same thing. As you can see, that good old reliable VT-100 is selected. However, if you open the drop-down list, you see that there are many others to choose from.

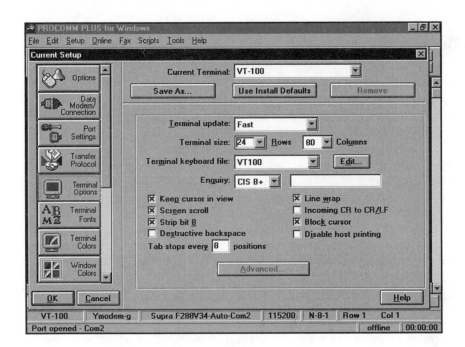

ProComm's terminal emulation settings.

Moving on down to the south side of this window, you can customize some specific features of your VT-100 (or VT-220, or whatever other terminal you selected—but I'd put my money on VT-100).

Terminal update   Not all terminal programs allow you to control the terminal update speed. I left it on Fast because I'm borne of a generation without patience for the finer things, such as screen updates.

Terminal size   The "standard" or "normal" terminal is generally 24 or 25 rows by 80 columns. Many of the UNIX programs on the remote machine assume this screen size and work best in it. If you feel deviant and want to be a black pixel, you can make the terminal size as big as your screen can handle. But you may have to instruct the remote computer about this change, and how you do that varies, so you'll have to ask your provider.

107

It's the Size That Counts

Some UNIX systems can and will determine the size of your terminal window upon log in. In those cases, if you've configured a 40 row by 100 column terminal window, the UNIX shell adjusts to fit it. However, some UNIX systems won't automatically notice this, and they'll make use of only a portion of your total window. This may not hurt anything, but one might prefer to greedily squish as much text onto her screen as possible. (I know I do!) The most common remedy is to use the UNIX **resize** command. If you type **resize** at the UNIX shell prompt, the shell attempts to determine your current terminal emulation and screen size. After it spews a bunch of strange characters onto the screen, the UNIX shell can take advantage of your entire terminal window.

The rest of the options in this window control changes you can make to satisfy your personal preferences (such as how to scroll the screen, what type of cursor, and so on). Feel free to fiddle with these until they're browned and seasoned to taste.

ProComm also contains settings windows for Terminal Fonts, Terminal Colors, and Window Colors. Of course, these are all cosmetic settings, some or all of which your own terminal program may or may not support. Hey, if you want purple letters on a green background, it's not my place to stop you. It's the government's.

The Path of Least Resistance

When you download files, the terminal program needs to know where to put them on your computer. The technical term for such a location is a *path*, and most terminal programs offer you the chance to configure path settings. Path settings are not crucial for a transfer to succeed, but it's very convenient if the files you download end up exactly where you want them. In ProComm, you can select **Setup**, **Extended Menu**, **Options**, **Paths** to access the configuration window shown in the following figure.

What About the Others?

The other path settings in this window refer to extra features of ProComm. They may or may not have analogues in your own terminal program, but they're not directly related to file transfers.

For our purposes, the only truly important path setting in this window is Download path. Obviously, you want to set the download path to indicate where you want incoming files to reside on your hard drive. Because most incoming downloads will be file archives that need further processing (such as dearchiving), it's convenient to have some sort of temporary "incoming" directory on your hard drive. If you do, that's what you should use as the download path.

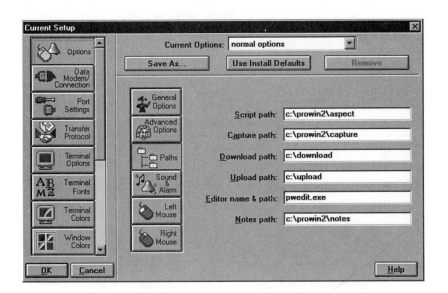

ProComm's path settings window: drop your downloads into the right bucket.

The upload path is a less concrete matter. When you choose to upload, your terminal program opens a dialog box in which you select the file(s) to send. If you define an upload path, the dialog box begins at that location. Convenient maybe, but not critical.

General Settings

Two other notable categories of settings remain. One is often known as General settings; the other is the transfer protocol.

The General settings enable you to configure some of the operations of the terminal program itself that are not related to the act of communications (such as scrollback buffers, logfiles, chimes or sound effects, and so on). You will notice the most variation between ProComm and other terminal programs here because these settings rely on how much icing the program offers you. None of these are vital to communicating via modem, but they can enhance the experience and offer many conveniences (such as keyboard macros, where one function key stands for some long command, and so on).

The other important communications-related setting is the *transfer protocol*. Chapter 11 explores the sticky depths of transfer protocols, which are vital to downloading. It also covers configuring a protocol.

Reach Out and Connect to Something

If you've made it this far in the chapter, there's a slight chance that everything is configured properly. Although much of the above information seemed very detailed and technical, many of those settings will turn out to be the defaults in your terminal program. Hopefully, most of the extremely technical information will serve useful as a reference in the future should you need to change something.

So, now comes the easy part: dialing into your service provider. Although ProComm, like many terminal programs, offers its own fancy phone book for shortcut dialing, you'll use the manual method, which is guaranteed to be consistent between terminal programs.

You need to send the modem the command that is used for dialing: **atdt** or **atdp**. If you have tone dialing, use **atdt**; if you have pulse dialing, use **atdp** (and then catch up to the rest of us here in the '90s, thank you). So dial up that service provider. (Of course, you'll probably use a different phone number.)

```
atdt 736-6001          [you'll hear the modem dial and then some strange,
                        alien burping sounds]
CARRIER 14400
PROTOCOL: LAP-M
CONNECT 115200
User Access Verification
Username:
```

Not too difficult, that. The information in the Carrier, Protocol, and Connect lines tells you about the modem connection. (Your modem may or may not offer this information.)

➤ Carrier tells you the actual baud rate of the connection. If you own a 14.4kbps modem, the best you can hope for when connecting to another 14.4kbps modem is a carrier of 14400.

➤ Protocol is less important than Carrier. It gives you information related to compression and error correction.

➤ Connect tells you the maximum baud rate that can be achieved and usually mirrors what you configured in your terminal program.

After those bits of information is the actual text from the service provider. You're ready to log in and have at it.

The New Term on the Block: HyperTerminal

Prior to the 95 version, Windows came with a terminal program inspiringly called Terminal. It was not very comprehensive and worked pretty much like the generic terminal programs I've been describing—but with far fewer features. At best, it was useful for logging onto the Net and downloading a real terminal program.

Somewhat more enthusiastic about online communications this time around, Microsoft included a more extensive program with Windows 95: HyperTerminal. If you install Windows 95 using the Typical installation option, HyperTerminal is installed on your system. While I still prefer the third-party terminal programs (whether they are commercial or shareware) over anything included with an operating system, HyperTerminal can get the job done.

HyperTerminal works somewhat differently from the "prototypical" terminal program I've been discussing thus far. To launch HyperTerminal, click the **Start** button on the Windows 95 taskbar, select **Programs**, and select **Accessories**. Click on **HyperTerminal** on the Accessories submenu, and the HyperTerminal opening screen appears.

Microsoft sees Windows 95 more as an all-inclusive *environment* than strictly as a terminal program. Apparently, Microsoft intended HyperTerminal to fit into the greater environment of your Windows 95 experience instead of being just another discrete stand-alone program. What that means, essentially, is that HyperTerminal recognizes Windows 95 and uses some of its settings. Let me explain.

Even in previous versions of Windows, you could use the Control Panel's System settings to configure some of the same elements we discussed earlier (baud rate, com port, and so on). However, programs such as ProComm and most other stand-alone terminal programs basically ignore all those system settings. They only care about the settings you set within the terminal program itself. Not so for HyperTerminal. It cares a lot about your related Windows 95 settings. In short, it sees itself as an extension of the operating system.

Windows 95's HyperTerminal program: not too fancy but it does the job.

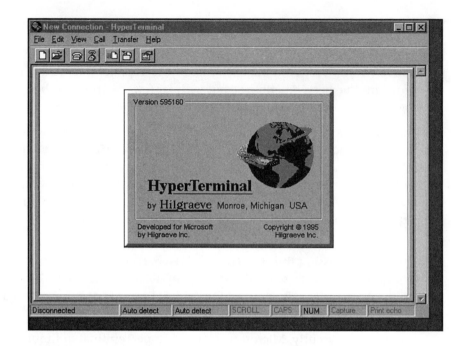

Settings, Settings, Settings...and Configurations

Because of this bond between HyperTerminal and Windows 95, to configure the serial and modem settings we discussed earlier in the chapter, you have to go into the Windows 95 Control Panel. To do so, open **My Computer** and double-click the **Control Panel** icon. In the Control Panel window, double-click on the **Modems** icon, and a configuration window appears (see the following figure).

The General Tab displays a list of the modems that are already set up on your computer. Because Windows attempts to recognize your modem during installation, there is probably already an entry there for your modem. If so, select the modem entry now. If the entry is incorrect, click the **Add** button, and Windows walks you through selecting the correct modem. After you select the correct modem entry, click on the **Properties** button. The Modems Properties dialog box displays the options shown in the following figure and described in this list.

> **Port** The communications port will probably already be set correctly; it's likely to be Com1 or Com2 (or possibly even Com3).

Set up and configuring a modem in Windows 95.

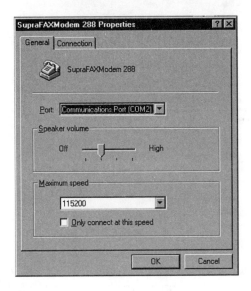

Set communications port, volume, and baud rate properties for the Windows 95 modem.

113

Speaker volume This controls the volume of the dialing and connection sounds that come out of your modem. (If there are naggy people or curious cats in your environs, you may want to keep the volume low.)

Maximum speed This is basically the same as the "baud rate" option in traditional terminal programs. We've been over it: 57,600 and 38,400 are common selections for a 14.4kbps modem, and one step up from each of those are common selections for a 28.8kbps modem. If you check the Only connect at this speed option, the modem refuses any attempt to connect to a slower modem or a poor connection. Generally, you don't want this enabled; it limits your flexibility to connect to a variety of modems.

The Connection tab of this dialog box contains even more configuration settings. Click on the **Connection** tab, and you see the options shown in the following figure. (They could've just used one big window if you ask me.)

More modem settings.

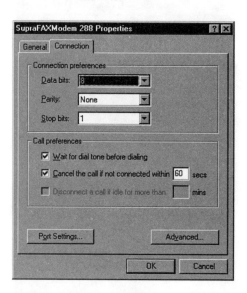

This tab's Connection preferences area contains the traditional data bits/parity/stop bits settings. As I've stated several times already, set these to **8**, **None**, **1**. In the Call preferences area, the first check box enables the modem to recover the line before accepting a dial command; leave it checked. The second check box controls how long HyperTerminal must wait for a connection before giving up. I find the default sufficient, but if you connect to a modem that takes several rings to answer, you may choose to lengthen the delay or disable the option entirely.

At the bottom of the window are two more buttons, each of which takes you to another configuration window. (Can anyone spell "labyrinth?") Click on the **Port Settings** button to see the Advanced Port Settings dialog box shown in this figure.

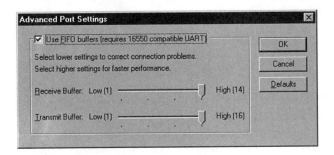

A more advanced setting, this turns the 16550 buffer on or off. Most users should leave this alone.

This setting regulates our old friend the FIFO buffer. If you remember, this is also known as the 16550 UART, and it buffers incoming data to aid in high-speed communications. Most importantly, you should enable this option if you have a 16550 (even though Windows 95 probably configured it properly upon installation). Leave the two sliders alone. In most circumstances, you shouldn't have to change anything in this window, but it's nice to know you can.

Click **Cancel**, and HyperTerminal returns you to the Connection tab. Now hit that button in the bottom right: **Advanced**. HyperTerminal displays the Advanced Connection Settings dialog box.

The setting to note here is Use flow control. Definitely enable it, and select hardware style (preferably).

The only option I want you to look at in this window is in the upper-right corner: Use flow control. Make sure this is checked, and then select one of the styles. As you can probably recite in your sleep, Hardware is preferable. Leave everything else in this dialog box alone, and click **OK** to move back a window. In the Connection Settings window, click **OK** again. You're returned to the original Modems Properties window, and you're done. Click on **Close** to save the settings.

Opening a New Connection in HyperTerminal

When you first launch HyperTerminal, it asks you to create a new connection (as opposed to simply displaying a terminal window in which you can enter **at** commands). As you can see in this figure, you choose an icon to represent your connection and give the connection a name. Then you can adjust the communications settings. HyperTerminal adopts the settings you have configured for your active modem in the Modems option in the Control Panel folder.

Opening a new connection in HyperTerminal.

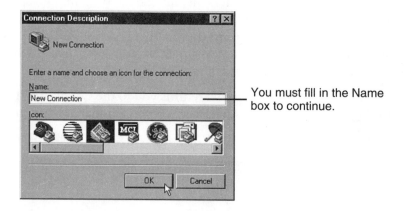

You must fill in the Name box to continue.

After you select an icon and name for the connection, HyperTerminal displays the Phone Number dialog box shown in the following figure. In the third text box, enter the phone number you want to dial. Below that, the Connect using box should contain the name of the preconfigured modem.

You choose a port in HyperTerminal just as you would in any prototypical terminal program. If you choose a Com port (the appropriate one for your modem), Hyper-Terminal prompts you to configure all those lovelies such as baud rate, parity, stop bits, and handshaking. If you want to access the modem directly with **at** commands, choose one of the Com settings instead of a preconfigured modem—that seems to be the way HyperTerminal is. If you keep the preconfigured modem, you have to enter a phone number to dial. If you choose a Com port instead, you don't enter a phone number; after configuring the port settings, you can access the modem via **at** commands.

With the phone number entered, you're about to dial. The adrenaline builds.

Your configured settings for country and area code appear in the Phone Number dialog box even though they really have no relevance to dialing out to a local number. If the modem in the Connect using box is correct, enter the phone number of your service provider and click **OK**. HyperTerminal displays the Connect dialog box to confirm the connection.

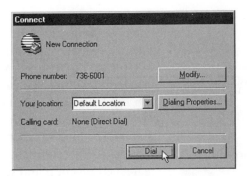

One last confirmation before you dial. Excitement peaks.

Click **Dial**, and the process begins. When you're connected, your provider's machine prompts you to log in (see the following figure). Enter your login name and your password. That is that. Not so bad, was it?

Make a Mistake? If you type a mistake in the phone number, you can change it by clicking the **Modify** button in the Connect dialog box.

117

Connected! The service provider asks you to log in, and you're on your own.

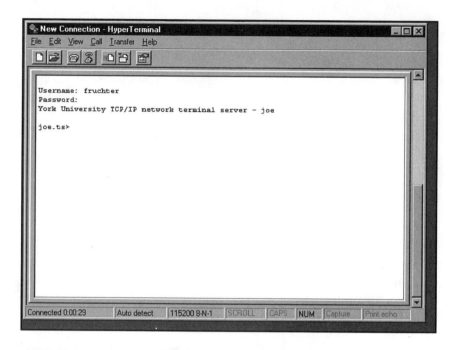

```
Username: fruchter
Password:
York University TCP/IP network terminal server - joe

joe.ts>
```

Know Your Icons If the icons in the HyperTerminal icon bar seem to be somewhat cryptic, remember that you can point to any icon to see its description label.

HyperTerminal does not have a plethora of features that make it different from other terminal programs. There isn't, for example, much more to configure than the connection settings. However, you can alter the font with the View Font menu option. In addition, Hyper-Terminal has good transfer protocol support (see Chapter 11), and it provides an icon bar to simplify your tasks. The essential difference is in the way you create a connection and set configurations, which is because of HyperTerminal's ties to the Windows 95 operating system.

How to Meet the Right Terminal for You

Any reader who is still awake is surely asking, "But how do I know which terminal program to use? Where do I get it?" One question at a time, please.

In the cosmic sense, you can use any terminal program you want. As with any other product, they vary in terms of features and quality. Follow these guidelines when you're choosing a terminal program:

➤ At the very least, you want your terminal program to support the major terminal emulations, such as VT-100 and VT-220.

➤ Because we have yet to discuss transfer protocols you may not understand them, but you will want a terminal program that supports Zmodem and Ymodem. Some of the lesser programs out there only support the protocols Kermit and Xmodem (see Chapter 11). Those are not desirable.

➤ A scrollback feature, although not mandatory, can be very convenient. Scrollback enables you to move back through previous screens to see what happened.

➤ Session capture is a handy feature that enables you to save the entire contents of an online session to a file for future reference (it's like tape recording a conversation, but it's not as sneaky).

➤ Macros and other shortcuts can be nice for lazy fingers.

As is true of the fancy radio and leather steering wheel sheath in your car, the usefulness of these things depends largely on how much you're going to use the terminal program. If you are going to spend hours a day using it, bells and kazoos can save a lot of time. For 10-minute e-mail checks, they're probably not worth paying for.

Some terminal programs, such as ProComm Plus, are standard commercial off-the-shelf software (I'm not endorsing that particular product; it's just what I have). Those commercial programs are generally going to be fairly capable. Some terminal programs are included or "bundled" with modems or computer setups, and some perfectly capable terminal programs are available as shareware or even freeware on the Internet and other online services. To find out about available shareware and freeware programs, check out Appendix A.

One Bundled Program... One popular example of a program that comes bundled is COMit. My experience with this program has shown it to be somewhat less-than-adequate in the terminal emulation and transfer protocol areas.

Check This Out...

If you want to tap into popular opinion before you indulge (especially if you're considering a costly commercial product), check out the UseNet newsgroups **comp.os.ms-windows.apps.comm** for Windows users or **comp.sys.mac.comm** for Mac users. There you can solicit recommendations from more veteran terminal addicts.

The Least You Need to Know

The terminal program is your all-around vehicle for dumb terminal emulation. Terminal programs come in all manner of size and capability, from tiny programs that basically just let you dial the modem, to large applications with many icons, buttons, and options. The basic point remains the same: they handle communications between your computer and the remote computer via your modem.

➤ Terminal programs allow you to talk to your modem using **at** commands. Most programs start up ready for you to begin entering commands. One notable exception is Windows 95's HyperTerminal, which requires you to do a bit of fiddling before sending modem commands.

➤ On the PC, the modem connects to the Com port. You must configure your terminal program to the right Com port, which is often Com1 or Com2.

➤ It is very important that the remote computer and your terminal program speak the same *terminal emulation*. Otherwise, screen formatting may be unreadable, and keystrokes may be interpreted wrong. The most common terminal emulations are VT-100 and VT-102, so select those if your terminal program supports them.

➤ Set the baud rate to 57,600 for 14.4kbps modems or 115,200 for 28.8kbps modems. Some older computers may not handle these speeds well, so if you lose incoming data, lower the baud rate to 38,400 or 57,600 respectively. If your modem is of any other speed and supports compression, set the baud rate to four times the modem's speed. If you have a bottom-of-the-barrel modem, such as a 2,400 baud modem with no compression, just set the terminal baud rate to 2,400.

➤ Hardware flow control, also known as hardware handshaking and RTS/CTS, is preferable over software flow control (aka Xon/Xoff). Always enable one or the other type of flow control, but never enable both of them.

## Chapter 11

Terminal Programs: The Sequel

In This Chapter

➤ Protocols and you

➤ King of the hill: Zmodem

➤ Ymodem-g groupie

➤ The truth about Kermit

So far so good. At this point, you can configure your terminal program to speak to your modem, choose pretty colors, and dial up your service provider. You still can't download, though. Oh, is that what this book is allegedly about?

Well, in the spirit of truth-in-titling, let's look at how to actually transfer a file. Doing so requires the use of aptly named *file transfer protocols*, which handle the dirty deed. Conceptually, this chapter is the second half of the previous chapter, so if you want to pass around photocopies, be sure to put both chapters together with a staple or one of those humongous mammal-sized paper clips or something. Oh yeah, and get permission from the publisher before you spend half your lifetime in front of the copier.

An Overview of Transfer Protocols: Party Time

The word "protocol" finds a lot of use in computing. Computers have to follow a rigid set of rules to accomplish any given task because they really aren't that bright. Sure, they can add more numbers in two seconds than you could in a George Burns lifetime, but other than that, computers don't have a clue about what's going on. A *protocol* is a set of rules that tells the computer (and people in the military—same idea but with camouflage) exactly how to behave in a given situation. In this chapter, that given situation is the transferring of a file from one computer to another by way of a modem. The purpose of a transfer protocol, then, is to make that transfer proceed smoothly and accurately.

Protocols have to be designed to account for a number of variables, including the capabilities of the computer and modem. For example, many protocols had to pick up the slack back when older, slower modems did not have the capability to perform "hardware error-correction." When a bit of data is sent from one computer to another, one of the components needs to check the data to make sure it was not damaged in the process. (If it is damaged, the resulting file will be corrupted and probably useless; therefore, the data needs to be sent again.) In the older days, software—specifically, the transfer protocols—had to take care of this verification. However, the recent technological stomp forward has brought us modems that can perform this error-checking before they ever pass on the data to the computer. Basically, any 14.4kbps or 28.8kbps modem available today has this feature built-in (with the possible exception of extremely cheap bottom-of-the-barrel brands).

Transfer protocols vary in how many features they offer. Here are some important ones to consider.

➤ Can the transfer protocol find out the total size of a file before transfer or the total size of all files to be transferred? If so, the estimated time of transfer can be calculated.

➤ Can the protocol resume a transfer that has been interrupted? This will become important later, as you'll learn in Chapter 20.

➤ How fast can the protocol pump data through the modem? Depending on the design of the protocol, you may or may not be able to reach the full speed capabilities of the modem itself.

Needless to say (but I will), it's essential that both computers involved in the transfer use the same protocol. Pragmatically, this means that you must use a protocol that both your terminal program and the remote computer support.

There are far more protocols around than are covered in this chapter, but only a few are in common use and could be considered "necessary." The most common protocols include Zmodem, Ymodem, Xmodem, and Kermit. You can see which protocols are available to you by accessing the transfer settings of your terminal program. In ProComm, for example, you can open the Transfer Protocol setup window (shown in the following figure) to see a list of possible protocol options.

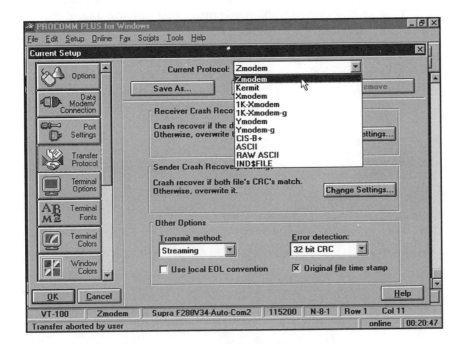

So many protocols, so little time.

As it happens, ProComm offers a number of choices. But you'll probably use only one protocol most of the time, and that will probably be one that's discussed in the following sections. The first up, Zmodem, is always a solid player.

The Popular Choice: Zmodem

Zmodem is quite possibly the most widely used transfer protocol. It includes such important features as error-correction and the capability to resume interrupted transfers. It handles batches of files well (enabling you to transfer several files in an automated manner) and can even report on total file sizes and total batch sizes. Another nice feature is Zmodem's capability to initiate a transfer automatically. That is, if you tell the remote computer to begin a Zmodem download, your terminal program automatically recognizes this and begins accepting the data without any instructions from you.

As far as throughput goes, Zmodem does a good job of transferring data given a modem's speed. However, Zmodem automatically implements error-correction, which may be superfluous over a connection with error-correcting modems on both ends.

Because it's complicated to implement, lower-end terminal programs often don't have built-in Zmodem support. That's a bad thing unless you transfer files only on a rare occasion—in which case, this is the wrong book for you.

Good terminal programs allow you to control the configuration of certain options to affect Zmodem's behavior. The following figure shows ProComm's Zmodem configuration screen. Other terminal programs may offer more or fewer settings that you can change.

Zmodem Configuration options.

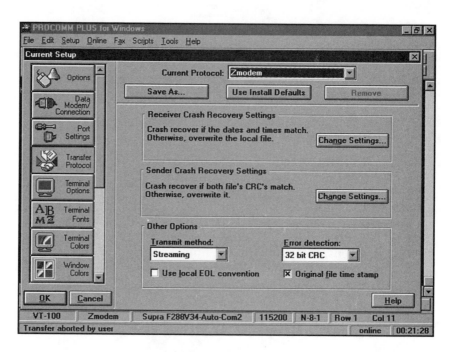

The first two options regard how the protocol handles crash recovery. Essentially, they tell the modem what to do if you try to download a file that has been partially downloaded already. The previous download may have been interrupted for any number of reasons, ranging from computer error to someone picking up the telephone receiver. You can usually configure Zmodem to recover from crashes on all occasions, or only when the file you're currently downloading has the same time and date stamp as the partial one on your computer.

In the Other Options section of the window, you see the Transmit method drop-down list. Notice that in the preceding picture it is set to **Streaming**. That means data will continuously be sent into your computer. (The other options—2k window and 4k window—request that data be sent in segments of 2k or 4k each.) Although some slower computers do not handle the continuous streaming data well, most users should do fine with streaming.

To the right of the Transmit method option is the Error detection drop-down list. Remember that Zmodem provides error correction even if your modem does, too. Your options are 32-bit and 16-bit. Try 32-bit first; it is the better choice because it ensures more secure correction. However, on a very old and slow computer (the corner dust box kind), you may have to use 16-bit to avoid errors.

Last in this window are these two check boxes:

> ➤ **Use local EOL convention**   You may find this useful if you are transferring an ASCII text file from a system different from your own, where the "End of Line" (EOL) characters are different. If you download a text file and find that the line feeds are messed up, try enabling this feature if your terminal program supports it. (For more information on this subject, turn to Chapter 19.) Do note, however, that if this feature is on, you cannot use crash recovery. Normally, I leave EOL convention disabled.

> ➤ **Original file time stamp**   If this box is enabled, the file that's transferred will contain the same date and time stamp on the receiving end that it did originally. If this box is disabled, the resulting file's date and time stamp will reflect the date and time of the transmission. This may or may not matter to you, depending on whether you want to retain the file's original information or its transfer information.

If all these options seem daunting, take heart that in most cases, the defaults are fine for most setups. But after going through them this way, if you want to fiddle with them, you'll have some idea what might happen. (Good things, you hope.)

As I said at the beginning of this section, Zmodem is one of the most commonly used transfer protocols because it does the job reliably and quickly. Frankly, if your terminal program and the remote machine both support Zmodem, there is little reason to use anything else. However, there are some other protocols worth mentioning....

My Personal Choice: Ymodem-g

There is another transfer protocol with the purely coincidental name (believe it or not) of Ymodem. In most cases, Ymodem is not as good as Zmodem. However, there are several subclasses of protocols within the Ymodem family. One of those, known as Ymodem-g, is especially worth noting.

What makes Ymodem-g special (besides its colorful mane and unusual mating call) is that it works essentially the same way as Zmodem, but without the error-correction. This can be a good thing because performing error-correction in software is a waste of processing time if it has already been done in hardware (the modem). And dropping the software error-correction enables you to achieve even higher *throughput*.

Now, although Ymodem-g doesn't have a lot of Zmodem's nifty features, such as crash recovery, it's a wee bit faster. Depending on the speed of your computer, you may be able to transfer data 15–20 bytes per second faster using Ymodem-g than you can using Zmodem. You don't think that's much of an improvement? Well, when a very impatient person is downloading very large files, every little bit counts.

The following figure shows Ymodem-g's few options, each of which is discussed below.

Ymodem-g offers far fewer features than Zmodem does, but they're easier to understand.

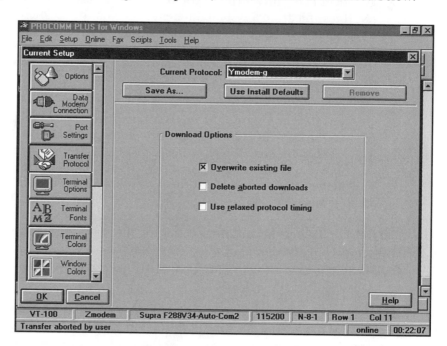

Overwrite existing file   If you check this option, Ymodem-g automatically over-writes any file that has the same name as the one you are downloading. If you do not check it, Ymodem-g asks you before it overwrites such a file.

Delete aborted downloads   This option enables you to control whether Ymodem-g deletes partial files that result from an interrupted file transfer. Although you can't crash recover using Ymodem-g, you can crash recover an interrupted file transfer using Zmodem. For example, if you transfer 65% of a file using Ymodem-g and then the modem disconnects, you can complete the transfer using Zmodem with crash recovery, and it's not a total loss. Therefore, you may not want to have a partial file automatically deleted.

Use relaxed protocol timing   This is one of those options that doesn't seem to make any difference (*I* can never tell a difference anyway). The idea is that if your modem and computer can't keep pace with rigid timing, you enable the protocol to cut some slack. This is probably more useful on older and slower computers; I keep it disabled.

The best way to determine which protocol you like the most is to try them with the same file. See which works fastest on your own machine. If the difference between Zmodem and Ymodem-g is negligible and you like the added features of Zmodem, that's your answer.

Technosludge: Kermit

All right, okay, perhaps the above adjective is a little harsh. I must admit, I haven't had good experiences with Kermit. Perhaps this is due to the fact that it was more widely used in the older days of networking when things were much slower.

Kermit is, in fact, not "just" a file transfer protocol; it allows for a wide variety of communications between a local and a remote machine—and it dices onions, too! It works on a server/client philosophy where the local machine "requests" actions and/or files from the remote machine. However, as I said, it was much more popular in older days and tends to be slow compared to the throughput of Zmodem or Ymodem-g.

To scare you away from Kermit a little more, look at ProComm's Kermit configuration window, shown in the next figure. Look at all those settings! Most of them are not going to yield interesting results, but they have to be set correctly for anything to work. As in most cases, the defaults should work with the defaults of Kermit on the remote computer.

To put it bluntly, I simply can't recommend using Kermit in any of today's modern environments unless that is the only transfer protocol that your program supports—and you're just trying to download a new terminal program.

This picture is mostly meant to scare you away from Kermit. With a working Zmodem, why bother with this stuff?

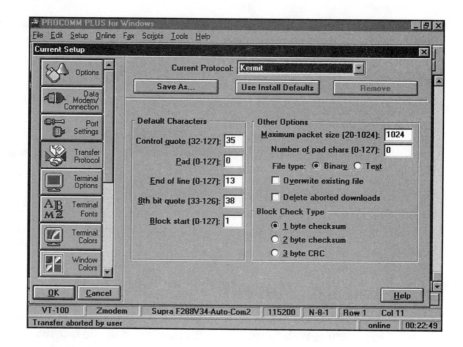

The Least You Need to Know

To successfully transfer a file between two computers, both computers must have their stories straight. Enter transfer protocols, which tell both machines how to properly behave themselves. But some protocols do this better than others.

➤ The most popular protocol is Zmodem. It gets excellent throughput, performs reliable error-correction, and provides a host of extra features such as crash recovery and automatic download initiation. I recommend that you use a terminal program that supports Zmodem.

➤ Ymodem-g is a variant strain of Zmodem that does not perform error-correction. This allows for slightly higher throughputs between reliable connections, such as modems with built-in hardware error-correction (which includes most modern, fast modems). Although Ymodem-g doesn't support Zmodem's other handy features, it can be useful. And if a Ymodem-g transfer is interrupted, you can switch to Zmodem to crash recover the remainder of the transfer.

➤ Kermit is more than just a file transfer protocol: it enables one computer to control the behavior of a remote. However, it tends to be slower than Zmodem and Ymodem-g, and if defaults don't work properly, configuration is more difficult. Some older or more minimal terminal programs may support only Kermit. If that's true of your terminal program, use it only long enough to download a better terminal program (of course, that's my humble opinion).

Pay Attention: The Download

Well, it all comes down to this chapter. If this one fails, the reviews will be harsh. The dumb terminal users, at least, will rip me to pieces; I might be able to redeem myself in the eyes of the SLIP/PPP users later in Part 4.

This chapter and the next are specific anatomical looks at transferring a file. This time around the carousel, I talk about *downloading*. After that, *uploading*. It's all so logical. Hang on....

Preparing to Download

Everyone has them: those friends who, whenever they speak about a visit to someone, say they went "up" to see Mary and Alice. And Mary and Alice are the types who always say, "Oh yes, Bob and Frank came down to see us last weekend." It seems these people pay no regard to geographical situations; the person doing the visiting is always going up, and the person being visited always has people coming down. Frankly, I find it very annoying.

Don't make the same mistake when you're talking about downloading and uploading. They are two very different things, and that distinction needs to be recognized—or I'll whine and moan and cry.

When you *download* a file, you transfer it from a remote computer to a local computer. When you *upload* a file, you move it from the local computer to the remote computer. For most people, downloading is far more common than uploading. We're all hoarders by nature.

Before you download, you need to consider what sort of system the remote computer is. If you're using an Internet account, which is one of the assumptions of this book as far as dumb terminals go, the remote system is probably a UNIX machine. That's a good bet.

The next consideration is whether you use your account with a menu-based system or from a UNIX shell prompt. If you use a menu system, you need to find the option for downloading a file. If such an option exists, hopefully it offers you a choice of transfer protocols or at least tells you which one it plans to use. The Zmodem protocol is most likely what you'll use. If you use a UNIX shell (or choose to drop out of the menu into one), there are several commands for initiating a download. Three worth knowing are **sz**, **sb**, and **sx**, which download a selected file (or group of files in some cases) using Zmodem, Ymodem, or Xmodem transfer protocols, respectively. Thus, you are most likely to want to use **sz** (which, semi-obviously, stands for "send Zmodem"). The basic format for the **sz** command is:

```
%sz filename(s)
```

Note that *filename(s)* can be a series of files (as in the **sz** command file1.zip file2.zip file3.gif), or it can be a wild card (as in **sz** *file*.**zip**, which downloads all files in the current directory whose names begin with "file" and end with .zip).

If you are using a menu system, your provider will have designed some way for you to select the files to download. I prefer to use the UNIX shell because it gives me more control; in most menu systems, you can quit to a UNIX shell if you want.

Start Your Transfer!

Now, before you actually go ahead and try this downloading thing, make sure your terminal program is set up properly. That means, for instance, that you have selected the proper transfer protocol (Zmodem for our example). Also be sure to note or choose where your terminal program is going to save the files it receives. (You do this by checking the Path settings, as discussed in Chapter 10.)

When your terminal program is ready, begin the download using either the menu commands or the UNIX shell. If you use the shell, you will see something like this:

The Automatic Downloading Option Some terminal programs have an option with which you can enable or disable automatic downloading of files when using Zmodem. If you have this option, you might as well enable it.

```
%sz file1.zip
***B400001222
```

The strange numbers that appear after you hit **Enter** are notes to your terminal program. Depending on your terminal, you may or may not see them at all, but don't worry about it either way. About a second after you enter the **sz** command, your terminal program displays a window that shows the downloading status. The following figure shows ProComm's downloading status window.

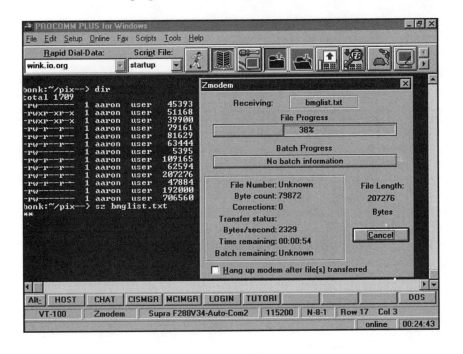

Initiating a download from a UNIX account with sz.

This is a rather important window, so let's take a closer look at it.

Understanding the Diagnostics

Ah, very good. At the top of the window, you see the name of the file being downloaded: bmglist.txt. Simple enough. Below that is the File Progress bar, which gives you an idea of how much of the file has been transferred—or how much more time you have to eat pizza. The Batch Progress bar is intended to show the progress of a group of files being downloaded. Say, for example, that you told sz to download four files. In that case, when the first file approaches 100% completion in the File Progress bar, the Batch Progress bar reaches 25%. This one might show that you've got enough time to actually go and order a pizza. Seriously, this type of information is very useful for planning purposes.

The transfer status window gives you a lot of important info—and it's fun to watch.

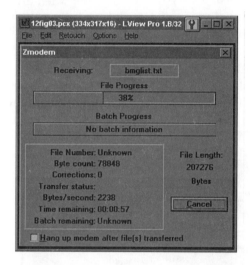

The box in the lower-left corner contains even more status information. File Number refers to which file in a batch download is being transferred. In our example, we down-loaded only one file. Apparently ProComm doesn't consider that a "batch of one," so it reports **Unknown**. Next is the Byte count, which is simply the amount of the file that has been transferred thus far. Corrections reports the number of damaged or broken pieces of data that were received and had to be resent. This is an important diagnostic because, in a proper setup, you really shouldn't be getting more than a correction or two from time to time. If you get a regular stream of them, you've probably got a problem.

Just below Corrections is the Transfer status. Here the terminal program gives a brief description of any problems that occur. These are usually paired with Corrections and could be considered an "explanation" of the error.

If you enable the **Hang up modem...** check box at the bottom of the dialog box, the terminal program disconnects when the download is complete. This may save you some time—and money—especially if you leave the download unattended.

Speed Limits

The Bytes/second statistic shows your throughput. (You might see this called something like Characters per second, CPS, or BPS, but it all means the same thing.) If you know what throughput you "should" be getting, you can use this information to figure out if something is not working properly. To know what you should be getting, you need to consider a number of variables (none of which include the phase of the moon, though it sometimes seems that way). The Big Three variables are:

➤ the transfer protocol you're using

➤ the speed of the faster of the two modems

➤ the type of file you're transferring

Most modern modems attempt on-the-fly data compression, which reduces the amount of data to be sent and (apparently) increases the transfer speed. However, all files do not compress equally. Specifically, you will get little to no compression on files such as ZIP and LHA that are already compressed. At the polar opposite extreme, you will get maximal compression on files that contain plain ASCII text. In terms of throughput then, a 14.4kbps modem using Zmodem transfer protocol to transfer an already-compressed binary file (such as a common ZIP file) will achieve an average of 1,630–1,650 bytes per second. I say "average" because it may take a little while to climb up to that speed, but it will reach it and will hover around it. Transferring a decompressed ASCII file with the same setup might yield throughput of anywhere from 2,500 to 3,000 bytes per second.

One Way or Another...

Does it really matter whether a file is already compressed or whether the modem performs the data compression? For example, an ASCII file appears to transfer at a much higher speed than a compressed binary file because the modem can compress it on-the-fly. But what if you compress the ASCII file prior to transfer using ZIP or UNIX Compress?

The answer is that the file would transfer at the 1,650cps average, but the file would be smaller. Overall transfer time is not going to be drastically different between a large decompressed file and a small compressed file (assuming the same file in each case). So it doesn't really matter where you perform the compression, as long as it's done. However, if you compress the file yourself, you have to decompress it yourself on the other end. If you let the modem compress the file as it transfers, it will appear at the destination already decompressed, which can save you some work.

Users of 28.8kbps modems can essentially double the above throughput numbers to estimate their appropriate speeds. What you should be most concerned about is having throughput rates that are lower than the averages listed here. If, for example, you have a 14.4kbps modem and are only achieving bps rates of 1,000, something may be wrong.

And if this is happening, you are probably getting a lot of corrections with appropriate status messages. That's why I included the next section, for your convenience.

Enter the CRC Error: Don't Panic, Just Weep

A number of factors may conspire to undermine a successful download. After all, there must be some checks and balances in the universe. Your terminal program is equipped to react to problems in one of two ways: to display appropriate error messages or to freak out (i.e., cease the download and spew junk characters onto the screen). First, let's consider the error messages.

Your terminal program reports error messages in some sort of "status" window. In ProComm, for example, it's the "Transfer status." The single most common error you will get, if you get any, will be what's known as a *CRC error*. (Yes, that does stand for Cyclic Redundancy Check. How did you know?) This nasty little booger means there was some sort of burp in the data flow that confused one of the computers.

When a stream of data rushes from one computer to another, both have to be able to process it in a timely manner. If one machine falls behind, the two lose coordination and incur errors. We'll look at some possible causes of this coordination loss shortly. The CRC error is often a signal of this problem. Normally, the two computers attempt to get back on track. Sometimes, though, this fails and the transfer is aborted.

Needless to say, you shouldn't be getting CRC errors. One or two are acceptable and not necessarily symptomatic, but if you get a string of them, you know you have a real problem.

Suspect #1: Overrun

What some people frequently encounter is a scenario in which they consistently transfer a certain amount of data, such as 1,024 or 2,048 bytes, and then the CRC errors start piling on. Fortunately, there is a good reason for this (well, it's not a "good" reason as such, but a sound one). The culprit is known as *overrun*. It means that data is coming into the computer more quickly than it can be handled, causing a sort of flood. A wide array of factors can cause your system to be susceptible to flooding. Fortunately, only a couple of these are common.

If you are using a PC, there is a wee little chip known as a UART on your serial card that has a buffer on it. This buffer helps prevent a data flood, or overrun, by cutting your computer some slack. On older PCs, the UART is known as the 8250, and it is generally incapable of providing enough slack for a high-speed modem in a processor-intensive environment such as Windows. Newer PCs, or serial cards, come with a 16550A UART chip, which is much improved. So, on the hardware end of things, you want to be sure you have a 16550A (or other letter, but not the plain 16550) UART chip. One simple way to find out is to run the MSD program (aka Microsoft Diagnostics) that is included with MS-DOS.

To check your UART chip, first be sure you're in MS-DOS alone and not a DOS shell within Windows. You do this by quitting Windows from the Program Manager in Windows 3.x, or by selecting **Shut Down** from the Windows 95 **Start** menu and selecting **Restart the computer in MS-DOS mode** from the shutdown menu that appears. Either way, you get the DOS C:> prompt.

MSD Didn't Work? You must run MSD from DOS alone; it doesn't work in a DOS shell within Windows.

At the DOS prompt, type **msd** and press **Enter**. After a brief pause, you see a screen that looks something like the one in the following figure.

From there, select the **COM Ports** option in the right column. The window that appears reports the status of your COM ports (see the second upcoming figure). The last piece of info, UART Chip Used, is what you want to know. In this case, it shows 16550AF for both COM ports; the one that matters is the port where your modem is (number 2 on this particular PC). As you can guess, this PC is A-OK for high speed transfers in Windows.

The main menu for MSD, the Microsoft Diagnostic utility.

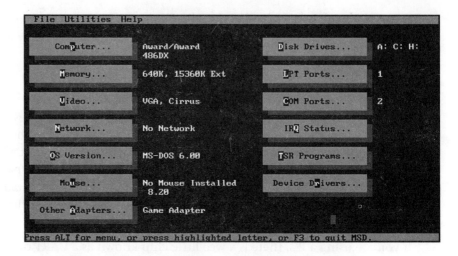

```
File  Utilities  Help

   Computer...      Award/Award        Disk Drives...    A: C: H:
                    486DX

   Memory...        640K, 15360K Ext   LPT Ports...      1

   Video...         VGA, Cirrus        COM Ports...      2

   Network...       No Network         IRQ Status...

   OS Version...    MS-DOS 6.00        TSR Programs...

   Mouse...         No Mouse Installed Device Drivers...
                    8.20

   Other Adapters...  Game Adapter

Press ALT for menu, or press highlighted letter, or F3 to quit MSD.
```

MSD's report of a PC's COM port.

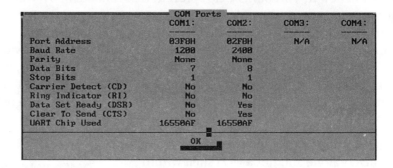

	COM1:	COM2:	COM3:	COM4:
Port Address	03F8H	02F8H	N/A	N/A
Baud Rate	1200	2400		
Parity	None	None		
Data Bits	7	8		
Stop Bits	1	1		
Carrier Detect (CD)	No	No		
Ring Indicator (RI)	No	No		
Data Set Ready (DSR)	No	Yes		
Clear To Send (CTS)	No	Yes		
UART Chip Used	16550AF	16550AF		

OK

In the interests of obligatory confusing terminology, the buffer that the 16550 UART supports is known as a *FIFO* (first in first out). Windows 3.x does not usually have FIFO-support enabled by default. So if you're using a 16550 UART, you may need to enable FIFO for use in Windows 3.x by adding the following line to your SYSTEM.INI file (which usually resides in C:\WINDOWS) in the section labeled [386enh]. Replace the *x* in this line with the number of the COM port your modem is on.

Inside Out

If you have an internal modem, you should be all set. They usually have their own 16550 UARTs built-in.

COMxFIFO=1

Windows 95 users don't have to worry about any of this; Windows 95 automatically enables the FIFO upon installation if it detects that you have the 16550 chip.

Suspect #2: The Phone Lines

Another culprit that can cause you to lose the coordination of data flow is the series of phone lines between your computer and the remote. A signal traveling by phone line may hit many "interchanges" on its way. Depending on the time of day and the speed of your modem's connection, these can throw off the data flow. If your phone lines are the source of these problems, possible solutions include reducing the speed of your connection (lower the baud rate in your terminal program before you dial) and attempting to make the call during off-peak hours.

You Can Fight CRCs Using hardware flow control helps eliminate CRC errors. Of course, obedient readers are properly using hardware flow control because I screamed about it so much in Chapter 10.

Suspect #3: The sz Command

In all the problems I've discussed so far, I've assumed your own computer was the culprit. However, it's possible that the remote machine and **sz** are the ones with an attitude problem. The **sz** command can take a lot of parameters, many of which are very obscure (the UNIX **man sz** command describes them for you). Two that many people find to be of help are worth noting here:

➤ The -e parameter changes the way **sz** handles escape codes, which may result in friendlier communications with your terminal program. You would use it this way:

```
%sz -e filename(s)
```

➤ Sometimes a transfer works better if the data is sent in "windows" (in smaller chunks, a certain amount at a time). As you may recall from Chapter 11, ProComm has an option to select a window size for a Zmodem transfer. You might try telling **sz** to send the data in either 2,048- or 4,096-byte windows. That would go a little something like this:

```
%sz -w2048 filename(s)
```

or

```
%sz -w4096 filename(s)
```

If your terminal program's transfer protocol setting has an option for selecting a Zmodem window size, choose one that matches the one you use with the **sz** command.

Last Ditch Effort Note that you can use the -e and -w options together if you get truly desperate, as in sz -e -w4096 *filename(s)*.

The Secret Chant of the Ancients

There are so many possible causes of CRC errors that I can't possibly tell you about all of them in this amount of space. So, if none of the fixes I've covered here solve your problems, you must attempt the secret chant of the ancients. While there is no accurate way to represent it in written form, it sounds something like this:

> "CRC go away, don't come back another day! CRC you've had your fun, cease this data overrun!"

Follow the chant by facing west and emitting a high-pitched wail. If even that doesn't solve the problem, describe your situation to the fine-feathered folks in a UseNet newsgroup such as **comp.os.ms-windows.apps.comm** or **comp.ibm.pc.hardware.comm**.

The Least You Need to Know

Downloading isn't too difficult if the computers on both ends are happy. If they're happy, it's just a matter of a few keystrokes. However, if they're unhappy, it's a matter of many keystrokes and often a trail of tears.

➤ Choose your protocol, gentlepeople. I recommend Zmodem if both your terminal program and remote machine support it.

➤ If you use a menu-based system, look for an option for downloading—preferably one that includes **sz** or some other form of Zmodem in its name. Otherwise, use the UNIX shell.

➤ Once you have set up your terminal program with the desired Zmodem settings and download paths, enter the **sz** command and file name(s) on the UNIX machine to begin the download.

➤ Take note of the information in your terminal program's status window. Watch for CRC errors and bytes per second counts, which signal problems.

➤ If the transfer runs into difficulties, investigate the possible causes on your computer. Make sure you're using hardware flow control and a 16550A UART chip. If you're seriously desperate, update your hardware drivers wherever possible and be sure FIFO is enabled if you use Windows 3.x.

➤ You can try adding parameters to the **sz** command to see if that alleviates the CRC errors. Try **%sz -e** or **sz -w2048**.

## Chapter 13

Going Up?
The Upload

In This Chapter

➤ Getting ready to rumble with Zmodem

➤ Let 'er rip with **rz**

➤ When Lady Luck is in the washroom... errors do creep

Presumably, you've already managed to successfully download a file from a remote computer to your own. Now the other way. Be sure to take deep breaths to avoid dizziness.

Prepare to Upload

Clearly, downloading and uploading are based on the same concept. Therefore, there's not much to explain about uploading if you understand downloading. In fact, if one was feeling especially relativist, one could say there is no difference between the two because whether or not you are uploading or downloading is an observer-dependent perspective. In my experience, however, uploading has traditionally been more problematic than downloading, so I won't leave you to find your way blindly.

You prepare your terminal program for uploading just as you do for downloading: make sure that both computers are using the same transfer protocol. Again, I recommend using Zmodem. On the UNIX side of things, you use **rz** (receive Zmodem) instead of **sz**. Unlike with downloading, you cannot set up an upload to initiate automatically. Why not? When you enter the **rz** command on the UNIX (remote) side, your terminal program doesn't yet know which file(s) you want to upload. As I'll illustrate in just a bit, you have to manually instruct your terminal program to upload and choose your intended files.

Other than that, uploading is pretty much the same as downloading. Let's run through the paces and attempt to upload a file. This should be cake, all other bugaboos being equal.

Fire When Ready

It's a good idea to know which file you want to upload and where it is located on your hard drive before you start the process. In a short while, you'll need to select that file. But first things first.

First, take note of your current directory in the UNIX account; the uploaded files will end up in that directory, so make sure you're in the one you want to be in.

Quick UNIX Tip #105

You can check your current path in a UNIX account with the **pwd** command. If you are at the top-level directory in your account, you'll see a result something like **/home/username** or **/u/usr/username**. So if you are within, say, the "pix" directory of your account, **pwd** reports that.

To move a file in your UNIX account from one directory to another, use the **mv** command. For example, let's say you just uploaded the margaret.gif file, and it ended up in your home directory instead of in "pix" where you wanted it. You can move the file using the following command:

mv ~*yourusername*/margaret.gif ~*yourusername*/pix/margaret.gif

Be sure to keep that tilde (~) in the command and to replace *yourusername* with your actual username, such as mikey or mary12 or whatever.

Then you must command the UNIX machine to receive the upload. If you're using the Zmodem protocol (as in the examples in this book), that requires the **rz** command (receive Zmodem). Assuming you're in the directory you want to be in, you should be all set. Isn't this exciting, like leaving for a camping trip early on a Friday morning?! In your UNIX account, either select the option for uploading from a menu or, at the shell prompt, enter **rz** and press **Enter**.

```
%rz
rz ready. Type "sz file ..." to your modem program
**B010000012f4ced
```

Although this says to type **sz** to your modem program, it really just means to begin the upload however you have to.

Next you tell your terminal program to begin an upload. To do so, you may have to select from a pull-down menu, hit a hot key, or click an icon. (In the case of ProComm, you select the **Online**, **Send File** command.) Regardless of what program and which method you use to start the upload, a dialog box like the one shown in the following figure appears.

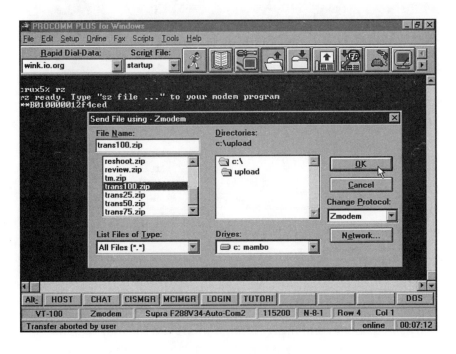

Select the file you want to upload.

Check This Out...

Seem to Be Dragging? You'll often get slightly slower throughput when uploading than when downloading. So don't expect cps/bps rates to be quite as high as you may be used to when transferring files in the other direction.

In the dialog box, select the file you want to upload. Then click on the **OK** button, and the magic begins.

The now-familiar transfer status window pops up, in which you can watch the progress of the transfer. The diagnostic information it shows is the same for uploading as for downloading, so you want to watch for the same yellow flags.

When the whole shebang is done, well, you're done! When it works, it's just not that difficult. When it doesn't work, uhhh, errr....

Uploading in progress. Watch out for errors—and pray.

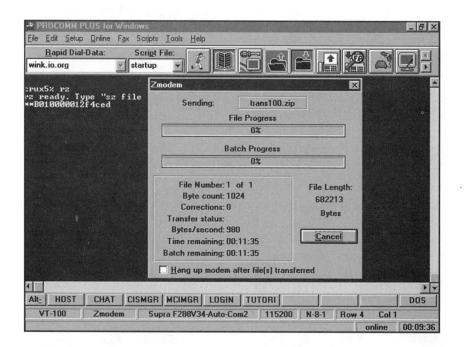

More Friggin' Errors! Arrggg!

One thing that can't be denied about computing is that it keeps you on your toes. If you're using a machine whose only capability is precision, there can be an amazing amount of frustration. If you thought that just because the download went smoothly with no errors, an upload would be the same, I have one grunt for you—HA!

Again, the culprit will be the conspicuous CRC error. (If you recall the CRC problem from your downloading experience, it essentially had to do with data coming in too quickly.) CRC errors during uploading are also often caused by a pacing problem.

Pacing problems can definitely be caused by improper flow control, and CRC errors (while uploading) can be a sign of that. However, let's assume that you have checked your flow control situation, and it's set for the proper cable and the proper terminal program configuration. In that case, the problem may be on the receiving (remote) end of the transfer.

One definite cause of this problem is uploading to an account on a different system from the one you dial into. For example, some people dial up a number to connect to the Net and then telnet from there to an account located somewhere else. If you attempt to upload to that account, you may very well encounter CRC errors because the route from your computer to your dial-in account to your UNIX account may not be able to sustain a fluid pace. If you upload to an account that you are directly placed into upon dialing your provider, the route is more direct (your computer to theirs), and an upload is much more likely to succeed without a basketful of CRC errors.

Short Chapter

Isn't it ironic that the two chapters about actual file transferring are among the shortest? But there is, in fact, good reason: the act of hitting a "download" icon and typing a two-letter UNIX command is not the meat of the dinner. Understanding the issues surrounding the transfer of files (from compression to terminal program settings) is where the real work is. That's my self-defense argument, anyway.

The Least You Need to Know

There aren't too many things you need to know about uploading once you've mastered (or at least succeeded in) the art of downloading. So there.

➤ Be sure you're using the same transfer protocol on both sides. Again, I recommend Zmodem. It's just easier that way.

➤ In UNIX, you begin an upload (to the UNIX account) with the **rz** command. Then you must use a menu command, an icon, or a hot key to tell your terminal program to begin the upload.

➤ You select a file to upload from the dialog box your terminal program presents.

➤ Watch for CRC errors, which may indicate flow control configuration problems or circuitous routes to the ultimate destination computer. Try to keep the number of computers in the loop to a minimum; two (yours and your service provider's) is optimal.

The UNIX Two-Step

Get out your fiddles, it's hoedown time. Or perhaps one should say "line dancing time" to sound contemporary. Users of dumb terminals connecting to UNIX or menu-based accounts don't have the luxury of downloading files directly from Internet sites to their computers. So, much as you would cross a rapids without Birkenstocks, you have to find the stepping stones in between shores. This chapter details the common two-step that you dance when you want to retrieve a file from, say, an FTP site to your local hard drive.

Leapfrogging Around the Net (One Step, Two Step)

Awhile back we spoke about the "middleman." The middleman is your service provider's computer, which essentially does the Internet communicating for you. That's why you use a dumb terminal (and that's why you're reading this section of the book). So, if you want to reach out there and grab a file from the Net (from an FTP site or even UseNet, for example), you can only do so with your service provider's computer, i.e., your Internet account. To get that file to its ultimate destination—your personal computer—you'll then need to transfer it from your account to your local PC. When you do so, you may think that it's because we put the file transfer concepts in this book together in such a beautiful and elegant way that a rainbow forms in your office. Of course, that could just be too much sugar.

There is a plethora of ways to get a file from the Internet to your account. (I can't really cover them all in detail here, but there are whole books that do just that.) I've mentioned the World Wide Web, Gopher, and UseNet. However, FTP is the most common way to retrieve files, so in the examples in this book, that's what I'll use.

The general outline of the concept is this:

1. Use a UNIX account to ftp a file from an Internet site to your Internet account.

2. Download the file from your Internet account to your local PC.

Simple enough? It actually is, and you may already know how to do this from your existing knowledge of the Net and from having read the earlier chapters in this book. For that reason, this chapter is essentially one big walk-through example for clarity's sake (clarity appreciates that sort of thing).

Before you begin with FTP, I should point out that two different versions of FTP are available on some UNIX accounts. Some have "plain old" FTP, which is what I illustrate here because it is a standard. Systems with more hip administrators may also have a program called *NcFTP*, which is a more modern, easy-to-use, feature-rich FTP client. If you have NcFTP on your system (it will say so when you run **ftp**), I recommend that you use it; the commands I use here for plain old FTP also work in NcFTP.

Dance-Thru: FTP to UNIX Account

First things first: you need to choose a site to ftp from. Well, for argument's sake (clarity doesn't like that so much), let's say you don't have a specific file in mind, but you want to see what's the latest software available for your PC. "WinSite" is the nickname of a popular FTP site for Windows software, and via some other means, I've learned that its address is **ftp.winsite.com**. So starting at the UNIX shell prompt in your Internet account, run FTP and open a connection to Win Site.

```
% ftp
ftp> open ftp.winsite.com
Connected to winftp.winsite.com.
220-
220-          You have reached winftp.winsite.com [129.79.26.27].
220-
```

```
220-      All anonymous ftp transactions are logged. If you find this
220-         policy unacceptable, terminate your connection NOW.
220-
220-      If you cannot login due to lack of connections, please try again.
220-
220- !!!!!!!!!!!!!!!!!!!!!!!!!!!!!!!!!!!!!!!!!!!!!!!!!!!!!!!!!!!!!!!!!!!!
220- !!!!            We are now accepting Windows95 uploads          !!!!
220- !!!!   This server will be your Windows95 software archive      !!!!
220- !!!!   Put your Windows95 software in /pub/pc/win95/uploads      !!!!
220- !!!!!!!!!!!!!!!!!!!!!!!!!!!!!!!!!!!!!!!!!!!!!!!!!!!!!!!!!!!!!!!!!!!!
220-
220-
220-
220-
220 winftp FTP server (Version wu-2.4(9)Wed Jun 28 19:35:10 EST 1995)ready.
Name (ftp.winsite.com:aaron):
```

At this prompt, enter the name **anonymous**.

```
331 Guest login ok, send your complete e-mail address as password.
Password:
```

At the above prompt, enter your e-mail address in the form
myusername@myemail.address.

```
230-**   You have reached winftp.winsite.com [129.79.26.27]
230-**   Micron P5-90 PCI PowerStation+ Linux 1.2.10 64MB memory 6GB disks
230-**
230-** To request automatic help, e-mail:  ftp@winsite.com
230-**         To contact us via e-mail:  ftp-admin@winsite.com
230-**      Windows files are located in:  /pub/pc/win3
230-** Your current working directory is:  /
230-**
230-** !!!!!!!!!!!!!!!!!!!!!!!!!!!!!!!!!!!!!!!!!!!!!!!!!!!!!!!!!!!!!!!!!!!!
230-** !!!!            We are now accepting Windows95 uploads          !!!!
230-** !!!!   This server will be your Windows95 software archive      !!!!
230-** !!!!   Put your Windows95 software in /pub/pc/win95/uploads      !!!!
230-** !!!!!!!!!!!!!!!!!!!!!!!!!!!!!!!!!!!!!!!!!!!!!!!!!!!!!!!!!!!!!!!!!!!!
230-**
230-**            You are user number:  138 (of a possible 160)
230-**               Local time is:  Tue Aug  1 08:51:48 1995 [EST]
230-**
230-
230 Guest login ok, access restrictions apply.
Remote system type is UNIX.
Using binary mode to transfer files.
```

The above is mostly system information, some of which you may or may not find interesting. You do need to note one important piece of information, however. The last
output line, which says Using binary mode to transfer files, will be important in a
few minutes. Remember it.

Now that you are connected to WinSite, you need to get a directory listing to find where the Windows software is:

```
ftp> dir
200 PORT command successful.
150 Opening ASCII mode data connection for /bin/ls.
total 7
drwxr-xr-x   7 0        1            1024 Jul 26 00:46 .
drwxr-xr-x   7 0        1            1024 Jul 26 00:46 ..
dr-xr-xr-x   2 0        0            1024 Jul 11 23:19 bin
drwxr-x--x   5 0        0            1024 Jul 31 09:34 ftpd
drwx--x--x   2 0        0            1024 Jul 20 09:19 msgs
dr-xr-xr-x   3 0        0            1024 Jul 26 00:45 pub
drwxr-xr-x   3 0        0            1024 Jul 11 23:20 usr
226 Transfer complete.
```

Presumably, the directory you want will be inside **pub** because that is the traditional Net convention. Move into **pub** and get another directory listing.

```
ftp> cd pub
250 CWD command successful.
ftp> dir
200 PORT command successful.
150 Opening ASCII mode data connection for /bin/ls.
total 5
dr-xr-xr-x   3 0        0            1024 Jul 26 00:45 .
drwxr-xr-x   7 0        1            1024 Jul 26 00:46 ..
-r--r--r--   1 0        1             127 Jun 26 09:57 .cache
-r--r--r--   1 0        1             171 Oct 13  1994 menu
dr-xr-xr-x   7 0        0            1024 Jul 31 00:15 pc
226 Transfer complete.
```

Okay, you're getting warmer: there's a **pc** directory. Move into that.

```
ftp> cd pc
250 CWD command successful.
ftp> dir
200 PORT command successful.
150 Opening ASCII mode data connection for /bin/ls.
total 9
dr-xr-xr-x   7 0         0           1024 Jul 31 00:15 .
dr-xr-xr-x   3 0         0           1024 Jul 26 00:45 ..
-r--r--r--   1 0         1            242 Jun 26 09:57 .cache
dr-xr-xr-x   2 30        0           1024 Jul 11 23:20 borland
-r--r--r--   1 0         1            270 May  2 00:30 menu
dr-xr-xr-x   3 0        31           1024 Jul 11 23:20 misc
dr-xr-xr-x   2 0         0           1024 Jul 11 23:20 starter
dr-xr-xr-x  26 0         1           1024 Jul 31 00:57 win3
dr-xr-xr-x  21 0         0           1024 Jul 23 09:43 win95
226 Transfer complete.
```

Bingo! For the time being, make believe you're a Windows 3.1 user (there is actually more software there for Windows 3.1 than for Windows 95 right now, so it makes for a better example). Go into the **win3** directory and get another listing.

```
ftp> cd win3
250-** Welcome to the Windows Collection at WinSite.
250-
250-Please read the file README
250-   it was last modified on Fri Jul 28 22:15:06 1995 - 4 days ago
250 CWD command successful.
ftp> dir
200 PORT command successful.
150 Opening ASCII mode data connection for /bin/ls.
total 1173
dr-xr-xr-x  26 0          1             1024 Jul 31 00:57 .
dr-xr-xr-x   7 0          0             1024 Jul 31 00:15 ..
dr-xr-xr-x   4 0          0             1024 Jul 21 11:52 .admin
-r--r--r--   1 0          1             2667 Jun 26 09:57 .cache
-r--r--r--   1 0          0               46 Jul  5 09:08 .message
-r--r--r--   1 0          0             1162 Mar 23  1994 BECOME_A_MIRROR
-r--r--r--   1 0          1             2107 Feb  2 10:08 CDROMS.TXT
-rw-r--r--   1 0          0           341971 Jul 31 00:57 INDEX
-rw-r--r--   1 0          0           145200 Jul 31 00:57 INDEX.ZIP
-rw-r--r--   1 0          0            98410 Jul 31 00:57 LS-LTR.ZIP
-r--r--r--   1 0          0            22997 Jul 28 22:15 README
-r--r--r--   1 0          0              756 Jul 28 22:17 SYSTEM.TXT
dr-xr-xr-x   2 0          0             2048 Jul 31 00:55 access
dr-xr-xr-x   2 0          0             5120 Jul 31 00:55 demo
dr-xr-xr-x   2 0          0            16384 Jul 31 00:55 desktop
-r--r--r--   1 0          0              496 Dec  6  1993 dirtree
dr-xr-xr-x   4 0          0             1024 Jul 12 01:22 drivers
dr-xr-xr-x   2 0          0             1024 Jul 31 00:55 excel
dr-xr-xr-x   4 0          0             3072 Jul 31 21:04 fonts
dr-xr-xr-x   2 0          0             9216 Jul 31 00:55 games
dr-xr-xr-x   2 0          0             2048 Jul 31 00:55 icons
-rw-r--r--   1 0          0             6546 Jul 31 00:57 last100uploads
```

In truth, this isn't even the entire list, but that would be too long. Suffice it to say that there are many directories of Windows 3.x software here. But the file you're most interested in on this particular seek and find mission is the final one: **last100uploads**. That file will fill you in on what's new around here.

Before you retrieve that file, think back to when FTP told you that you were in binary transfer mode (I told you to remember it!). Well because this file is an ASCII file, you need to switch to ASCII mode before you retrieve the **last100uploads** file or it may not display properly.

```
ftp> ascii
200 Type set to A.
```

Good, that worked. Now go get the file.

```
ftp> get last100uploads
local: last100uploads remote: last100uploads
200 PORT command successful.
150 Opening ASCII mode data connection for last100uploads (6546 bytes).
226 Transfer complete.
6647 bytes received in 0.63 seconds (10 Kbytes/s)
```

Very nice. You don't need to download this particular file to your PC to view it; UNIX can handle that. If you just use the Ctrl+Z key combination, you can temporarily leave the FTP program and view the file. (In fact, you're just putting the FTP on "hold," not breaking the connection.) So hit **Ctrl+Z**, and this happens:

```
ftp> ^Z
Suspended
%
```

Back at your shell prompt, view the file:

```
%more last100uploads
**  This File Last Updated:     Mon Jul 31 1995 at 12:57:33 AM EST
winsock/yawtel07.zip    950721  Yet Another Windows socket Telnet v0.7 Beta
nt/sp3i86_3.exe 950721  <REMOVED, The file was corrupt>
nt/sp3i86_2.exe 950721  <REMOVED, The file was corrupt>
drivers/printer/d5w3us.exe      950721  <REMOVED, The file was corrupt>
util/wnmai251.zip       950710  WinNET Mail v2.51 <ASP>
games/727_11.zip        950629  A Hi/Low Betting Card Game w/Sounds
wpwin/searchwp.zip      950627  CommTech PowerSearch v3.0 for WpWin QuickFinde
winsock/xplan03.zip     950627  Update .plan file through winsock
winsock/xfing025.zip    950627  XFinger v0.2 Winsock finger client
winsock/smtsrf11.zip    950627  SmartSurf V1.1 Windows Online Costs Monitor
winsock/autown16.zip    950627  Automated Internet for Windows 1.6
util/wcpd20.zip 950627  Windows Complete Program Deleter 2.0 uninstaller
```

Again, I cut the full list short. As you can see, it includes each new file, the subdirectory in which it resides, the date it was uploaded, and a small annotation about it. Let's say you've scanned this file and decided that **SmartSurf V1.1** looks like the greatest thing since all-night Bingo. You want it.

To return to the FTP program, type **fg** at the shell prompt (and hit **Enter** a couple of times).

```
%fg
ftp
ftp>
```

Okay, now change to the subdirectory (**winsock**) that contains the file you want.

```
ftp> cd winsock
250 CWD command successful.
```

Before you get the file, consider the transfer mode. You switched to ASCII transfer mode earlier, remember? But this is a ZIP file, and as such, it's binary. You must use binary mode to transfer this file to the UNIX account, or it will be useless.

```
ftp> binary
200 Type set to I.
```

Great. Now for the booty.

```
ftp> get smtsrf11.zip
local: smtsrf11.zip remote: smtsrf11.zip
200 PORT command successful.
150 Opening BINARY mode data connection for smtsrf11.zip (207969 bytes).
226 Transfer complete.
207969 bytes received in 9.9 seconds (20 Kbytes/s)
```

Yahoo! That's it—you got the file! Now it sits happily in your UNIX account.

From here you can quit FTP (with the unintuitive **quit** command), or you can get more files. Or you can just sing for joy.

Dance-Thru: UNIX to PC

Now that you've completed phase one of your mission, it's time for the final blaze of glory. This should be easy because it's the same exact procedure you went through in Chapter 12.

1. Proceed with a dumb terminal download. Once again, Zmodem gets the nod as the file transfer protocol of choice.

2. Make sure the terminal program is properly prepared and configured. (If you've done this before, it should be just fine already.)

3. Then from your Internet account, issue the ol' **sz** command.

```
%sz smtsrf11.zip
**sz 3.36 04-23-94 finished.
```

The transfer status window pops up on your terminal program, and in the happy end, it all looks like the following figure (on the UNIX side of things).

The second step in the hula: download complete!

And that, as they say in Brooklyn, is that.

Don't Forget About Zmodem

Remember that you can perform a batch download with Zmodem. So if you have ftp'd multiple files to your UNIX account, you can download them all in one swill. If you do, the files wind up on your local PC wherever you've defined the download path settings in your terminal program. When you do a batch download, you can go about your business and do other more productive things (such as watch your favorite daytime talk shows) while your computer does the work.

The Least You Need to Know

Users of dial-up UNIX accounts have to deal with the middleman. It's not particularly difficult, but it does require a little dance.

To transfer a file from an Internet site to your local PC, you must work through two steps:

Internet site -> UNIX account

UNIX account -> local PC

When using FTP, this means you ftp to the Internet site from the UNIX account and retrieve the file. Then you use **sz** from UNIX to download the file to your local PC with your terminal program.

## Chapter 15

Somewhere In Between: Commercial Online Services

In This Chapter

➤ The whats and what-nots of online services

➤ America Online

➤ The Microsoft Network

➤ A spot of CompuServe and Prodigy

If there are any good arguments for one world government controlling every aspect of people's lives, one would be that confusing technology situations such as the one discussed here might be avoided. Of course, there would also be disadvantages, such as a lack of personalized "UKIS4ME" license plates.

It's easy to get confused about the differences between the *online services* and the Internet. (And in some cases, it's in certain parties' self-interest to maintain that confusion.) First I'll clear the air about what an online service is exactly, and then I'll show you how file transfers under the wing of online services are often much simpler than those we talk about elsewhere in this book.

Everybody Get Online Now

Due to the extremely dynamic state of these still-emerging technologies and their assimilation into our culture, many people use words that have very ambiguous meanings to newcomers. In the strictest sense, any time you connect your computer to another computer, you are *online*. But that's not exactly what people mean when they use the term *online service*. To explain by means of contrast, let's consider what this beast known as the Internet actually is.

The *Internet* is not a "thing." The word refers to the entire set of computers that can communicate with one another using shared communications lines, protocols, and so on. This *set* may change daily, depending on who installs a computer one place in the world or removes one somewhere else. In a sense, the Internet is like a nation: it does not have one static face. At any given snapshot in time, either is defined by the individuals (people for a nation, computers for the Internet) who connect to make it up. This is called a *network*. There are two major differences, though, between the Net and a nation. First, in a nation, the set of participants is bounded by geography; on the Net, the set is bounded by shared technology. Second, a nation has a "head" that leads it (presumably); the Internet has no such head but is merely a collection. On the Internet, the facilities available and uses thereof are only a matter of what any participant decides to create.

An *online service*, by contrast, is both a network and a governed nation. Consider any of the popular online services, such as America Online. At the technological level, America Online is also composed of a set of computers that can communicate with one another. So it is a network. But, unlike the Internet, the network of America Online is centrally controlled and regulated. That is, every bit of it is owned by one company, perhaps even one person. That "head" has total control: he determines what may or may not be done using the network and offers the service's users whatever facilities he wants. Online services such as America Online, CompuServe, Prodigy, and The Microsoft Network are national and even international in scope, and they sell you access to their privately owned—*privately controlled*—networks.

A Costly Way to Access the Internet
Unless you find the online service's private offerings attractive, paying their rates merely for the opportunity to rent Internet time is much more expensive than starting an account with most local ISPs.

In a financial sense, you pay an online service for the use of their facilities and for the costs they bear in creating an environment that you presumably find comfortable and productive. On the Internet, you pay to "rent time" from the provider's Internet connection. (For this reason, Internet accounts tend to be cheaper than online services.) A large number of providers (called Internet Service Providers or ISPs) who rent time in the form of either UNIX shell accounts or SLIP/PPP accounts, have sprung up. They're located all over the place, and each one serves one or several particular regions.

To make matters even less clear-cut, the online services have begun to add and advertise a new twist: *Internet access*. Each of the online services now offers at least some access to Internet-based facilities, be it FTP or the World Wide Web or UseNet. In those cases, you are paying the online service *both* for using their privately controlled resources and for renting time on the Internet.

This chapter assumes you do have an account with one of the above-mentioned services (otherwise there's little point in reading it when you could be out pricing 2 × 4's instead). Because the online services are in complete control over how you accomplish any task, transferring files tends to be relatively straightforward. You don't need to worry about protocols, configuration settings, and so forth. It's all taken care of already—automatically. Now let's look at each major service and breeze through how they handle that all-important act... (transferring of course, what else?).

Swinging with America Online

I'm willing to place odds that a good 40% of every AOL payment goes to hiring graphic artists (this is a baseless joke; please don't sue me). Seriously, AOL does sport a very slick and very easy-to-navigate interface.

But we're here to talk about downloading, right? Well, America Online offers two major sources of files to download: FTP via the Internet and software *forums*.

FTP by AOL (and Other Tales of Alphabet Soup)

When you connect to AOL, its glitzy main menu appears. The following figure shows the main menu, which gives you access to all of AOL's features.

From America Online's main menu, head for the Internet Connection.

The Internet connection

Click on the **Internet Connection** button. In the Internet Connection window, you see the net-related facilities that AOL provides. The largest source of files on the Net comes by way of FTP. So click the **FTP** icon and zoom to the next menu, the main FTP menu shown in the next figure.

You can get further info about this FTP thing straight from the horse's mouth.

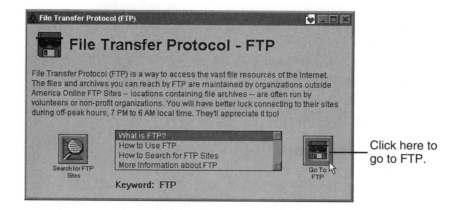

Click here to go to FTP.

From this main FTP menu, you can get more information on the subject itself. In brief, you can click on the options in this list to learn about the topics I discuss in Chapters 9 and 16 of this book. To jump directly into the mud, click that little **Go to FTP** icon that shows the street-cool floppy disk. Oh, and pause to smile. The dialog box that appears contains a list of popular FTP sites.

From here, you can select the FTP site on the Internet that you want to connect to. America Online provides a brief list of sites that contain much of the popular software you may be looking for. For example, the first site listed is WinSite, the major Windows software repository. If none of the choices offered are appealing (or if you just enjoy typing), click the **Other Site** button and enter the name of any FTP site in the universe that you want to visit. Yep! Type in your own, be your own person! That's exactly what you're gonna do.

Find Mac Files Here, Too
AOL even maintains their own Internet FTP site that contains mirrors of popular archives for both the PC and the Mac (**mirrors.aol.com**).

For example, enter the **ftp.netnet.net** site (largely because I happen to find myself there a lot and its address has been imprinted into my neural ganglia). This site consists mostly of mirrors of other sites, but, it is often easier to access during the day than many others are. Note the check box labeled Ask for login name and password. If you leave this unchecked, AOL attempts to log in to the FTP site as **anonymous**, which is the standard method for all public sites. Therefore, if you want to access a private FTP site, such as your own personal UNIX account on another system, you need to check this box so you can enter a username and password. Then click the **Connect** button. The behind-the-scenes negotiations begin, and if they're successful, the FTP site's message-of-the-day greeting appears. Click **OK** to move past the message and into the site's contents. What appears next is AOL's prototypical FTP navigation window (see the following figure).

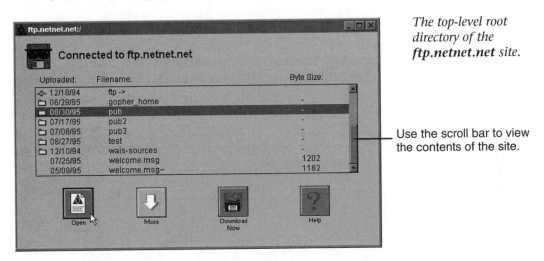

*The top-level root directory of the **ftp.netnet.net** site.*

Use the scroll bar to view the contents of the site.

Browse through the contents of the FTP site by clicking the scroll bar. If necessary, click on a subdirectory folder and click **Open**, or just double-click a folder to open it. For now, enter the **pub** subdirectory. After you do some searching (and for the sheer sake of getting on with this example), enter a subdirectory called **peoples** within **pub**. I have no idea what this topic is about, but there are several files here, as you can see in the next figure.

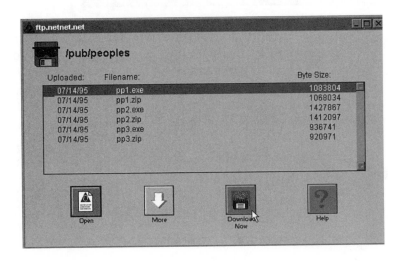

Inside the peoples subdirectory (but who knows what that is).

Multiple File Downloading Is Not an Option

It is not possible, at present, to select multiple files for download in AOL. What you can do as a workaround to downloading a batch is to go around and select each of the files you want, and then click **Download later**. But as for immediate transfer, it's one at a time.

Now we'll begin to download. Select the **Download Now** button and click on the **pp1.exe** file. (Regardless of what the file is or where you got it, this is a good reason to remember to scan for viruses on downloaded files!) The Download Manager dialog box appears (see the following figure), asking where you'd like the file downloaded to. Select a destination path and file name for the file. The AOL default path is fine for right now so click **OK**. AOL starts the download and displays the download progress in the File Transfer status window for your convenience.

Choose a destination for this download.

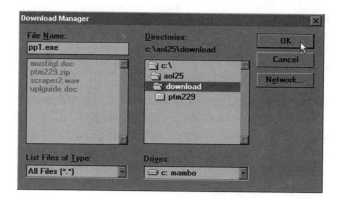

Do Two Things at Once You can continue to use other AOL facilities while a file downloads, but response time may be slow.

The status window provides vital details about the transfer—namely how close it is to being complete! If you click the **Sign Off After Transfer** button, you are signed off and disconnected from AOL at the end of the download. This is just (just??) a way of saving some money; it takes a little longer to manually log off. Of course, this is only useful if the download is the final activity you want to engage in before logging off AOL. At any time during the transfer, you can click the **Finish Later** button to temporarily pause the download (which you can resume later).

Something Funny Transferred on the Way to the Forum

Now you know how you can use AOL to reach Internet-based resources, FTP specifically. But America Online also provides its own file libraries from which you can download. The advantages of using AOL's file libraries are that they include informative file descriptions, well-maintained organization, and preventative virus scanning (although this can never be 100% perfect).

To get to AOL's file libraries, click the **Computing** button on AOL's main menu (from which you previously jumped to the Internet Connection). This time you land in the Computing forum, shown in the next figure. There should be some goodies in here.

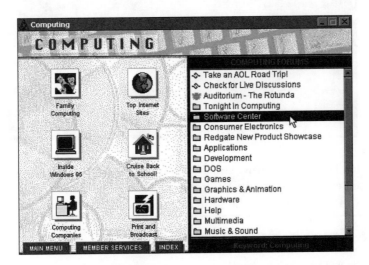

The software center in the AOL Computing forum.

On the right side of the window is a list of computing forums, one of which has the attractive name Software Center. And where better to retrieve software than the Software Center? Exactly. So give it a quick double-click, and you find yourself at the Software Center main menu. Click the **Forum Libraries** button, and AOL displays a list of software libraries you can choose from. This place is like one of those smorgasbord restaurants!

Because you're a Windows user, head the ol' mouse pointer in that direction. Double-click the **Windows** forum name to see what's available in the way of Windows software files. The list that appears should look something like the following figure. From there, go for **Utilities for Win95 & NT**.

You'll notice that the rest of the process is much like that for using FTP. AOL presents a list of available files, each of which has a description you can read by clicking the Read Description icon. You also have the familiar Download Now and Download Later options and an option for uploading. For the time being, disregard the delayed downloading and uploading options; we'll discuss those in a few sentences.

159

You're sure to find something interesting here—at least if you have Windows 95 or Windows NT.

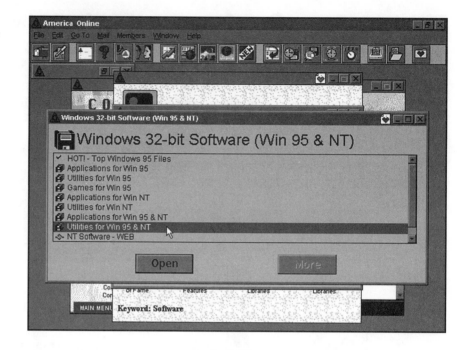

For this example, click **Download Now**. From here on out, everything is the same as it was for FTP (discussed earlier). The main difference between downloading files via FTP and downloading from AOL forums is the source of the file, not the procedure you use.

Not Now AOL, I Have a Headache

One neat feature (which I've already mentioned a few times) is the Download Later option. When you select a file to download later, AOL stores it in a queue that you can manipulate at any later date. To do that, you use AOL's Download Manager (see the following figure), which you access by selecting **Download Manager** from the **File** menu.

The Download Manager dialog box shows you previous downloads and enables you to finish delayed ones. In the figure, for example, you can see two downloads in-waiting. The first is one that I selected from a software forum, and the second is the file that I walked you through the process of downloading earlier in this chapter (which I interrupted by clicking Finish Later mid-transfer).

You use the buttons across the bottom of the Download Manager dialog box to work with files you've selected for downloading. Click the **Show Files Downloaded** button to see a log of your past actions. To complete any of the downloads in the queue, select them by holding down the **Ctrl** key and clicking their names. Then click the **Download Now** button to start the transfers again.

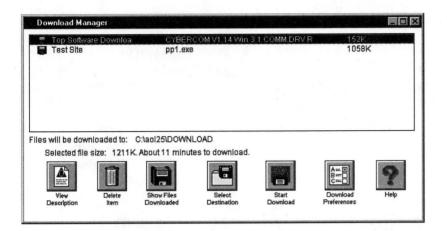

Using AOL's Download Manager, you can complete delayed downloads.

Another button worth further explanation is the Download Preferences button. Click **Download Preferences**, and a window opens, displaying the following options:

Display image files on Download   If you download a GIF or JPEG-format graphic file with this option enabled, AOL launches a viewer to display it. You may or may not want this enabled.

Automatically decompress files at sign-off   If this option is enabled, any ZIP files that you download are automatically decompressed when you log off of AOL. You may find this convenient, or you may prefer to control unzipping using WinZip (in which case you deselect this option).

Delete ZIP and ARC files after decompression   If you enable the previous option and enable this one, the original ZIP (or ARC) file is deleted after it's decompressed. I would not recommend using this option; you'd better keep the ZIP around just in case you need it again. You can delete it yourself when you're sure you don't need it.

Confirm additions to my download list   Select this option if you want AOL to ask your permission before adding files to the download list. It's safest to leave this option enabled.

Retain information about my last *X* downloads   Use this option to indicate how large a history log you want to keep. It's completely up to you. I just stick with the default 100.

Lawful Uploading

You can also upload software to AOL, and the service encourages you to do so. In fact, they don't even charge you for the online time it takes to upload an archive. However, you do have to follow a fairly strict set of rules. Those rules and the uploading instructions vary from forum to forum, so my advice to you is to read AOL's own information files.

You can start by entering the **Computing** area, followed by the **Software Center**, and then the **Free Upload Center**. Read the first file, **Uploading Tips**, and then read any further information in the specific forums to which you want to upload files.

New Kid on the Block: The Microsoft Network

Jumping into the online service fray, Bill Gates and Co. launched their own service along with Windows 95. Intended to rival all of the other online services, MSN has the advantage of being well-integrated into the Windows 95 work environment. Thus it's very system-friendly. On the other hand, it's only useful to people with PCs. On the third hand, that's quite a few people.

To sign up with MSN, and to access it forever thereafter, just double-click **The Microsoft Network** icon (shown in the next figure) on your Windows 95 desktop. If you don't seem to have such an icon, you probably did not install MSN with Windows 95. You can use the Control Panel's Add/Remove Programs function to install MSN if you didn't do so upon initial installation.

The Microsoft Network icon. Pretty, isn't it?

Sign Up for MSN Signing up with MSN is not entirely relevant to this chapter, so I'm not going to walk you through it. However, the service holds your hand the entire way.

When MSN starts, its main menu opens in a window (see the following figure). Given the flashy artwork MSN sports, Microsoft either found some starving artisans whom AOL overlooked, or they simply cloned some new ones.

Like Prodigy, MSN does not directly support Internet FTP. There are, however, plenty of files available in MSN's own libraries. But before we begin digging into them, it's helpful to understand the metaphor that underlies everything we do in the Microsoft Network.

162

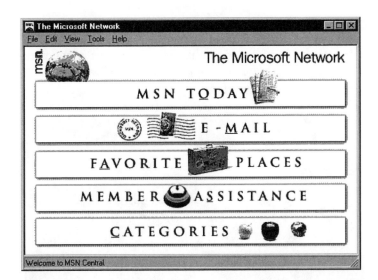

The main slate of options at The Microsoft Network.

Does It or Does It Not Support Internet?

In all honesty, the situation is about as clear as mud. Newer versions of the MSN software (such as version 1.05, current at the time of this writing, or the version that comes with the Microsoft Plus! commercial package) support two types of MSN connection: "The Microsoft Network" and "Internet and the Microsoft Network." The latter has fewer access numbers in place than does the former; however, that will change over time. If you choose only The Microsoft Network when using the New Connection setup in MSN, you can use only the facilities provided within the MSN folders. In that case, there is no explicit FTP capability. If you configure an Internet and The Microsoft Network connection, you can use any Windows clients discussed in this book in addition to MSN's own offerings. Granted, this is a somewhat confusing scenario at this point in time; it will make more sense after you read Chapter 16.

In constructing the network to be integrated with the Windows 95 environment, the MSN is designed as if it were another hard drive on your computer. That is, you move around MSN by opening up folders, which may contain files or more folders. A file can consist of anything: a plain text message from another user (similar to a UseNet posting), a binary file, or a combination of both. So whether you are in a file library or a discussion forum, all information is stored in files that you can double-click to access. Should the files contain binary data such as an archive, a button appears that you can click to initiate a download. That is the concept, anyway. You'll see it in practice as the pages turn.

Words into Actions

To paraphrase a certain singing rural Austrian character, let's start at the very beginning. Click the **Categories** button of the MSN main menu to move toward some files. The following figure shows the Categories window.

Categories of interest at MSN are organized like file folders on a PC.

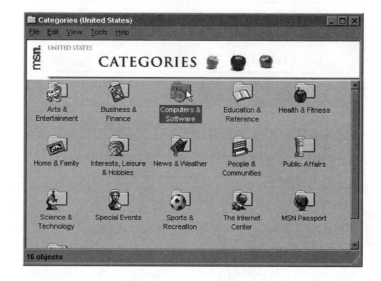

As you can see, each area of interest is represented by a folder in MSN. In this case, double-click on the **Computers & Software** folder to open a window that contains yet another series of folders. As I said earlier, navigating MSN is a lot like navigating around your own computer in Windows 95—and that's no coincidence (of course, I can't prove it empirically, so don't ask me to).

In the Computers & Software folder, double-click the **Software** folder, and then click on the **Electronic Games** folder. Within that folder, click on the **Computer Games Forum** folder to reveal yet another set of folders, including the one you want: Computer Games File Library. Click on **Computer Games File Library** to find some daytime distractions. The following figure shows the available folders full of games.

These folders are arranged slightly differently, but the concept remains the same. As you scroll up and down to see what's available, the Puzzles folder viciously grabs your attention. Double-click on **Puzzles**, and you see MSN's amazing list of puzzles (shown in the second upcoming figure).

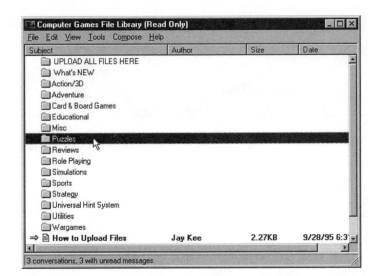

Hopefully there are some good ones; there's only one way to find out.

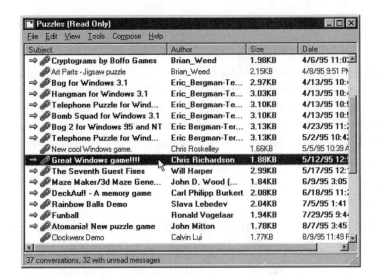

All the puzzle games. Select the Great Windows game and hope the hype is true.

Here's the meat of this whole dinner: files. Remember that on MSN, each file appears as a message. Accessing the "messages" is intuitive enough—another double-click. In this case, you are taken in by the message claiming to be a "Great Windows game." Double-click on the message, and MSN reveals a window like the one in the next figure.

This is what a "message" on MSN looks like. The icon represents the downloadable file.

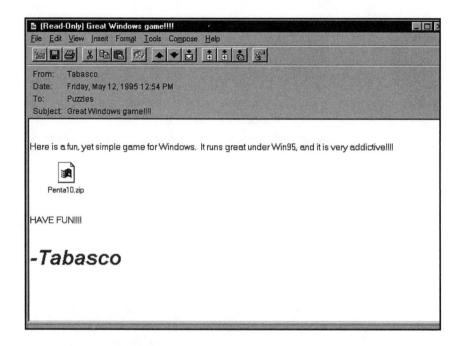

The MSN displays what appears to be an electronic mail message, with **From:** and **To:** header lines and some text, which turns out to be a brief description of the program. An icon represents the ZIP file archive itself. Thus, if you want to download the file—and this goes for most anything on MSN—you simply double-click the icon that represents it. Doing so brings up a window that shows the following information about the file you're about to download:

File size   In this case, you learn that it is almost 102KB in size (not terribly large by today's standards).

Download time   MSN estimates the length of time the download will take based on the type of modem you're using. This download will take less than one minute.

Be Wary of the Status
Unfortunately, even the manager can scan only for *known* viruses. Therefore, it's possible that new ones may escape his examination.

Status   This indicates whether or not the file has been approved by a manager. It should provide reassurance that the archive is not corrupted and that it was scanned for viruses.

Price   This file's price is listed as 0.00, which is nice. However, watch out for files in forums run by third-party companies; they may cost you.

At the bottom of this window are two action-oriented buttons. The Download File button starts the transfer; the Download and Open button transfers the file and attempts to execute it. (The capability to execute the file depends on how you've configured for automatic decompression. See the next paragraph for more on that.) For this example, click on **Download File**.

A file transfer status window opens to update you on the play-by-play (or should one say "bit-by-bit"?). It's not quite as informative as, say, a Zmodem transfer status window, but the important information is there. In this file transfer window, you can configure the preferences for automatic archival extraction. To do so, open the **Tools** menu of the File Transfer Status window and select **Options**. (You can do this while downloading.) The File Transfer Options window shown in the following figure appears.

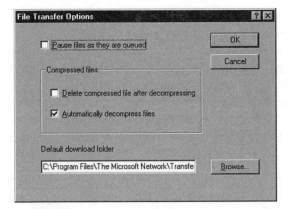

You can configure these options to control how MSN handles downloads.

The first check box regulates whether MSN pauses the operation between the files in a batch download. If you really want an automated download, leave this disabled.

The next two options control how MSN handles compressed archives (usually ZIP files). Skipping to the second check box, indicate whether MSN should attempt to decompress the archive automatically. This works fine if you want extreme automation. However, some people (such as yours truly) prefer to handle these tasks on their own with WinZip. (I guess we need that feeling of control.) Anyway, if you do enable automatic decompression, the first check box takes on significance. You've seen a similar option before. (Remember: Delete the original ZIP file once extracted?) Select it for total automation, but be aware of the risk: if the decompression fails for any reason and the ZIP is deleted, you have to download the whole thing from scratch. I prefer to keep the ZIP around for a little while on the side of prudence (she lets me).

The final control in this window is a text box in which you type the download path. In other words, you tell MSN where the downloaded files should end up on your hard drive. Choose anywhere you like—although it's traditional practice to create a specific directory for such things. (You wouldn't want to break tradition, would you?)

That's largely how file transfers work on the Microsoft Network. Although you may encounter files in locations other than the specified "file forums," the paradigm is the same. There are messages that contain icons representing files, and you double-click the icon for retrieval. That is the basic theory underlying everything on the MSN, and it works fairly intuitively. I suppose that was the point. Take that, you detractors. Somewhere, a Bill smiles.

Other Services

As does America Online, the CompuServe network relies on a straightforward point-and-click interface. In fact, the procedures for retrieving files by Internet FTP or CompuServe's own forums are largely similar to those for AOL. One advantage to using CompuServe is that it has a reputation of having the largest file libraries, and some programs available there cannot be found elsewhere. Another nice feature of CompuServe is that it enables you to register certain shareware programs online. However, insofar as moving files between your PC and the CompuServe network goes, the America Online procedures are highly preferred.

Another very popular online service is Prodigy. Prodigy tends to be more suited to retail-style business than do the other services. For example, none of the Internet-style file libraries are available on Prodigy. Instead, it includes forums dedicated to specific software makers, from whom you can download software for a price. While Prodigy does not include specific FTP access, it does offer a Web browser that, by its very nature, can access Internet FTP sites. You'll learn more about that browser in Chapter 17.

The Least You Need to Know

Online services tend to cost more than straight Internet accounts, but for those who find commercial online services satisfying environments, the good news is that transferring files is relatively straightforward. Much, if not all, of the gritty work has already been taken care of by the designers, and the dirt was swept under the rug.

➤ Online services are discrete networks separate from the Internet. They are centrally owned, operated, and regulated. Today these networks often offer facilities that you can use to connect to the Internet for certain functions.

➤ In America Online, you can access Internet FTP sites in the **Internet Connection** area. From there, you have the same options as anyone else using FTP (as described in Chapter 16).

➤ Downloading a file in America Online generally involves locating the file and clicking the **Download Now** or **Download Later** button.

➤ You can manage interrupted or delayed downloads or view a log of past downloads using AOL's Download Manager (select **Download Manager** from the **File** menu).

➤ The Microsoft Network does not provide a direct FTP facility, but it has many file libraries of its own. Users who are configured for what Microsoft calls "Internet and Microsoft Network" can use standard Windows FTP clients, as described in Chapter 16 and Appendix B.

➤ You navigate through MSN in the same way you move between folders on your hard drive in Windows 95.

➤ Files on MSN appear as messages, which can contain anything from plain text to binary files. Double-click on a file icon in a message to initiate a download.

Part 4
Doing the SLIP/PPP Thing: File Transfers via TCP/IP (Smart Terminals)

or "Real Net folk do it with SLIP."

By day, by night, and even by early evening, more and more people are connecting to the Net as real participants. A whole array of file resources awaits them, some of which we'll climb our way through in the following chapters. And I'll explain in glorious yet sensible detail the curious acronyms FTP and WWW as well as UseNet. Come one, come all.

OOOOOH.

FTP
THE WH STOR

## Chapter 16

All About FTP

In This Chapter

➤ Talking clients

➤ Setting up for fun and transfer

➤ Take the files and run

➤ Up(load) through the pipes

➤ A problem or two

FTP is the Babe Ruth of file transfer facilities. Okay, realistically, FTP has almost nothing in common with the aforementioned baseball hero except its wide popularity. Failed analogies aside, though, the hearty File Transfer Protocol has been in use on the Internet for a long while—and it hasn't yet lost its legs.

In practice, FTP is the de facto standard for transferring a file from one computer to another across the Internet. If you have any sort of TCP/IP connection (such as a SLIP/PPP account), all of this will benefit you greatly. You can now transfer files from any Internet computer directly to your own PC without a middleman, a transfer protocol, or anything else I told you about in Chapter 15. What's more, FTP isn't even particularly difficult to use. So while this is a crucial chapter of this book, it is also a relatively straightforward one. Rejoice.

The Client That's Right for You

When we talk about FTP, we're looking at a classic client-server scenario as Aristotle first wrote about in his seminal work, "Air, Fire, Client, Server." Much of the Internet is based on this model. For our discussion, the focus will be on using the client. It enables you to grab booty from other sites.

A Spot of Theory

Computers are allegedly very obedient. Although it may not always seem so (okay, it rarely seems so), they enjoy doing what they're told to. The purpose of the client/server concept is to allow one computer to command another one. The client's job is to request some sort of information or data from a remote computer. The remote computer must contain a server, which is programmed to understand and process a client's requests.

Both the client and the server require special software to perform their roles. In addition, each client/server pair has to agree on what protocol they will "speak," such as FTP or HTTP (the Web). Different protocols allow for different, more- or less-complex capabilities. One aspect of the complexity of a protocol is how much latitude the client and server have in communications. For example, a very simple client/server protocol might allow for only one command: **send me file *x***. A slightly more advanced protocol might allow for two commands: **send me a list of available files** and **send me file *x***.

Most Internet facilities work with client/server pairs such as FTP, Gopher, and the World Wide Web. You should primarily be concerned with obtaining client software for your own computer. (Server software is often a more advanced beast.)

Basically, you might encounter two styles of FTP clients:

➤ **Command-line clients**   This sort of client requires you to navigate and work on the Internet by entering keyboard commands as you would from the UNIX shell or the MS-DOS prompt. You'll most certainly encounter this type of client in a UNIX account, but there are also some command-line based clients for the PC. The major disadvantage of a command-line client is that it has a higher learning curve for a new user. However, users familiar with command-line environments might prefer one of these. As well, in some cases a command-line client offers the user more control than the graphical client alternative does.

➤ **Graphical point-and-click clients**   Most of the clients and other programs discussed in a book like this are graphical: you navigate and work in them using point-and-click techniques. These types of programs often have tamer learning curves and are, therefore, quite popular with novice users. The major advantages of point-and-click clients are that the concept of what you are doing is more tangible, and that the "how-to" of accomplishing a task is usually more obvious. Even for more experienced users, graphical clients are often just plain quicker to work with.

The major disadvantage of using a graphical client is that they often offer a user less potential power. For example, imagine that you want to transfer a group of files via FTP. Let's say all the files match the wild-card expression **dogf*.*** (meaning every file name begins with **dogf** regardless of what it ends with). In a command-line client, you could transfer all those files with one command; but in most graphical clients, you would have to find all the files that matched that wild-card pattern yourself and manually click on them.

We danced through an example of using a command-line client in Chapter 14. If you are on a PC or a Mac, chances are you'll go for a graphical client. A fine choice. For each platform, you can choose from a few graphical FTP clients, all of which behave similarly. If you are a PC user, the most popular FTP client is WS_FTP, so we'll use that as our detailed example. Other clients are going to be very, very much the same. Even Fetch for the Mac is basically the same, but we'll give it a quick look too because of its popularity. As with any other product, there are several alternatives to WS_FTP that you can choose from (see Appendix B). Feel free to try them all on for size. In the end, it's a matter of personal preference, just like a Speedo.

Setting Up Your New Client

You can find WS_FTP on the Internet at any major Windows FTP site, such as **ftp.winsite.com** (see Appendix B). Of course, then you run into that yolky chicken-and-egg problem because you don't yet have an FTP client to retrieve with. There's no single answer to that, but perhaps the simplest solution is to retrieve WS_FTP to a UNIX account and then download it using a dumb terminal transfer protocol. Otherwise, coax a friend into downloading it for you and slap it onto a trusty floppy.

Once you have the WS_FTP archive, of course, you'll have to dearchive and install it. Note that there are actually two versions of WS_FTP: one for 16-bit TCP/IP software and one for 32-bit. If you're using Windows 95's Dial-Up networking, you want WS_FTP-32; otherwise, get the 16-bit version. Decompress the ZIP file into wherever you'd like the WS_FTP program to reside on your hard drive. Once that's done, just execute the main program file, ws_ftp.exe, using Windows' **Run** command (you may choose to add an icon for this program to a program group for convenience). When the program starts, you see the opening welcome screen shown in the following figure.

The first role of any FTP client is to get you connected to an FTP site. Usually, you can configure a list of sites that you prefer, so you can choose from them quickly whenever necessary. Most FTP clients come with a few sites preconfigured, which makes this manic trampoline called life a wee bit easier. WS_FTP calls each particular site configuration a "Session Profile."

175

WS_FTP's opening screen. Notice the session profile window.

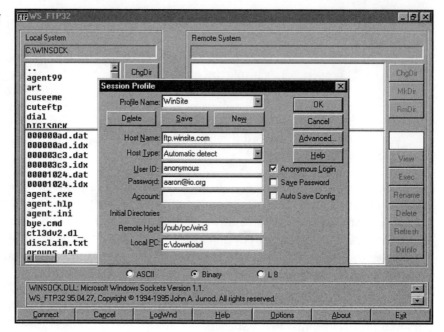

For any given site, you can configure a number of parameters and login parameters.

Profile Name   Type in whatever you'd like to name this site configuration.

Host Name   Enter the actual Internet address of the FTP site you want to connect to.

Host Type   Tell WS_FTP what sort of computer the remote machine at this site will be. In almost all cases, Automatic Detect works just fine. It's unlikely that you'd even know what sort of computer the remote host is, anyway.

User ID   Most public FTP sites are anonymous, which means you should enter **anonymous** as the User ID. Note that you can check the Anonymous Login check box to the right of the User ID entry to have WS_FTP perform anonymous login automatically.

Password   Enter your e-mail address.

Account   If you are connecting to a personal UNIX account, enter the username for that account here. It will most likely be the same as what you entered for User ID.

At the bottom of the Session Profile window are two entries that allow you to specify start-up directories. You can determine which directory path to open for both the remote computer and your local PC. For example, if you prefer that all downloads reside in your local path (C:\DOWNLOAD), enter that in the **Local PC** text box.

When you finish setting these parameters, save the configuration you created for a site by clicking the **Save** button near the top of the window.

If you follow these steps for other sites, you can wind up with a long list of preconfigured sites to choose from (as is touchingly portrayed in the next figure). Simply select the one you want to connect to on any particular occasion.

I Am Who I Am   The only time you wouldn't use anonymous login is if you are connecting to an FTP site on which you have an account (such as your UNIX account). For example, if you wanted to ftp files from your UNIX account, you would enter your account ID and password and set the Host Name to the machine your account is on.

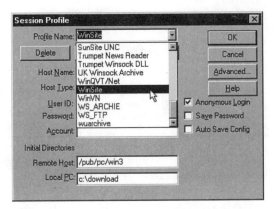

Each item in the list of preconfigured session profiles corresponds to an FTP site.

The Download: Theory and Examples

Finally, an educational experience where the theory is the easy part. In the case of FTP, there isn't a heck of a lot of theory at all. Your client connects to a server, it requests directory listings from the remote computer, and it might request files. If it does, the files pump from the remote computer to your own. Operation complete. Endorphins released. You don't need to tense up about all the sorts of error horrors you suffered through using dumb terminal emulation. If you've managed to get your TCP/IP connection to work in the first place, FTP should function just fine.

In the spirit of predictable fun, though, let's make an example out of WS_FTP connecting to WinSite. Open the connection, browse some directories, and retrieve a few files. After the ride you may feel slightly queasy, but you will know almost everything you need to about using FTP. Please keep your hands inside the book at all times.

177

Do you recall the session profile for the WinSite connection? Come on. You just saw it. Don't tell me you've forgotten so quickly. If this were a pop-up book, you'd have been hit in the face with a screenshot by now, but Que rejected the idea of a pop-up book outright. Anyway, when you select a session profile and click **OK**, the connection opens, resulting in a bifurcated window (good word, huh?). The left window shows the local PC; the right one shows the remote site (see the following figure).

WS_FTP with an open connection to WinSite.

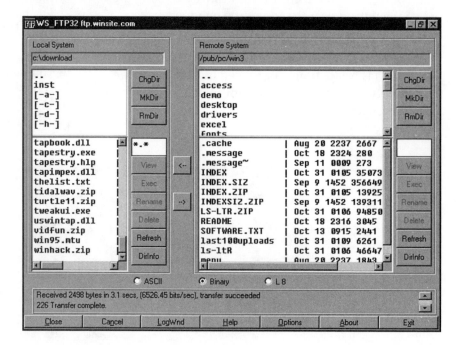

On the left ventricle—er, in the left window—you see the Local System contents. The top half of the window contains directory paths, while the bottom half contains the names of files in the local directory (C:\DOWNLOAD). The right window contains the same sort of information, but for the remote computer (that is, the FTP site).

To the right of each window are operation buttons, which you use to manipulate files between the two computers. You'll learn more about tinkering with those shortly. Below all the windows are buttons for ASCII, Binary, and L8. I'm sure you recall the very important distinction between ASCII and binary files. (You should. I've talked about it enough that I'm starting to sound like a broken record.) Ignore the L8 option. Because most files you transfer will probably be binary, it's safest to leave binary selected. If you do transfer a file that is just plain ASCII text, click the **ASCII** button prior to transfer. If you're not sure, binary is the safer bet.

At the very bottom of this window is a small area where server messages appear. These usually include some information about the system you are connecting to and so forth. Sometimes there is also important information about changes to the site. Unless you have eyesight just short of Superman's, you'll be hard pressed to read the messages that scroll by in that little teeny window. However, most FTP clients offer you a way to see a full log of the server messages. In WS_FTP, for example, you can click the **LogWnd** button in the bottom button bar to see the full window of messages (shown in the next figure).

Where's My Line Break?
If you do transfer an ASCII file as binary, you may lose the line breaks, in which case the resulting file will look funny. The quickest solution is to just go back and download the file again with the **ASCII** button selected.

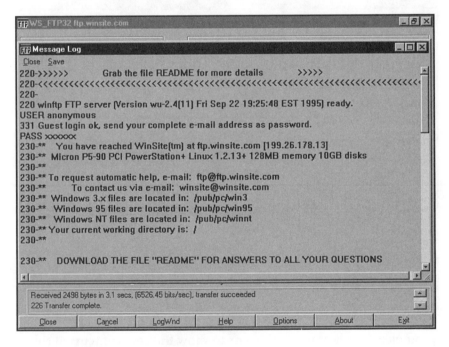

The message log window contains everything the server wants to tell you.

Bringing the Remote Up Close

The right window is the main focus of this example. It lists all that's available on the remote FTP site. As you did in the UNIX example, you'll view the list of new uploads, and then you'll download one of those files.

179

Only for ASCII You can only use View with ASCII files. Because of that, when you use View, you often don't have to worry about switching to ASCII mode; the FTP client handles it.

Scrolling down the list of files in the right window, you see the file last100uploads. You can use the hard-labor method to view this file: switch to ASCII mode, retrieve it, and launch a text viewer to read it. Nothing wrong with that. But many FTP clients offer a shortcut that's often called View. This shortcut enables you to view the contents of an ASCII file immediately without having to go through all the above steps—but be sure to use this only on plain ASCII files. In this case, select the **last100uploads** file and then click **View**. During your reenactment, the screen should look like the one in the next figure.

View the contents of a file the quick 'n' easy way.

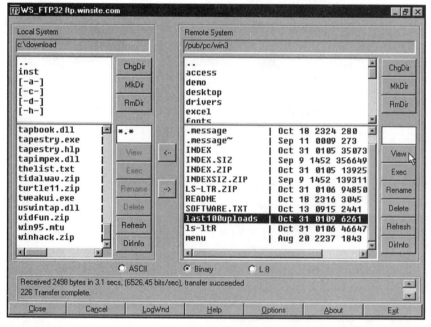

When the transfer is complete, a viewer window opens to show the gory contents of the file. Browse awhile to find some files of interest. Do keep in mind that if you remain completely inactive for a few minutes while connected to a site, you will probably lose the connection. If that happens, just reconnect when you're ready to go on. Let's say that when you're browsing the list, you find three interesting-looking games: CyberTarot, SpaceWar, and CalcuMemory. Given that the boss is going to be in Honolulu next month, these might be worthy downloads. You can see they're in the games/ subdirectory in WinSite. So close this text window, and then scroll down the directory list in the remote window (as shown in the following figure) until you find the games subdirectory.

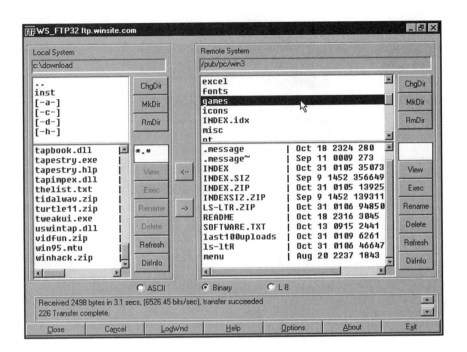

Select the games subdirectory at WinSite.

Double-click the **games** subdirectory to see a new list of files from the server. To select multiple files to retrieve, use the standard technique of holding down the **Ctrl** key and clicking on the desired files. In this case, select the files **tarotw.zip**, **spacewar.zip**, and **calmem10.zip**. After verifying that **Binary** is checked, you begin the transfer by clicking on the arrow pointing in the direction the file should go—that makes sense. In this case, you click the left-pointing arrow because you want these files to go *to* your local PC.

All's Wild in Love and Cards

Remember earlier when I said that graphical FTP clients lacked some of the flexibility of a command-line client? My primary example was that of a wild-card download. However, I should note (in the interests of fairness and of evading litigation) that WS_FTP does, in fact, support wild-card file listings. Adjacent to each window is a small box that, by default, contains the characters *.*. That is a total wild card that means "all files." If necessary, you can modify that pattern (you can make it **dogf*.***, for example) to get a list of only the file names that match the pattern. Not all graphical clients support this useful feature, though, so "yours truly" is not a total liar.

With three games selected, you're about to click the download button. Excitement builds.

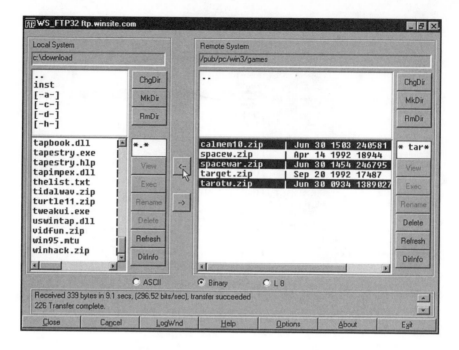

Click the arrow and call the neighbors; the download has begun! You see a transfer window (shown in the next figure) that's similar in concept to the ProComm transfer window. WS_FTP displays a progress bar that reports the percent completion of the files being transferred, the throughput rate, and the time that's passed. Expect slightly less speed when transferring by FTP than when using Zmodem with the same speed modem. While you can certainly perform "batch" downloads with FTP (simply select multiple files), you won't see batch total reports for estimated time and size.

Shhh... transfer in progress.

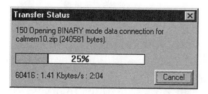

Because you don't have to worry about the errors during an FTP transfer that you do during a Zmodem transfer, that's basically it. When the transfer is complete, the file is on your local PC's hard drive, and you can have your way with it.

Where's the Speed?

The question remains as to why an FTP transfer takes longer than the transfer of the same file on the same modem using Zmodem. The answer is the same one salespeople use to excuse gouging prices: overhead. While there are lots of advantages to using a complex protocol such as TCP/IP, doing so requires extra processing that isn't necessary for "dumber" protocols.

The basic transfer philosophy for using TCP/IP is to break data up into many small "packets," send each packet to the destination via the Internet, and then reassemble the packets in order at the receiving end. This philosophy is responsible for making the Internet the incredibly flexible and robust system that it is. However, it also demands more calculations by your CPU than does the continuous stream of data pumped by Zmodem. You see the results of this extra time in FTP's slightly slower data throughput. Yet this slowdown is minor compared to the advantages of using TCP/IP and FTP. There's a life metaphor in there somewhere.

A Quick Fetch

Fetch for the Macintosh is very similar to WS_FTP for Windows. We'll breeze through it here just to cover its major features. The details about performing transfers (described in the previous section) apply to all graphical FTP clients.

When you launch Fetch, you see the Open Connection dialog box, which is somewhat akin to WS_FTP's Session Profile window (as you can see in the following figure). Here you enter the information for your FTP connection: the name of the site, the login info (usually **anonymous** as the User ID and your e-mail address as the password), and the directory on the remote site to start in. Fetch offers a Shortcuts button with which you can access preconfigured sites (just like session profiles).

Open Connection...
Enter host name, user name, and password (or choose from the shortcut menu):
Host: sumex-aim.stanford.edu
User ID: anonymous
Password: ••••••••••••••
Directory: /info-mac
Shortcuts: ▼ [Cancel] [OK]

Open a new FTP connection with Fetch.

Click **OK**, and you're connected. Fetch shows the list of remote directories and files. The next figure shows the main directory for Info-Mac (the directory you specified in the Open Connection dialog box).

Well, look at that.
You're connected to
Info-Mac.

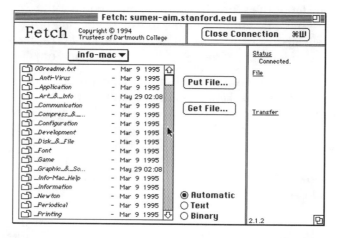

To look for something interesting in the Communication directory, double-click on it. Then work your way into the MacTCP directory and look for nifty clients. Ultimately, you might see a list like the one in the following figure. Suppose you're interested in downloading the file anarchie-16.hqx, a popular alternative to Fetch. Select that file, and you can take it for a test drive.

Where's My Local System?
Unlike WS_FTP, Fetch does not contain a window that shows local directories and files.

Select the anarchie
file to download it.

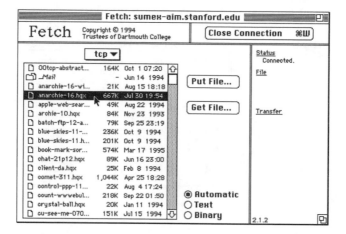

Before you download, however, note a few things about the Fetch window. At the bottom are the option buttons for the file transfer modes. You learned about the Text and Binary options earlier in this book. If you select Automatic, Fetch determines whether the file is text or binary. Automatic usually works, but from time to time you may hit a stubborn file that requires you to specify Text or Binary. Note also that Mac files are commonly stored in ".hqx" format, which is not that of a compressor or archiver, but something more like uuencode. Fetch will automatically "de-hqx" files as it downloads them so you are left with just the archive (such as .sit or .cpt).

Now that you know all that, begin the download by selecting the file and clicking **Get File**. Fetch opens a dialog box in which it prompts you to name a save location. After you provide that information, transfer status information appears along the right side of the window (see the next figure).

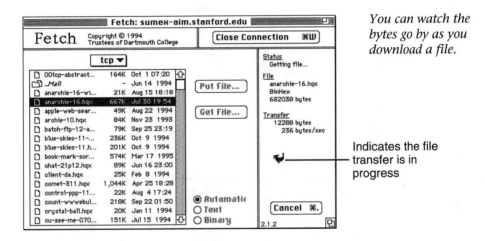

You can watch the bytes go by as you download a file.

Indicates the file transfer is in progress

If you want to select a range of files to download in Fetch, hold down the **Shift** key and select the desired files. Aside from that, you can see that one graphical FTP client is not terribly different from another.

And an Upload, Too

Let's take a minute and put it into reverse. Although they occur less often, there will be times when you want to send a file from your computer to a remote site. For example, perhaps you authored a new program and would like to make it available on a public FTP site. Or maybe you scanned in a picture that you want to place at a public graphics site for others' use. Or maybe you want to move a file from your local PC to your UNIX account.

Before you can upload a file, you need to know whether you have permission to do so. For example, consider the games directory at WinSite that you just downloaded a few bundles of joy from. You cannot simply upload a game of your own into that directory. If they let everyone do that, chaos would be the order of the day. Many public FTP sites have a directory called uploads to which you can send submissions. Someone at the site then screens the files for viruses, copyright infringement, corrupted archives, and so on.

Follow the Rules

As you might expect, public FTP sites often have rules regarding the format of submissions. For example, some require that you submit a ZIP file, accompanied by a text file containing a brief description of the software. Read the various README files at each public site to learn about specific rules for that site.

Okay, okay. Enough talk, let's get started. Assume you have found a site and directory to which you want to upload files. The first step is to connect to the site, which you do just as you did when you downloaded files. In fact, you do just about everything the same as you did earlier. So move into the directory in the remote site that you want to upload to. This time, though, you select a file (or files) from your local PC window and send them in the other direction by clicking the right-pointing arrow. The following figure shows exactly that.

You have multiple files selected for an upload. Hang on tight.

Click here to upload the selected files.

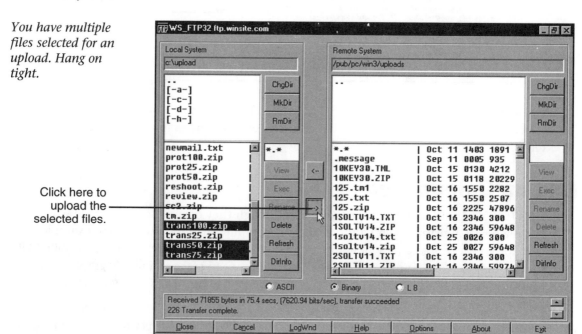

Once again, remember to check the ASCII/binary transfer mode *before* you begin the upload. If you don't, you might waste a lot of time (and possibly money). When you click the transfer arrow, the files are sent from your machine to the remote site, and the very familiar transfer window appears, keeping you abreast of the action.

Whatever Could Go Wrong?

Fortunately, as I've stated a few times in this chapter, you'll run into very few errors in an FTP transfer. However, I have to give it to you straight and tell you about the two "bad things" that occur most often.

Slow Transfer

It's true that an FTP transfer will be slightly slower than a comparable Zmodem transfer, but sometimes your FTP might be *very* slow. There are a few possible reasons for this, the first of which is beyond your control.

➤ **The network traffic between you and the remote machine, including the load on the remote machine.** If, for example, many people are transferring files from that site at the same time, everything is going to bog down. As a general rule of thumb, FTP from busy or geographically distant machines during peak times of the day is going to result in slower-than-normal throughput. There's not much you can do about it per se, but you can attempt to circumvent it by ftping during nonbusiness hours (depending where the remote site is located). Another alternative is to use a mirror of the FTP site. Many popular sites have *mirrors* (other sites that share the same data), and one of those mirrors might be less crowded or closer to you geographically. The main FTP site in question will have a list of available mirror sites.

➤ **Improper TCP/IP configuration on your computer.** Unfortunately, it's impossible to go into the ins and outs of each TCP/IP package available (and that's beyond the scope of this book anyway). Besides the manual or the documentation, the best sources for configuration advice are appropriate newsgroups such as **comp.os.ms-windows.networking.tcp-ip**, **alt.winsock.trumpet**, or **comp.sys.mac.comm**.

Interrupted Transfer

It's also possible that something may happen to interrupt a transfer midway. Perhaps someone lifted the phone extension off the hook and knocked the modem offline, or perhaps a lightning bolt hit your house and turned your computer into sawdust (this is not a good thing, unless you own a sawmill). Regardless of why it was interrupted, it may be impossible for you to complete your transfer without starting from scratch. (You'll find an explanation of that predicament in Chapter 20; a real page turner, this is.)

The Least You Need to Know

FTP is the way. Enlightenment, wisdom, computer files; it's all there when you're down with FTP. And it's not too difficult to use. This is how you do it.

➤ Get yourself an FTP client. You have several to choose from, but the popular picks are WS_FTP for Windows users and Fetch for Macin-types. Both are available on the Net (see Appendix B).

➤ After you install the client by decompressing its archive, launch it. Then you can configure some FTP sites, or simply try some of the ones already configured.

➤ You want to log in to most public FTP sites with the **anonymous** user id and your e-mail address as the password.

➤ Once connected, you can scroll around the files and directories available on the remote site and select any files you'd like to download.

➤ Don't forget to check the transfer mode setting (ASCII vs. binary). Make sure it's correct for what you intend to download; it will usually be binary.

➤ Uploading is the same thing in reverse, but be sure that you have permission to upload to a particular directory on the site before you do it. If you don't have permission, your file will be rejected at the door.

That Crazy World Wide Web

If anything can be blamed for transforming the Internet from a geekalot hangout into a hip, street, billboard-deserving consensual medium of cool, it's the World Wide Web. While not a file-transfer resource per se, the World Wide Web is an all-encompassing information retrieval system. Although you are not likely to use the Web for mass batch file transfers, you may often download particular files available from a Web page.

File Transfer and the Web: A True Story

The World Wide Web's calling card is its premise of *hypertext*. The simple idea behind hypertext is that any particular piece of information can be linked to another related set of information, which can be linked to another set of information, and so on. "Information," in this case, might be anything that can take the form of digital data: text, graphics, or sound, for example. You, the user, decide whether to follow or not follow any link within a Web document (also known as a *Web page*).

All Part of the Program
Most file transfers that take place during your time on the Web are not transfers that you instigate; they are part of the necessary mechanics of using the Web itself.

When you open a connection to a Web page, which is also called *opening a URL*, the file that contains that page is downloaded to your computer. Your Web client (or *browser*), such as Netscape or Mosaic, reads the file and displays the results in your browser window. From there, every time you click on a link, the same thing happens: the file the link points to is downloaded to your computer and is interpreted and displayed by your browser. In this technical sense, the World Wide Web is always about file transfer.

However, that's really a broader sense of the term "file transfer" than we're using in this book. In this book, we've dealt with intentional file transfers, which you instigate by indicating a specific file or group of files that you want to move between computers. Yet there will be times when you want to intentionally transfer a specific file from the Web, in the sense of the file transfers we've been discussing. Therefore, I'll walk you through the process, which starts at a web page like the one in the following figure.

This is a Web page with files that you can download. Any questions?

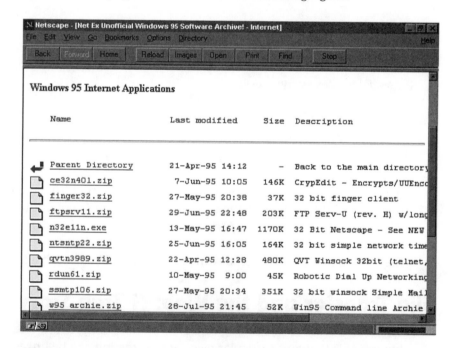

This Web page lists several available programs for Windows 95, some of which you may want to download. That's the sort of file transfer we're focusing on in this chapter.

You'll encounter such download opportunities in two areas:

➤ Public sites that either hold files or contain links to the files

➤ Private sites (such as your personal UNIX account)

Uploading files using the Web is a less-supported action than downloading is. Although some newer Web browser releases offer support for uploading, that is not a feature you should just assume exists. In fact, one should never assume anything according to my grade school teachers, year after year after year.

Because downloading isn't all that complex in the first place, and Web clients offer limited file transfer capabilities compared to dedicated FTP clients, the contents of this chapter aren't too involved. That's a good thing—and a rare thing in computing.

Check This Out...

URL?

A Web address is more commonly called a URL by those in the know. Some people pronounce that as three letters ("U-R-L"), while some people say it like the name Earl. (The latter sounds pretty silly, though.) Phonetics aside, the acronym stands for *Uniform Resource Locator*, although some stalwarts may insist it's "Universal" or "Ugubugu" or something. A URL looks like this:

http://*name.of.site/some/dir*

The first part (http://) indicates which protocol to use. Other URLs might include ftp:// (for FTP sites), gopher:// (for Gopher sites), and news:// (for UseNet news). After the double slash comes the machine name of the remote site, and after that are any directory paths that lead to the file. Now that URLs are being plastered all over movie billboards, it's nice to know what they mean. (Somewhere, sometime, a UNIX geek laughs.)

Tender, Juicy Cuts of Web Clients

Before you can access a World Wide Web site, you need appropriate client software. A large number of Web browsers are available these days for every platform. Some are free; some are shareware; some are exclusively commercial products. But of all the browsers available, three stand above most others in terms of sheer popularity.

Check This Out...

Client vs. Browser For whatever reason, people began calling Web clients "browsers." So I will use the two words interchangeably in this book for variety.

Lynx

Lynx is a text-based Web browser. While most proponents of the Web push its multimedia capabilities, some people, by choice or because of hardware limitations, use a text-based browser. (With a text-based browser, you can't see any of the graphics or hear any of the sounds that a Web page might sport, but all the text is there.) Lynx is the most popular and capable of the text-based browsers. It is mostly used in UNIX accounts by people dialing in with dumb terminal emulation, but there is also a version of Lynx for MS-DOS for those who love it so.

A candid shot of Lynx in action: in this case, it is browsing its own Help page.

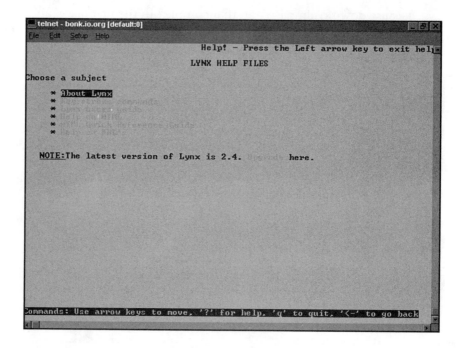

NCSA Mosaic

Mosaic was the first Web browser to reach big-time popularity, and many would argue that Mosaic is responsible for bringing the Net to the masses. As a result, many people use "Mosaic" as a generic term for a Web browser—much as they use Xerox, Kleenex, and Band-Aid to encompass all products similar to those. (In my opinion, such people should be slapped.) Violence aside, NCSA Mosaic is one particular Web browser that fully supports graphics and sound. Versions are available for the PC and Mac, for those users who have TCP/IP connection to the Net (such as a SLIP or PPP account).

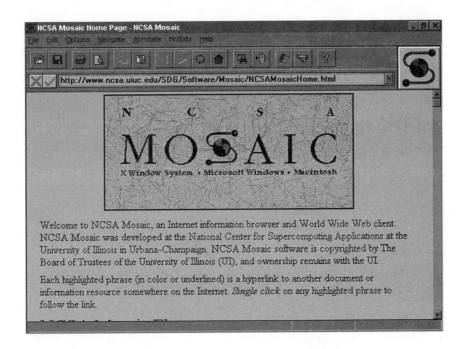

Mosaic is considered by many to be the mother of all Web browsers.

Netscape

Although NCSA Mosaic brought fame to the Net—and the Web—Netscape has since stolen the stage. In many circles, it has replaced Mosaic as the de facto Web browser of choice. Of particular note are the clever techniques its authors have used to become a "standard." When developing Netscape, the manufacturers continuously added features (and they are still adding features) that Web authors can use to enhance their pages in a number of ways. The catch has been that for users to profit from these "extra" Web capabilities, they have to use Netscape.

Many Web sites now display the claim "Netscape Enhanced" as a way of telling you, in short, that "This site will look better if you use Netscape." While other Web browsers can always play catch-up with the new features, Netscape clearly has the pole position on this matter at present.

Web Browser Limitations

Whichever client you choose, they're all capable of downloading files. Keep in mind, however, that you must work with these common limitations when you're downloading files with a Web browser:

➤ You can't select multiple files for a batch download.

➤ You can't search for available files using wild-card patterns.

➤ There often isn't much status information during file transfers via the Web.

➤ You usually can't upload files (and even if you could, the above constraints remain).

Down the Chute

A very hackneyed teacher I once had said that it's best to teach by example. (She's the same one who warned against assuming—and taught us to lead a horse to water.) Ultimately, though, she gets her due credit here because "teaching by example" is precisely what this situation calls for. That'll learn her to fail me.

Mosaic Users Can Follow Along There's no reason to walk through using both Mosaic and Netscape because they are so similar, especially in this respect. I'm going to use Netscape for the example, but the instructions apply even if you're using Mosaic.

Because this book can't pretend to be a complete tutorial on using any particular Web browser, I have to make the assumption that you have some experience with whichever browser you use. (I would like to think that even if you haven't used the browser before, you'd find enough help here that you could figure out how to download a file. I hope my teaching by example is adequate....) We'll start with downloading a file using Lynx, and then we'll move on to Netscape.

For each example, you'll use the same Web site: the Consummate Winsock Apps List. Created and maintained by Forrest Stroud, this site maintains a catalog of applications for use by Windows TCP/IP users. Besides being handy for keeping you up-to-date with the newest programs, it serves as an excellent example for downloading files. Its URL at the time of this writing is **http://cwsapps.texas.net**, but that has a tendency to change.

The Lynx Way

In most cases, you launch Lynx from a UNIX shell just by typing **lynx**. Users of menu-based accounts might have an option for Lynx (or Surf the Web, which probably means Lynx in non-hipspeak). However you do it, launch Lynx, and then press **Shift+G** to tell Lynx to open a new URL. At the bottom of the screen, Lynx displays a prompt asking you which URL you want to open (see the next figure).

At the prompt, enter **http://cwsapps.texas.net** and hit **Enter**. If all is well in the universe, the Web page is transferred, and it appears on your screen. As you can see in the second upcoming figure, it's a bit messy-looking in Lynx because of the limited layout capabilities of a text-only browser. To move between the links (which appear in a different color from the plain text), you use the up and down arrow keys. To follow a link, you highlight it and hit either the right arrow key or Enter.

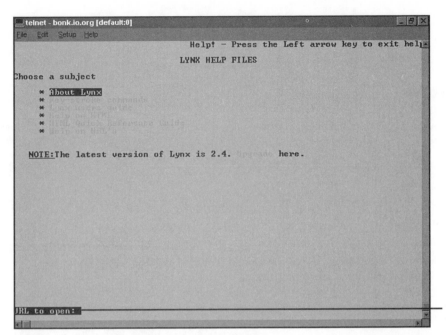

Lynx just sits around waiting for you to connect to a Web page.

Enter the name of the URL you want to open.

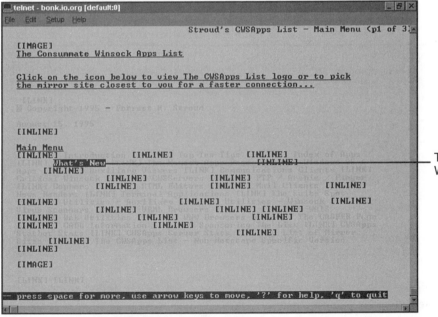

The CWS Apps main menu, opened in Lynx.

The link to the What's New page

For Text Eyes Only

Many Web pages that are graphics-heavy offer an alternative Text Only link. Choosing that link can be helpful when you're using a text-based browser such as Lynx because it makes the screen much less cluttered. All of those **[image]**, **[inline]**, and **[link]** symbols that you see on Lynx's screen indicate where graphics would be. When you select Text Only, those symbols disappear. If there is no Text Only link and you can't avoid the [] symbols, try to ignore them.

For our example, move to the **What's New** link by pressing the down arrow key until that link appears highlighted. Press **Enter**, and the What's New page appears. This page contains new or updated applications released on any given day. (Again, because this page was designed to look especially nifty in Netscape, it looks messed up in Lynx.) The What's New page resembles the next picture.

This list shows you the programs that are available on the What's New page.

The link to Eudora Light information

```
telnet - bonk.io.org [default:0]                                    _ | 8 | X
File   Edit   Setup   Help
                                  Stroud's CWSApps List - What's New (p1 of 5)

    [IMAGE]


    The Consummate Winsock Apps List

    [INLINE]

    New for August 15, 1995:
    [INLINE] [INLINE] Revised

    New for August 14, 1995:
    [INLINE] [INLINE] Added

    [INLINE] [INLINE] Added        0.53 Beta
    [INLINE] [INLINE] Updated  Eudora Light 1.5.2 Official Release --
    Thanks go to Jeff Beckley
    [INLINE] [INLINE] Updated            3.11 -- Thanks go to Jon Ort


    New for August 13, 1995:
    [INLINE] [INLINE] Added a page for
    [INLINE] [INLINE] Added                        1.0 Beta 1 --
    Thanks go to Joe Boyogo
    [INLINE] [INLINE] Added        1.1e
    [INLINE] [INLINE] Added             2.02 -- Thanks go to The BeasT
    Man
    [INLINE] [INLINE] Updated            2.02 -- Thanks go to The BeasT
-- press space for more, use arrow keys to move, '?' for help, 'q' to quit
```

Look through the links on this page for a new application. Humor me and pretend that Eudora Light catches your eye. Have you been looking for a new e-mail utility (which is just what Eudora is)? Are you hesitant because you're not yet sure what the "light" means? Perhaps it has fewer calories than Eudora Original and Eudora Dry. Well, there's one way to find out more about it: use the arrow keys to highlight the **Eudora Light** link and then press **Enter**. Then follow its lead to the screen shown next.

Version and release date of application

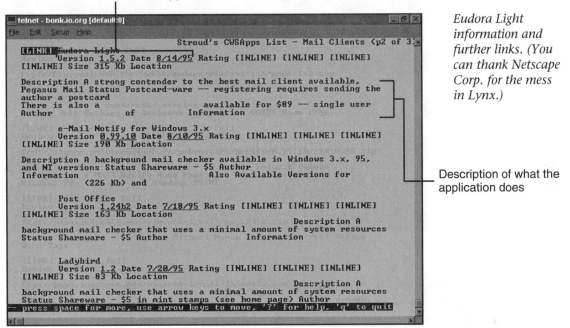

Eudora Light information and further links. (You can thank Netscape Corp. for the mess in Lynx.)

Description of what the application does

At the top of the page is the information for Eudora Light: release date, version info, blah blah blah. More important is the brief description that explains what this piece of wonder is all about. Of course you decide that it's worth a look, so you want to download the sucker (I can read your mind). Well, how handy! There is a link to the program archive just above the description.

To download the program using Lynx, highlight that link above the description and press **Enter**. Lynx displays some status messages at the bottom of the screen as it attempts to connect to the proper site where Eudora is located. When it makes the connection, you see the information shown in the following figure. At the bottom of the screen, Lynx displays the message **This file cannot be displayed on this terminal: D)ownload, or C)ancel**. In short, what Lynx is saying is, "Hey, this is a binary file! I can't display binary on the screen, so what should I do?" Always willing to lend a helping hand, you tell Lynx to download the file.

Lynx asks what to do with the selected binary file.

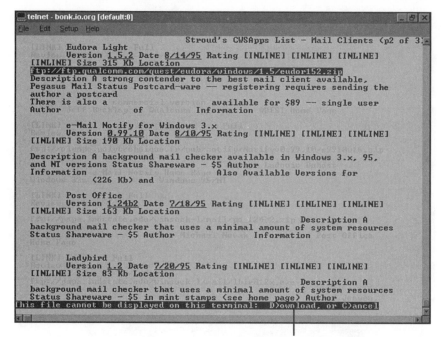

Prompt to download file

Press **d**, and the download begins. Lynx keeps you updated on the progress, and when the file is fully baked, Lynx gets right there in your face with another question: **Do you want to save the file or download it right now using Zmodem?** The choice is up to you. If you're prepared to begin a Zmodem transfer, choose that option. If you're not, save the file into your UNIX account and download it manually later.

Nag Nag Nag

In my best parental-impression voice, I offer this caution: If you choose to download the file immediately and something goes wrong with the transfer, you'll have to go all the way back into Lynx, back to CWSApps, and so on, and retrieve the file with Lynx all over again. The smart choice is to save the file first, and then download it on your own. That way, if something should spin awry, you've got the file in your UNIX account and you can resume the download. And by the way, tie your shoes—and brush your teeth....

Down with Netscape

Graphical pointy-clicky interfaces only make things easier. A few slides of the mouse and a click or two, and you'll be downloading that Eudora Light file in no time. First things first, though: you need to launch Netscape. (Of course, that's assuming you *have* Netscape. If not, there are plenty of books begging to help you with that "problem.")

Netscape gives you a couple of ways to open a new URL. You can open the **File** menu and select **Open Location**, you can press **Ctrl+L**, or you can click the **Open** icon near the right side of the toolbar. Regardless of which method you use, the following dialog box appears so you can tell Netscape exactly what it is that you want to open. Enter the CWS Apps address (shown in the following figure).

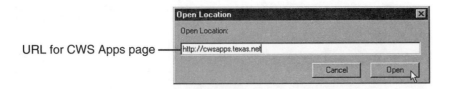

URL for CWS Apps page ——

In Netscape's Open Location dialog box, enter the CWS Apps address.

Click **Open**, and Netscape happily connects to the site and loads the opening page. As you can see in the next picture, this is much nicer-looking in Netscape than it was in Lynx.

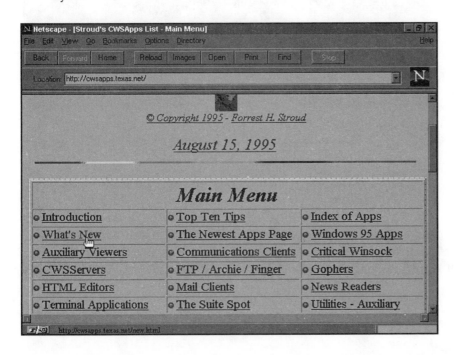

The CWS Apps main menu, displayed in Netscape. What fun!

In the table of options on the right side is the What's New link. Click on the **What's New** link, and Netscape retrieves said page (see the following figure). What do you know, but partway down the page is the **Eudora Light** link—in much prettier environs this time around.

The What's New page is far more impressive here than in Lynx.

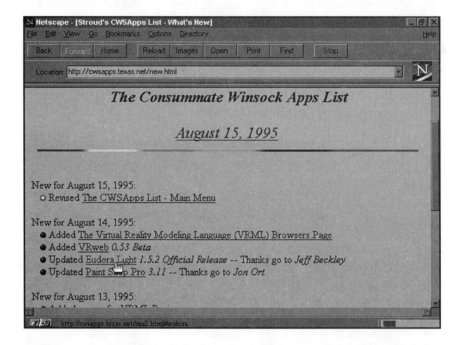

This is getting predictable. Click the **Eudora Light** link, and voilà! Honestly, "voilà" *was* a bit premature considering you have to scroll down the page a bit to get to the Eudora Light table. The very angular table offers a slew of info about the product (as you can see in the next figure), including a link to a full review.

But the link we're interested in at present is the one that downloads the archive itself. In this case, it's the Location: link in the table. Click on the **Location:** link, and Netscape displays a dialog box that says it can't identify the file type. When it asks you what to do with the file, select **Save to disk**. The Save As dialog box, shown in the second upcoming figure, makes itself known (as you might have guessed it would).

No Batches Here Because a download begins immediately when you click on an appropriate link, you can't select a batch of files to transfer.

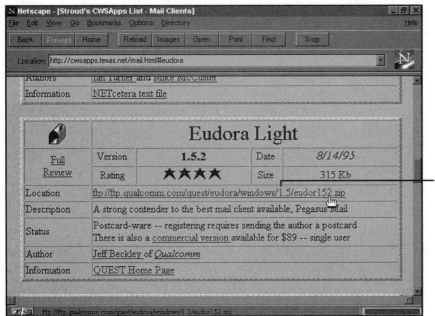

The Eudora Light info table contains several links; you're poised over the one to download the program.

Click this link to download the program.

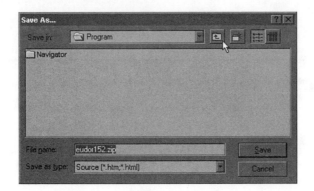

Netscape prompts you to indicate where to save the file.

Specify a name and a location on your local PC to which you want to download this file, and click the **Save** button. Netscape begins to retrieve the file. Because the file is being pumped down the same lines it would if you were using FTP or Zmodem, the download takes about the same amount of time (depending on its size and on your system). That could very well mean several minutes for a large file. The Saving Location status window keeps you updated on the progress of the transfer.

Eventually, the download is complete—and that's that. Not too many problems arise during these procedures. The most common obstacle is that the site a particular link points to is either down or extremely busy. In that case, you may just have to wait until another time.

In Private

The previous examples illustrated the most common sort of Web transfer: by way of a public Web page. If you have a UNIX account, however, you may want to access its files with a Web browser. Doing so is relatively easy. You simply open a URL by typing an address in this format:

> **ftp://*youruserid@yourhost***

In many cases, your e-mail address contains the two pieces of information you need. For example, if you are **sfreud@pillar.dreamy.org**, the URL to your account would be **ftp://sfreud@pillar.dreamy.org**.

Slasher Flicks

Although it is considered "proper" behavior to include the trailing backslash in a URL address (as in **http://bob.marley.com/~rasta/**), when connecting to a personal UNIX account, you want to leave that slash *off*. If you attempted to open that URL I just used as an example by typing **ftp://sfreud@pillar.dreamy.org/**, you would wind up in your service provider's root directory instead of your personal home directory.

When you open a new connection to this URL, the Web browser prompts you for a password (this *is* a private account, after all). Enter the correct password, and you jump to your home directory. You can move around from your home directory. Once you're in the account, you retrieve a file exactly as you did from a public Web page (described in the previous section).

Online Services Meet the Web

When the World Wide Web took over the earth like kudzu in a downpour, the commercial online services knew they'd better grab a hoe and start seeding. By now, each of the services I've discussed in this book has added its own Web browsers to their Internet services. Those browsers are very similar to each other and, in fact, are very similar to the graphical browsers you've already learned about in this chapter. However, we will take a brief look at how to use America Online's Web browser to download a file.

Launch America Online and enter the **Internet Connection** area (as you did when you used FTP in Chapter 15). From there, select the **World Wide Web** option shown in the next picture (in color where available).

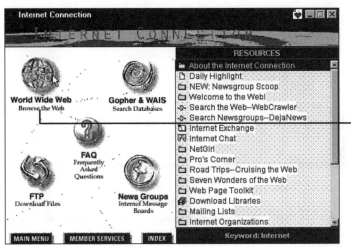

You access the Web browser from the Internet Connection area.

Click here to launch AOL's built-in Web browser.

AOL launches its Web browser, which looks like a typical graphical browser. At first, you see AOL's home page from where you could start exploring. However, in this case, you want to jump directly to a new page whose URL you already know: **http:// cwsapps.texas.net**. Click in the text box that displays the name of the current URL (see the following figure), and then enter the new URL directly into that text box to open the new connection.

The (Inevitable) Exception
The Microsoft Network's Web browser differs slightly from those of AOL and CompuServe. See the section "A Note About MSN" at the end of this chapter for more information.

At the top of AOL's home page, enter a new URL.

Enter the new URL you want to open here.

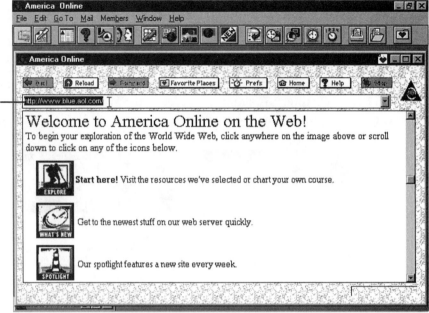

When you're connected to CWS Apps, click on the **What's New** link and (once again) scan for interesting goodies. This time around, you see that on October 1 a new version of HotDog Pro was released.

Ooh, look! A new HotDog Pro!

Click on that link to go to HotDog Pro info, where you learn that it's the best "HTML editor" available. (An HTML editor is an application for creating Web pages.) Try to contain your excitement! Click on the link to retrieve the file, and AOL opens that good ol' Save As dialog box (below). Specify where you want to save this file and click **OK**. That's the long and short of it. The download begins.

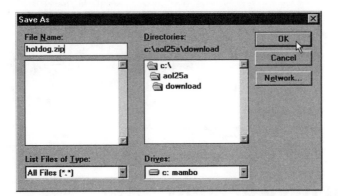

Tell AOL where to save the file. Pretty simple, huh?

Downloading from America Online's Web browser is pretty straightforward. And as I alleged, retrieving files from AOL's Web browser is the same as downloading with Netscape or any other graphical browser, including those on CompuServe and Prodigy.

A Note About MSN

The Microsoft Network works a little differently from AOL. On The Microsoft Network, you reach the Web browser by navigating through the **Categories** menu to the **Internet Center**. The following figure shows the window in which you find the icon for the Web browser.

When you click on The Microsoft Network icon, MSN actually launches a separate application, Internet Explorer, by default. The Internet Explorer, Microsoft's own Web browser, is included with the commercial Microsoft Plus! Pack and is also available on the Internet at **http://www.microsoft.com**. Internet Explorer works just like all the other graphical Web browsers. It is best described as a cross between NCSA Mosaic and Netscape; its file retrieval process is like that of Netscape (explained earlier in this chapter).

To the Web, courtesy of The Microsoft Network.

The Least You Need to Know

While it's not the premier way to download buckets full of files, the Web is a convenient, all-encompassing environment from which individual file transfers are very easy. With the spirited guidance in this chapter and the advice of a little leprechaun, it's not just easy, it's blarney!

➤ The address of a Web page is known as a URL. Web pages often contain links to other URLs.

➤ Some URLs point to files that you can download. Selecting one of those URLs starts the file transfer procedure.

➤ You cannot download a batch of files from the Web.

➤ In Lynx, use **Shift+G** to open a new URL. Then use the up and down arrow keys to navigate between links, and press **Enter** to select a highlighted link.

➤ In Netscape or Mosaic, you open a new "document" or "location" to reach a new URL. Simply click on a link, and if it leads to a downloadable file, the program leads you through the process.

➤ Use the format **ftp://*youruserid@yourhost*** to reach your UNIX account from a Web browser.

The News That Fits

At some point in recent geologic history, the moniker "UseNet News" was applied to the discussion groups that are carried, among other media, by the Internet. Of course, there is much more than "news" composting into the UseNet heap; some groups are dedicated to carrying files. And because UseNet is not the greatest facility for transferring files, many new users are left befuddled as to how to get files from UseNet onto their personal machines. The answers can be convoluted. In this chapter, we'll get all wound up in examining *some* of the possibilities.

Hey, How Did These Files Get Here?

As an architecture, UseNet is, in fact, all about transferring files. When you make a posting to UseNet, it is saved in the form of a file. That file is then transferred through the UseNet channels and distributed to readers around the world (in a process explained in that sidebar on the next page). In that sense, then, it is incorrect to say that UseNet is not designed for file transfer per se. However, because of the way in which UseNet distributes postings (that sidebar, nudge nudge), the expectation was/is that files would be relatively small. In most cases, that is true because plain text posts don't take up very much space and most posts are not terribly long.

"Post" Literacy I'm not trying to confuse you, but I use the word "post" as both a verb and a noun in this chapter. Within the verbiage of UseNet, both are correct. As a noun, a "post" in UseNet is any particular message available to be read. Sometimes I use the word "posting" instead; as a noun, a post and a posting are the same thing. As a verb, "post" is grammatical short-hand for "to make a post." Thus, it is valid to use the sentence "I posted a message." Of course, the "message" is in fact the "post" (noun), but "I posted a post" sounds idiotic. Granted, this is a little awkward grammatically, and perhaps it's even incorrect. But these are the conventional usages. Just don't tell William Safire, and we'll be okay.

In addition to the difficulties UseNet has transporting very large files, another aspect of its design stacks the cards against the transfer of most files: the binary vs. ASCII distinction (more accurately referred to as the 8 bits vs. 7 bits distinction). As you learned in Chapter 3, the 7-bit "alphabet" is a subset of the 8-bit alphabet. UseNet, designed on the 7-bit alphabet, cannot carry 8-bit data (which is what most large files are likely to be). On the surface then, it appears that UseNet isn't even capable of transferring binary files. And it's true: UseNet cannot. But with a bit of digital alchemy, you can overcome that barrier. All you have to do is convert 8-bit files into 7-bit files for transport and then convert them back afterward.

You can do this sort of thing using a few techniques. The most recent is called MIME; the older and more common is called uuencoding. The basic concept behind them is the same. They enable you to convert binary files to a temporary format that UseNet can transport.

Even if you can smush 8-bit data into 7-bit data, one problem remains: many UseNet systems simply refuse to accept files larger than a certain size. So while you may be able to post a 950k binary file from your system, many readers' systems will not accept it. The solution is to break the file up into slices and post each slice.

The reader can then reassemble the slices. In the end, if you're the reader, you have to accomplish three mighty tasks to bring a file from a UseNet newsgroup onto your own computer.

1. Piece together the file if it has been broken into bits.

2. Decode the file to convert it from 7-bit data back into 8-bit data.

3. Transfer the 8-bit file to your local PC.

For different users on different systems, the ease and/or automation of some of these steps varies. As we'll see later, steps 2 and 3 occur automatically behind the scenes in some cases. In other cases, all three steps occur automatically. In the rest of this chapter, we'll consider the most likely scenarios.

Techno Talk

blah blah
blah blah
blah blah

Pass It On...

When you access files from an FTP site, they exist in a *centralized* form. That means all the files exist on one centralized system (a single computer or a local network, for example) and are served out to the requesting remote computer. In essence, when we grab from any one FTP site, everyone is drinking from the same trough. UseNet does not work this way in the least. In fact, it works in the opposite way. There is no central UseNet server. Each individual Internet ganglion (usually your service provider) must keep its own server that feeds the news to the users on that provider. When someone makes a posting to UseNet, that post is sent from server to server to server (and hopefully all servers get the post within a short period of time). This is known as a *store and forward* system because each server saves the post as a file on its hard drive and then passes a copy on to another server that does the same.

This system has some definite disadvantages. It is extremely redundant that every post made to UseNet takes up space on every hard drive of every local news server. And, in getting there, every post must be passed as traffic across the network for every "forward," which means the same information is sent over and over across the Net. Multiply that by the number of UseNet newsgroups and the number of posts in them every day, and then imagine that all of that is being stored and forwarded, stored and forwarded, and so on. So disk space and Net traffic demands are both very high for UseNet.

I need to tell you, though, that this design is not an unintentional goof. In fact, the extreme redundancy of UseNet is also one of its strongest features. In a centralized system, if something goes wrong, nobody can take from the trough. Imagine what would happen if that one global UseNet server crashed. No one on the planet would be able to read news! And a centralized system is far easier to sabotage for the same reason. Another consideration is sheer usability. If everyone had to retrieve news from a centralized server, it would be impossibly slow. Lastly, the local server concept allows each particular site/provider to customize which slices of UseNet they make available.

Choose Your Weapon, Er, Newsreader

Love That UNIX Nomenclature UNIX programs are famous for having cryptic names. The ultimate achievement for a UNIX programmer is to devise a name that offers no apparent clue as to the program's function. "TIN" refers to "Threaded newsreader." I have yet to figure out where the "I" in the middle comes from. (A threaded newsreader follows the messages in a newsgroup by clumping them together by subject.) "RN" refers to the program "Read News," while "TRN" refers to its sibling "Threaded Read News." Finally, "NN" stands for either "Net News" or "No News (is good news)." Nobody really knows. We just use them.

It's client time again. To read UseNet news, you need a news client, which normal people call a *newsreader*. (Quite sensible, really.) You have quite a few newsreaders to choose from for every platform. You know, to a user, the freedom of choice is a plus. To an author, on the other hand, freedom of choice makes covering the topic in this chapter much more complicated.

Users who have UNIX accounts that they access by terminal program are likely to use one of the following newsreaders: NN, TIN, TRN, RN. (Nice names, eh?) Unfortunately, each of these has its own form of operation. While it's difficult to say for certain which of these newsreaders is the most common, I'm going to hedge my bets on TIN and use it for my example. The concepts apply equally to the other newsreaders, but the specific keystrokes and commands will vary. Refer to your program's online Help system for those details.

Remember that this section is for users who are using UNIX shell accounts or menu-based systems offering TIN; those of you on PCs or Macs with SLIP/PPP accounts will get your fair shake in a short while. As in other areas, I have to assume that you have some experience with these programs because this can't be a comprehensive newsreading tutorial. Significant restrictions apply. Some assembly required. Processed cheese.

Rin Tin TIN

Okay, readers, here's a what we're gonna do. I'll run TIN, and you find a newsgroup with suitable binary files, such as sound effects. Then Jerry here is going to cover the flank while we tackle a multipart uuencoded posting. No one looks back—no one gets hurt. And a 1, and a 2, and GOGOGOGO!

At the UNIX shell prompt, run TIN. Then hang back while it starts up.

```
%tin
tin 1.2 PL2 [UNIX] (c) Copyright 1991-93 Iain Lea.
Connecting to news.server.org...
Reading news active file...
Reading attributes file...
Reading newsgroups file...
```

On some systems this may take a long time. Me, I count the number of smudges on the wall. Fifteen so far. Okay, it's ready. Here we go. It'll sound something like this.

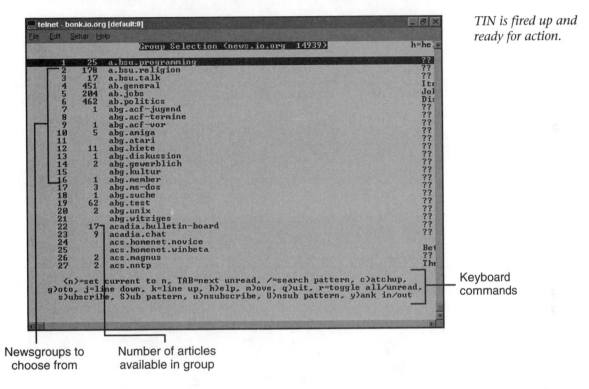

TIN is fired up and ready for action.

Keyboard commands

Newsgroups to choose from

Number of articles available in group

First, you'll go to a newsgroup that contains some binary posts. To do so, press **g**, and TIN prompts you for a newsgroup name. Enter **alt.binaries.sounds.misc** and hit **Enter**. That newsgroup's entry appears in the main list, as shown in the following figure.

Make sure the correct newsgroup is highlighted (use the arrow keys to highlight it if necessary). Then hit **Enter** to, well, see the newsgroup's contents. The second upcoming figure shows the contents of the alt.binaries.sounds.misc newsgroup.

TIN takes you to
the portion of the
newsgroup list that
you asked for. It gets
a bone.

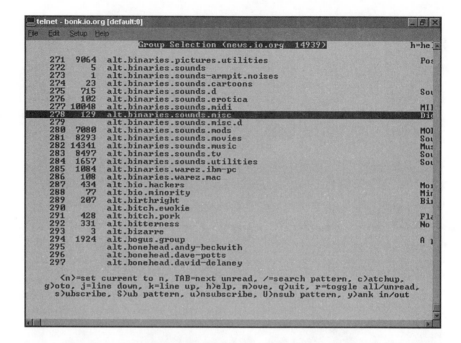

A list of available
articles. Not a bad
choice, huh?

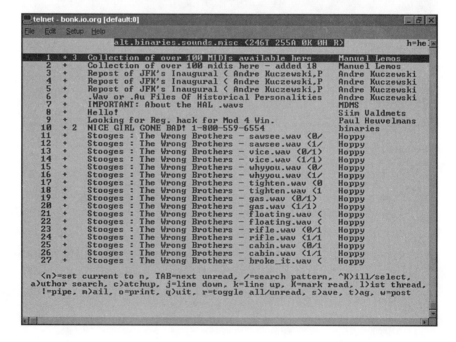

Scan the first page of postings and press the **Spacebar** to advance to the next page. Using patented time-elapsed publishing technology, I'm able to show you the results of your search for an interesting file. Take a look at the following figure to see what I mean.

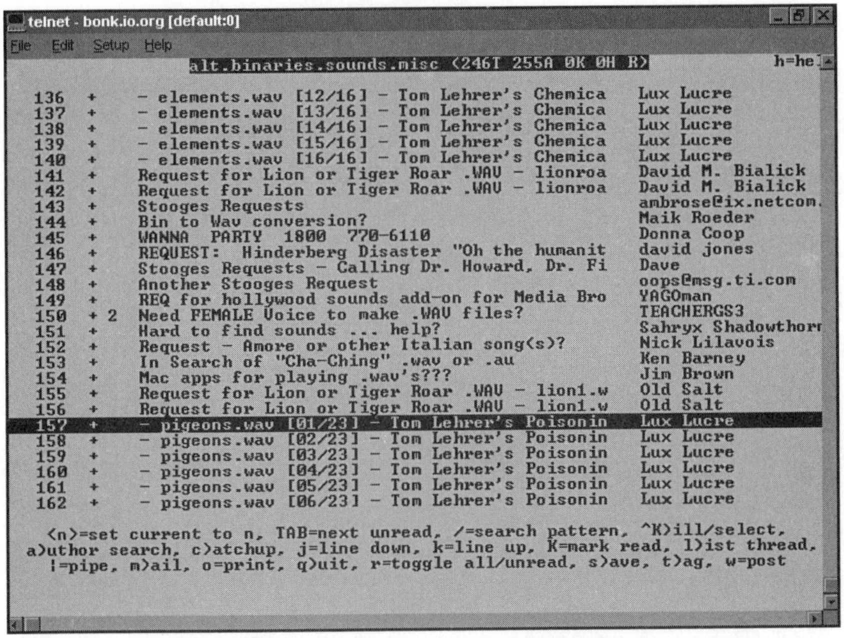

In the search for something interesting, you come across the start of a multipart post of a favorite old ditty.

Toward the bottom of the list is a multipart posting of that old romantic classic, "Poisoning Pigeons in the Park" by minstrel-professor Tom Lehrer. Each post has a number, such as [01/23], in the subject line. The number indicates that particular post's place in the sequence of the whole. This is a 23-part post, and it is probably quite a large file. Want to transfer it? No problemo.

The first thing you need to do to capture this sequence in TIN is "tag" each post. To tag a post, you highlight it and press **t**. It is important that you tag the posts in the proper sequence. In this case, the posts appear on the server in the proper sequence, so you just go down the list and tag each one. Sometimes, though, the posts don't arrive at your site in sequence, in which case you must use the numbers in the subject line to make sure you tag them in the proper order.

So what are you waiting for? Move down to the first part of the Pigeons song and hit **t**. When you tag the line, the plus sign in the second column is replaced with the number **1**. The line now looks like this:

```
 37   1     - pigeons.wav [01/23] - Tom Lehrer's Poisonin
```

This conveniently lets you see the order of your tagging sequence so you can verify that you get them tagged in the right order. Work your way down the posts, pressing **t** to tag each one. When you reach the bottom of the page, you see the next page, where the remainder of the pigeon posts are. Continue until you've tagged all of these files. The following figure shows your screen with all of the pigeon posts tagged.

All the pigeon posts are tagged in sequence.

```
telnet - bonk.io.org [default:0]
File  Edit  Setup  Help
          alt.binaries.sounds.misc <246T 255A 0K 0H R>                h=he
     163   7    - pigeons.wav [07/23] - Tom Lehrer's Poisonin    Lux Lucre
     164   8    - pigeons.wav [08/23] - Tom Lehrer's Poisonin    Lux Lucre
     165   9    - pigeons.wav [09/23] - Tom Lehrer's Poisonin    Lux Lucre
     166  10    - pigeons.wav [10/23] - Tom Lehrer's Poisonin    Lux Lucre
     167  11    - pigeons.wav [11/23] - Tom Lehrer's Poisonin    Lux Lucre
     168  12    - pigeons.wav [12/23] - Tom Lehrer's Poisonin    Lux Lucre
     169  13    - pigeons.wav [13/23] - Tom Lehrer's Poisonin    Lux Lucre
     170  14    - pigeons.wav [14/23] - Tom Lehrer's Poisonin    Lux Lucre
     171  15    - pigeons.wav [15/23] - Tom Lehrer's Poisonin    Lux Lucre
     172  16    - pigeons.wav [16/23] - Tom Lehrer's Poisonin    Lux Lucre
     173  17    - pigeons.wav [17/23] - Tom Lehrer's Poisonin    Lux Lucre
     174  18    - pigeons.wav [18/23] - Tom Lehrer's Poisonin    Lux Lucre
     175  19    - pigeons.wav [19/23] - Tom Lehrer's Poisonin    Lux Lucre
     176  20    - pigeons.wav [20/23] - Tom Lehrer's Poisonin    Lux Lucre
     177  21    - pigeons.wav [21/23] - Tom Lehrer's Poisonin    Lux Lucre
     178  22    - pigeons.wav [22/23] - Tom Lehrer's Poisonin    Lux Lucre
     179  23    - pigeons.wav [23/23] - Tom Lehrer's Poisonin    Lux Lucre
     180   +    - vatican.wav [01/21] - Tom Lehrer's Vatican     Lux Lucre
     181   +    - vatican.wav [02/21] - Tom Lehrer's Vatican     Lux Lucre
     182   +    - vatican.wav [03/21] - Tom Lehrer's Vatican     Lux Lucre
     183   +    - vatican.wav [04/21] - Tom Lehrer's Vatican     Lux Lucre
     184   +    - vatican.wav [05/21] - Tom Lehrer's Vatican     Lux Lucre
     185   +    - vatican.wav [06/21] - Tom Lehrer's Vatican     Lux Lucre
     186   +    - vatican.wav [07/21] - Tom Lehrer's Vatican     Lux Lucre
     187   +    - vatican.wav [08/21] - Tom Lehrer's Vatican     Lux Lucre
     188   +    - vatican.wav [09/21] - Tom Lehrer's Vatican     Lux Lucre
     189   +    - vatican.wav [10/21] - Tom Lehrer's Vatican     Lux Lucre

     <n>=set current to n, TAB=next unread, /=search pattern, ^K)ill/select,
     a)uthor search, c)atchup, j=line down, k=line up, K=mark read, l)ist thread,
     !=pipe, m)ail, o=print, q)uit, r=toggle all/unread, s)ave, t)ag, w=post
                                  Tagged thread
```

Great. All the parts are prepared for processing. Fortunately, TIN takes care of the rest for you. To start the magic, press the keyboard key that looks like a vertical dashed line (at the bottom of TIN's screen, it shows this key as ¦=**pipe**). To *pipe* means to send data to an external program for processing. TIN displays this message:

```
Pipe a)rticle, t)hread, h)ot, p)attern, T)agged articles, q)uit: T
```

In its own coy, roundabout way, TIN is asking you what data you'd like to pipe. For this example, you want to pipe the tagged articles, so you need to enter uppercase T—not lowercase t. TIN assumes T as the default; you can tell that because T already appears as the answer to the prompt. Press **Shift+T** and press **Enter** to pipe the tagged articles. You'll see this prompt:

```
Pipe to command []>
```

The ever-inquisitive TIN now wants to know what external program to pipe the data to. The answer is *uudecode*, the program on UNIX systems that handles converting all those parts into one 8-bit binary file. Yep, that's exactly what you want.

```
Pipe to command []> uudecode
```

TIN begins piping. When it's done, the finished file sits in your UNIX account ready for your use. That only leaves the last of the three steps—moving the file to your local PC—for you to complete. And don't you know, you already know how to do that. You download it using a transfer protocol with your terminal program (see Chapters 10 thru 12). Ta da! Voilà! Shalom! Fettucini!

Pointy and Clicky

Now you SLIP/PPP users out there needn't feel neglected. Just as there are FTP clients and Web browsers for the PC and Mac, there are also newsreaders for those platforms—quite a few in fact. I would have to write another whole book to go into detail on using every graphical newsreader out there. But Que hasn't asked me to write that book, so I'm going to have to choose one and go with it. As you can probably guess, the concepts of the graphical newsreaders are similar, but the procedures may vary. (Fortunately, you've got documentation, and that's what it's for.)

For this example, you'll use the popular Windows newsreader Free Agent. Its goal and general behavior are essentially the same as TIN, but it offers more options, flexibility, and ease of use. Start up Free Agent (assuming you've already configured it for your news server using the **Options Preferences** command), and then connect to the news server by clicking on the little lighthouse icon.

You can connect to the news server in Free Agent via the toolbar.

Click this button to connect to the news server.

Open the list of available newsgroups by selecting the **Group, Show All Groups** menu command. Scroll through the list to find **alt.binaries.sounds.misc** as you did in the previous example (or you can use **Ctrl+F** to search for the group). Double-click the highlighted group to enter it, and Free Agent asks whether to grab 50 sample articles, grab all articles, or subscribe to the group officially. The easiest answer is all articles. Click on **Get All Article Headers** (as shown in the next figure).

Before you enter a newsgroup, you have to make some decisions.

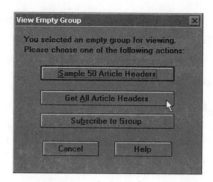

Free Agent displays a window like the one shown in the following figure. On the right side of the window are the article headers, in this case, the pigeon articles.

The contents of the selected newsgroup.

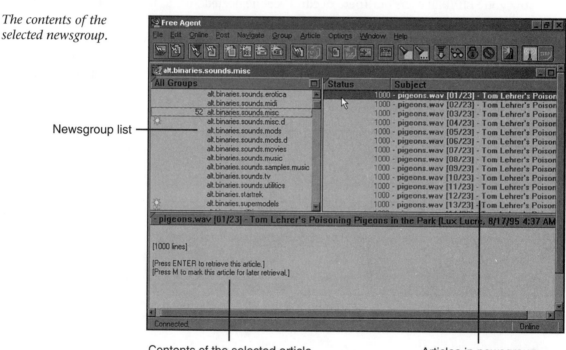

Newsgroup list

Contents of the selected article

Articles in newsgroup

Unlike TIN, Free Agent can attempt to figure out the proper sequence of a multipart post. So you don't have to select the articles in the proper order if they are not listed that way. Note, though, that not all graphical newsreaders can boast this feature; it depends on how advanced they are. Some may require you to select the posts in proper order and may not work at all if they're not. In this example, however, the matter is (as they say on Court TV) moot because the pigeon song is already posted in order.

In Free Agent, you can select the files for downloading using any of these techniques:

➤ Click on the first post with the left mouse button, hold down the button, and drag the mouse downward until you've highlighted all the posts.

➤ Press and hold down **Ctrl** and click on each post you want to include.

➤ Click on the first post you want to include, press and hold the **Shift** key, and click on the *last* file you want to include. Those two posts and all the posts between them are selected.

Like the process of making a peanut butter and jelly sandwich, this process is much more difficult to explain than it is to execute. Try it, it's fun. One way or another, make sure all the pigeon posts are selected.

You can do a number of things with the selected posts. Open the **File** menu, the beauty of which I handsomely captured in the following picture.

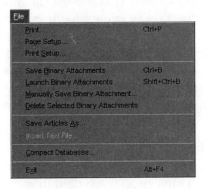

Use these options to work with attachments. Some newsreaders may offer fewer options.

The File menu contains these commands, which you use to work with the posts:

Save Binary Attachments (Ctrl+B)   Choose this option to retrieve each of the selected parts, put them back together (in order if possible), and save them to the local hard drive. Note that the articles will be uudecoded, so the saved file will be all ready for use in whatever program it was intended for.

Launch Binary Attachments (Shift+Ctrl+B)   For the most part, this is the same as the previous option except that after Free Agent retrieves, decodes, and saves the file, it attempts to execute the file. In Windows and Windows 95, you can create "associations" to file types, so that if you attempt to execute a GIF file, for instance, a specified viewer is launched. This option takes advantage of that particular Windows feature.

217

Manually Save Binary Attachment   When complete automation simply won't work, use this option. Sometimes, Free Agent can't figure out the proper order of a series of posts that are out of order. You can select the posts to be retrieved and then use this option to manually rearrange their order for Free Agent. Then Free Agent can process and save them as it should.

Most newsreaders have at least some of these options, although they may have names like "Decode" or "Uudecode" or something along those lines. That is all there is to it, really. The newsreader takes care of appending the dismembered files and uudecoding them.

Because you're retrieving the posts directly to your computer over TCP/IP (instead of to a UNIX account), the final step of moving the decoded file to your PC is already taken care of! Convenient, modern technology.

Whatever Could Go Wrong?

Without errors, what of life? On the upside, it's helpful to blame others when possible. (I learned that in kindergarten.) That is often the case when it comes to UseNet postings. A lot of people who don't really know what they're doing are armed with these fancy-shmancy newsreaders. They end up making partial, incomplete posts; they end up with improperly formatted posts; they post in strange and unusual encoding schemes. There-fore, it is highly possible that if your attempt to retrieve a posted file is unsuccessful, it may not be your fault. There are quite a few corrupted postings on UseNet because of these posters' errors, so don't automatically assume you're the one with the character flaw.

Some posts are corrupted in other ways. For example, sometimes news servers don't receive every part of a multipart post. Very frustrating. If this happens frequently at your site, it might be worth knocking on a certain newsmanager's door. Likewise, some posts are present in all parts but simply refuse to decode properly. In these cases, it is possible that there is incorrect text (such as information written by the poster) between parts of the encoded sections. It will be relatively obvious which text is incorrectly placed: a properly uuencoded file should appear as a solid uniform block of characters. Often the only way to fix this is to manually save the posts and then load them into a text editor to remove all nonencoded text from the file. However, this is a desperate last resort and, even if truly necessary, is not for the inexperienced.

Post 'Er

Change your shoes; it's time to post a message to a newsgroup. More specifically, it's time to make a uuencoded multipart post. That is the focus of this chapter, you know.

If you didn't have the capability to automate this process, even with graphical newsreaders it would be too complicated to discuss here. Fortunately, most current and updated newsreaders are acquiring this feature. For my example, I'll use Free Agent, which handles such postings in a nice, easy way.

Begin a new post by opening the **Post** menu and selecting **New Article**. You don't have to position yourself on the desired newsgroup first because you can enter the name of the newsgroups(s) you want to post to in the New Article window (shown in the following figure).

> **No Go, UNIX**
> Because the common UNIX newsreaders have no facility for doing this easily, you need special UNIX scripts to handle splitting and encoding the file. We're not going to cover that advanced a topic in this book, so no posting from UNIX.

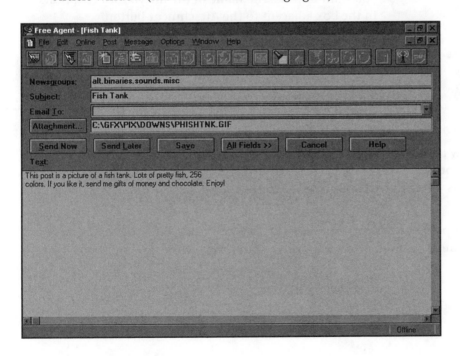

Compose a new article to post.

In this case, you're going to post a binary file by using the Attachment feature. In the **Newsgroups** text box, enter the name of the newsgroup you want to post to. You can post to multiple newsgroups simultaneously by entering all of their names on that line, separated by commas.

No Jaywalking! When you enter multiple newsgroup names to post to, it is called *crossposting*. This can be a convenient way to get the same message to multiple appropriate groups. BUT, note that word "appropriate." Crossposting unnecessarily is frowned upon in UseNet-land because it is a waste of space and resources. That goes many times over when you're talking about large binary files; you should crosspost a large binary file in very few instances. One newsgroup will suffice.

Next comes the Subject line of the post. Because you're making a multipart posting, Free Agent automatically adds the part information (such as *file*.jpg [01/10]) to the Subject line of each post. So if you enter **Picture of my dog** in the Subject line, the Subject line that appears on UseNet for each of those messages will read **Picture of my dog - dog.gif [01/04]** (*Your Name*). This time through, you're posting a picture of a fish tank, so **Fish Tank** appears in the Subject text box.

Click the **Attachment** button to access a dialog box in which you can find and select the file on the local PC that you want to post. The name of the file you select appears in the box adjacent to the Attachment button.

The bottom half of the window is the text message area. Normally, you'd write the contents of your post here. In this case, however, the contents is a file. You do have the opportunity to write any description of the file here, though, which is often appreciated by the UseNet reading community.

All set so far. Now to configure the multipart posting options. In Free Agent, you do this by opening the **Options** menu and choosing the **Preferences** command. The Preferences dialog box appears. Click the **Attachments** tab to see the options shown in the following figure.

These preferences pose two basic questions: How do you want to break up the message (message partitioning), and where do you want to put the text in the message box (message text).

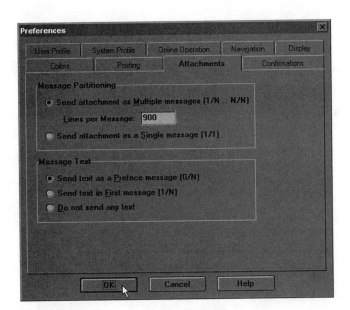

Use these options to tell Free Agent how to handle the attachment.

Message Partitioning   Select the first option: **Send attachment as Multiple messages**. Below that, indicate how many lines to split each message into. (The traditionally accepted value for UseNet is 900; it represents a message size that servers will accept.)

Message Text   The optimal option is the first: **Send text as a Preface message (0/N)**. That way, the first post in your sequence will be numbered 0 and will contain only the brief description. Readers can then easily and quickly see what the entire post is all about before they download it.

To finish the process, click the **Send Now** button, and the original file is uuencoded, split, and posted automatically. Just sit back and breathe in the glory.

Online Service Newsreading

It took some time for the commercial online services to get hip to the Net's approach to news. Eventually, they've all added their own flavors of home-cooked newsreaders, some of which are better than others. None of the newsreaders available on America Online, CompuServe, Prodigy, or The Microsoft Network are of the quality of the best stand-alone TCP/IP clients (such as Free Agent). However, AOL's and CompuServe's newsreaders are the best of the lot. Both can recognize uuencoded posts and decode them if necessary. Neither Prodigy's nor MSN's newsreader seems capable of auto-decoding posts. Instead, they just retrieve the uuencoded text. In such cases, you are forced to save the text in a file and use a separate utility (such as WinCode for Windows, available at the WinSite FTP site) to decode it.

The America Online and CompuServe newsreaders function similarly. We'll take a look at the AOL newsreader in terms of downloading a uuencoded file.

To start, navigate to the UseNet newsgroups in AOL by clicking the **Internet Connection** button, followed by the **Newsgroups** icon. AOL conjures up a screen something like the one in the next figure.

America Online's Newsgroups main menu.

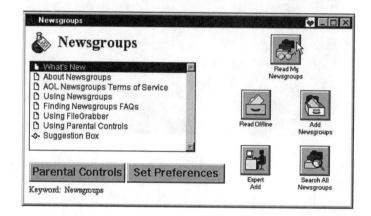

In this example, check out the newsgroup alt.binaries.sounds.misc again. To do so, you have to have already added this newsgroup to "My Newsgroups." (You can do that by selecting the **Add Newgroups** button in the previous picture.) Enter **My Newsgroups**, and then select the specific newsgroup you want: **alt.binaries.sounds.misc**. Guess what? You'll see a window of available articles (see the next figure).

The posted articles that are available to read. This one looks neat.

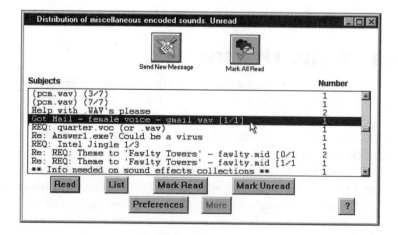

The post titled "Got Mail - female voice" might be a nifty sound to download. After all, every PC needs to express its feminine side now and then. Double-click on that post, and AOL begins the retrieval. In a few seconds, AOL realizes that this is no ordinary post—it's a uuencoded binary file. Therefore, it displays the dialog box shown next, which contains three options.

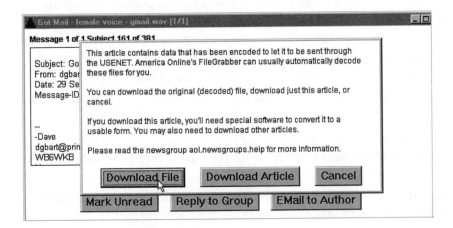

"Hey, this is a uuencoded file!," AOL quickly reports.

If you choose Download File, AOL retrieves the text and automatically decodes it. You'll be asked to choose a save location. (Note that in the case of multi-part posts, AOL seeks out all necessary parts.) If you choose Download Article, AOL saves the uuencoded text but does not decode it. And of course, if you select Cancel, AOL does just that.

Ultimately, that is all the user input that's necessary. As AOL retrieves the file, it displays that traditional transfer status window.

Always an Exception
There are always some instances in which AOL cannot auto-decode. When that happens, you may want to take a crack at it yourself, perhaps with another decoding utility such as WinDecode.

CompuServe's newsreader works in much the same way. However, instead of displaying a dialog box with the download/decode options, it provides three check boxes below the list of available posts. If you want articles uudecoded automatically, be sure to check the **Decode** box. Same idea, slightly different input.

None of the online services offers simple ways to post uuencoded binaries. To do so, one has to perform some acrobatics. In brief (it's too advanced to go into detail here), one has to uuencode the desired binary using an encoder such as WinCode. The resulting text file then has to be imported or pasted into the article composition window of the newsreader. This can be a real pain, and making multi-part postings is even more so.

The Least You Need to Know

While not an ideal resource for massive file transfers, UseNet offers people the opportunity to interactively exchange files. However, because of some limitations of the system, doing that requires some digital acrobatics.

➤ UseNet postings must be in 7-bit ASCII format; uuencoding is the process of converting an 8-bit binary file into 7-bit ASCII for the purpose of transport.

➤ Large UseNet postings should be split into several smaller messages, which any good newsreader can handle.

➤ Using TIN in UNIX, press **T** to tag, in order, the posts that make up multiple parts of a file. Use the Pipe key (¦) to send those posts for processing into the uudecode program.

➤ Using a graphical newsreader, you can often select all the relevant posts with the mouse and choose a decode or save binary option.

➤ When posting a large binary file, attempt to use your newsreader's file-splitting capability to ensure that each part contains fewer than 900 lines.

Part 5
(Somewhat More) Miscellaneous But Still Useful Topics

or "Don't ignore me please."

You can always count on miscellany, and here it is. These are not unimportant issues. Although some have more practical value than others, all are directly related to the matters discussed throughout this book. From strange file transfer voodoo, to reviving the (not quite) dead, to creating one's own archives, it's stuff worth an evening by the Radiovox.

## Chapter 19

Strange Little M's: Transferring Text Files Between Platforms

In This Chapter

➤ Invisible marker—the end of line

➤ Platform mix-up

➤ Stop stinky mistranslations before they appear

➤ Okay, then, after it's too late

The truth is, the how to's of transferring files do not make a vast topic. Therefore, in the luxurious pages of this full-grown book, I have the space to extend my elbows and yap about some more esoteric topics. So this part is sort of like those last few days of school: when the curriculum has essentially been completed and you learn about the interesting stuff.

In this first of the "esoteric" chapters, I'll cover some topics that are less critical, but nonetheless useful. They're all of a *slightly* more advanced nature than the topics in the earlier chapters, inasmuch as a novice user doesn't *need* to know them to function. But don't be frightened; this is no computer science thesis. It's likely that you'll run across at least one of these topics during your computing travels, and if you've read this chapter, you can tackle it with suave coolness and a steady brow.

Dealing with plain text files is one area of file transfer that can be a particular bugaboo. Because of a subtle difference between the major platforms, you could end up with oddly mutated text files when you move them between computers. We're going to put a stop to that—and lower taxes to boot.

End-of-Line Conventions

Most of what computers do is quite arbitrary. That is, what appears to be a set of rules and regulations is more often just a set of decisions that some people made once for no other reason than the sake of consistency. Not really much different from most any human institution—currency, units of measurement, or the BMV, for example. The same goes for the internal organization of files.

A long, long time ago on a page far, far away, I taught you about the two common file alphabets: 7-bit ASCII and 8-bit binary. First, let's recall binary. The task of representing, say, a picture of a banana using datapoints in a computer file doesn't have a very obvious solution. How would you capture the shape, color, or light reflections of that image using a set of numbers? Of course, it can be done, but how it's done is completely irrelevant to this book. Yet knowing that that difficult task is possible may help you see why representing plain text in a file is relatively simple.

How does the computer represent the letter A in a file? How about with an A? Okay, okay, it's true that a number is actually used to represent the letter, but still that is only one step removed from the final representation. (I'm referring not to the representation of the aesthetic shape of an **A**, but to the concept of an **A**.) In the ASCII alphabet, each character is assigned a number, and A's alter ego is known as 65. So imagine a text file that contains only one letter: **A**. If you display this file on the screen with a text editor, you would just see this:

```
A
```

Simple enough. However, one aspect of representing a textual message doesn't have such an obvious solution: the end of a line. Let's say that you create a text file containing the following message:

```
Dear Sue,

I am writing to you with a simple request:
You have been my neighbor for over a year, and in that time I've come to
despise you more every day.
```

```
The rest of the co-op is in agreement that you're not suited for living with
other human beings.
Please move out.

Your neighbor,
Mark
```

If there were no way to represent the end of a line, one could not preserve the structure of the text above. It would just be one long sentence. And because Sue wouldn't understand it, she wouldn't pack her bags. To eliminate this problem, the secret society of computing people decided to pick one of the unused ASCII values to represent the end of a line. That way, when the computer encounters that special character, it can skip a line on the screen (or printer, or whatever other output device is in use). Of course, that leaves us with the 64-bit question: "What is that special character?" Come on, everybody now; I can't hear you in the back. "What is that special character?"

Go Their Own Way

Yes, well, that's the problem. It depends who you ask. Here's the short explanation. If you ask a UNIX-person, he'll tell you that the value "10" represents an end-of-line. If you ask a Mac person, he'll tell you that "13" represents an end-of-line. And if you ask a PC sort, he'll insist that an end-of-line must take the form of *two* values in the proper order: 13 and 10.

I suppose we can salvage some hope out of this. At least everyone seems to agree that 10 and/or 13 make nice end-of-line characters. In fact, someone even gave the two values names (because humans don't like to refer to numbers—with the exceptions of C3P0 and R2D2). The value 10 is known as a *linefeed*, while 13 is nicknamed a *carriage return*.

Each major platform prefers to handle this situation differently, as the following table shows:

For a text file created in	The end-of-line is represented by
UNIX	a single linefeed
Mac	a single carriage return
MS-DOS/Windows	a carriage return followed by a linefeed

The following figures show a text file created in UNIX. It was then downloaded to a PC and opened in a Windows-based text editor. Watch closely.

BEFORE

An ASCII text file, created in UNIX and displayed in UNIX. Looks okay.

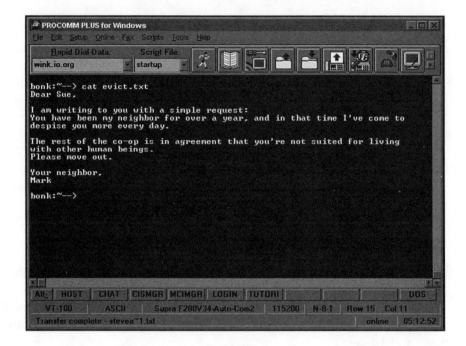

AFTER

Same ASCII text file, created in UNIX, but displayed on a PC. Looks less-than-okay. It's now one long line.

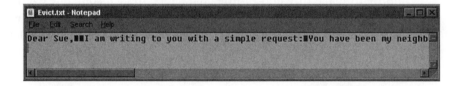

Clearly, something hideous has happened. It's not the fault of the transfer; none of the data in the file was changed. But the PC interprets the UNIX-created file differently—incorrectly.

Although it's not the case in this picture, many times an incorrect interpretation of linefeeds causes little ^M's to appear scattered throughout the text. Without a doubt, that is a tell-tale sign of cross-platform poisoning.

Preventing the Little M's Before They Strike

The biggest reason to avoid this whole confusion is the same reason why I should kill this fly on my keyboard: it's very annoying! Although these mangled files can be fixed (see the next section), it's worth the extra step it takes to prevent them in the first place.

Dumb Terminal Emulation

How you avoid linefeed dyslexia depends on how you download or upload a particular file. First, let's consider the dumb terminal emulation scenario. In that case, if you recall, you used a transfer protocol such as Zmodem to download a file from a UNIX machine to a local PC or Mac.

Scenario I: UNIX - PC via sz

If you use **sz** in UNIX to download via Zmodem to your PC's terminal program, the conversion is easy. Add the parameter **-a** to the **sz** command, as in:

```
%sz -a filename.txt
```

The UNIX end-of-lines are converted to DOS-style end-of-lines as the file is transferred. Danger averted (mop your brow). You must remember, though, that you can only use the **-a** on files that are ASCII, not binary.

Scenario II: UNIX - Mac via sz

The world is full of prejudice and discrimination, and computing is no different (hey, just read UseNet). The Mac doesn't quite get the fair treatment from **sz**'s creators that the PC does. While the PC needs to have a carriage return inserted in front of UNIX's own linefeed character, the Mac needs the UNIX linefeed to be replaced with a carriage return. Unfortunately (to quote Homey the Clown for all you FOX viewers), "**sz** don't play that game."

So what's a Mac user to do? Use the popular Mac terminal program Zterm. Open that program's **File** menu, select **Transfer Convert**, and check the **Text** option. Just like that, Zterm converts the file appropriately, and the Mac is happy. Whether or not other Mac terminal programs have such a feature, I'm honestly not sure. However, at the very least, you can always convert the UNIX (or MS-DOS) file into a proper format using a converter, which I'll cover next.

> **Check This Out...**
>
> **What About Mac to PC?** Although it's technically possible to transfer a file between a Mac and a PC, you're unlikely to encounter that scenario when using any type of Internet service (and the online services usually take care of protocols their own way).

TCP/IP Connections (SLIP/PPP Accounts)

Now the other common way to download a file is by way of FTP, especially for those users with TCP/IP connections such as SLIP/PPP accounts. In these cases, you use an FTP client such as WS_FTP in Windows or Fetch on the Mac. The key here is to be sure to select ASCII transfer mode instead of binary before you start the download. Some programs (such as Fetch) offer an "auto" mode, which lets the program attempt to decide how to handle the file properly. This usually works, but for certainty's sake, you can manually select ASCII and shut out any room for an error in judgment on the part of the program.

EOLs Are More Than Screen Deep

For most users, as long as a file's end-of-lines appear to be correct on-screen, that's enough. However, to the programmers out there, this warning is for you.

Some programming editors may display ASCII text properly even if imperfect end-of-line codes are used (such as a linefeed in place of a carriage return on a Mac). The problem is that even if the code you have loaded into the editor *looks* right, the incorrect EOLs (end-of-lines) may confuse the compiler when you attempt to turn your code into object code. If this happens, it's very possible that you'll be terribly confused because you, the human, won't see *anything* visibly wrong with your program. The moral is that if you transfer program code between platforms, be sure to figure out which conversion method is reliable and accurate for your situation. Otherwise, your compiler may drive you batty!

On the Rise: Uploading Text

All the same potential problems apply when you send text to another system. Once again, because most providers use UNIX machines, the assumption here is that you'd be sending the text from a PC or Mac to a UNIX system. Whether or not you need to deal with converting the end-of-lines depends partially on the intended use for the file. This may get a little weird, so hang with me for a second.

If you upload a Mac-created text file to a UNIX system in binary mode (either by FTP or Zmodem), it resides on the UNIX system with Mac end-of-lines. So what you have to ask yourself is this: Do you intend to read that file on the UNIX system? Or are you just using the UNIX account to store the file for download to another Mac at a later time? In the first case, the end-of-lines will matter to UNIX; in the second case, they won't because

UNIX is just holding onto the file, not trying to interpret it. If you do upload the file to UNIX in text format, you can display it from within UNIX. However, if you want to download it to a Mac again, you have to get it back into Mac format as explained in the preceding section. (This does make sense after the eighth read-through.)

Because some situations are unpredictable, the best way to determine if you can upload a text file from your computer to UNIX and have it remain usable is to try it. We've been using Zmodem for such transfers throughout the book, so attempt to use Zmodem to upload a text file you've created in a text editor (such as TeachText on the Mac or Notepad in Windows). Then, in the UNIX account, attempt to display the file using either the **more** command or the **cat** command, as shown here:

> **Go to Plan B**
> If that doesn't work, the more reliable method for uploading a text file with Zmodem is to use the command **rz -a** in the UNIX shell (instead of just **rz**). That way, the UNIX side takes care of converting the EOLs properly.

```
%more filename.txt
```

Does the result look correct? If so, you have your answer.

Finding a Cure

In any number of cases, you may find yourself sitting cozily at home with a nice fire going, popcorn on the stove, and a UNIX-format text file on your PC. But the file has already been downloaded, and the EOL problem wasn't taken care of. Must you download the file all over again? Fear not!

Because this whole EOL situation is a common thorn-in-the-side of computing and compatibility, a number of people have blazed paths by writing little utilities to take care of it. After all, the problem is essentially a simple one: change the end-of-line characters from whatever they are to whatever they should be. As a result, you can use certain utilities to correct EOL mistranslations on files that are already on the wrong platform (such as a UNIX-format text file you've improperly downloaded to your PC).

PC users can try out any of these fine utilities:

flip1exe.zip

dos2unix.zip

crlf15b.zip

They're all relatively teeny little programs that can get the job done, and they can all be found at a major PC FTP site such as Simtel (which is mirrored, for example, at **ftp.cdrom.com** in **pub/simtel/msdos**). Or you can use Archie. Each of these programs includes simple instructions. Note that they're all ZIP files, which you must decompress before use.

Mac users might try text-to-mac-12.hqx, which is available at any Info-Mac mirror (see Appendix B). Another very comprehensive Mac text converter is add-strip-302.hqx. I had some difficulty tracking down this program on the Net. It is allegedly at Info-Mac sites, but many of them no longer had it. Some did, though, so try an Archie search for it, and some good sites will come out of the woodwork.

Armed with the capability to avoid text-transfer mix-ups and to correct them post hoc, you should find that this long-standing flea on the computing community's rear end itches a bit less.

The Least You Need to Know

Every now and then when you attempt to transfer an ASCII text file, some strange voodoo may occur. Lines may get frayed ends—not unlike one's hair on an East coast summer day. No biggie. With this knowledge base, you can handle it.

➤ Computer designers had to choose a code to represent the end of a line of text, and they had to tell the computer to recognize it as such. Unfortunately, each major designer chose a different code.

➤ UNIX likes to end lines with ASCII code 10, which is called a linefeed.

➤ The Mac likes to end lines with ASCII code 13, called a carriage return.

➤ MS-DOS and Windows like to end lines with 13 and then 10, a carriage return followed by a linefeed.

➤ When downloading a file from UNIX to the PC via Zmodem (**sz**), use **sz -a** *filename* to perform an automatic conversion.

➤ When downloading a file from UNIX to the Mac via Zmodem, tell Zterm to use Text mode. (Open the **File** menu, choose **Transfer Convert**, and select **Text** mode.)

➤ When downloading to either a Mac or a PC with an FTP client, be sure to check either **ASCII** transfer mode or **automatic** (if available) before initiating the transfer.

➤ As a last resort, use one of the several utilities for the PC or Mac that can convert the wrong end-of-lines to the right ones.

## Chapter 20

Transferus Interruptus

In This Chapter

➤ My download has fallen, and it can't get up

➤ Zmodem to the rescue

➤ The sad truth about FTP

Oh, the pain. The death of a download can be a wrenching experience. After all, these things can be so exciting—like that electric race car set you had as a kid that invariably shorted out and melted the track. In this relatively brief chapter, I'll tell you about some of the (few) things you can do to resurrect file transfers that die in transit. After that, there will be a brief service, and then refreshments will be served.

When a Zmodem Dies

There are two basic scenarios in which you'll discover the dreaded problem.

Scenario I: Right Before Your Eyes

Suppose you found a 3-meg file filled with wonderful new clip art that you need. You've done everything necessary to get to the big moment, and now you are ready to download that file to your PC. Because this will take a while with your 14.4kbps modem (25–30 minutes), you've prepared the surroundings appropriately: dim lights, a chilled bottle of Mountain Dew, and a single white rose atop the monitor. You type **sz** in your UNIX account, hit **Enter**, and lean back to relax.

Your first update looks good:

> Estimated time of transfer: 28:30

> CPS: 1648

Smooooth...so you chill...you zen out to the pixels at the very edge of the monitor that seem to sway...

> Estimated time of transfer: 20:21

> CPS: 1655

When technology works, it is a beautiful thing. But then... "Hmm," methinks, "this download does not look so healthy" turns into "**AAAAAAAHHHHHHHHH!!!!!!!!** What the heck is going on?"

A transfer gone haywire.

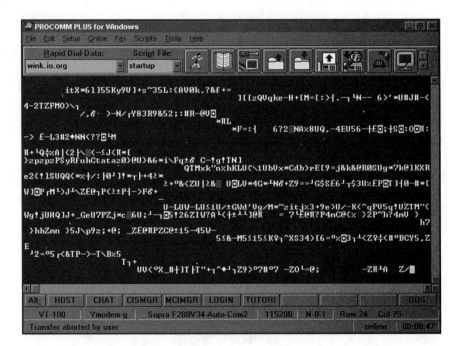

Let's consider the possible reasons for such a thing:

➤ The transfer window disappeared, and garbage just spewed all over the screen.

➤ The power went out due to a huge thunderstorm, and your computer blackened.

➤ Your kid brother Jake picked up the phone to call the NINJA hotline ("I'm a turtle, call me").

➤ Marlot, your adopted stray cat, saw a fly on the modem cable and yanked it clear out with one powerful swipe.

You sit in a state of numb shock.

Zapped

Although I presented it humorously, there is good reason to watch out for severe weather or storms when you're using your computer. Many people are aware of the dangers of power spikes and buy surge protectors to defend against them. Remember that your modem is also plugged into the wall by a phone line. An unfortunately placed lightning strike can very possibly launch a surge down the phone line that can completely bake your modem. What's more, because your modem is hooked up to your computer by its serial cable, that same strike could sizzle your PC, too. This is not a good thing. Do not use your modem during storms with lightning; that is often the reason why modems must be repaired or replaced.

Scenario II: The Arrival Home

Consider the same story as in Scenario I, but say that, instead of hanging around to watch the monitor glow, you go out to exchange "thoughts" with "actual people." When you return from this awkward yet refreshing experience, you see that the transfer window is gone, and you assume the download is complete. Then you check the file on your hard drive and see something like this:

```
C:> dir clipart.zip
 Volume in drive C is MAMBO
 Volume Serial Number is 1D06-3D3F
 Directory of C:\

CLIPART ZIP        948,128  08-14-95 11:53a
        1 file(s)         948,128 bytes
        0 dir(s)      266,928,128 bytes free
```

Oh no! 950KB? But the original was 3 megs! Welcome to transferus interruptus.

Super Protocol Saves the Day

As I mentioned in some other chapter (several actually), when you use Zmodem, not only are the computer gods appeased, but you are empowered with the "resume" capability. Because Zmodem keeps track of what it has done, it can pick up and continue a transfer that was interrupted—which can save you time and capillaries. Although I did briefly go into this earlier, I want to look closer at the Zmodem resume options here.

To jar the imagination (which is different from "canning" the imagination), I give you the following figure. It shows ProComm's Zmodem configuration screen. Here you can set the options that make it possible for you to resume and recover interrupted file transfers.

You can configure Zmodem's crash recovery settings.

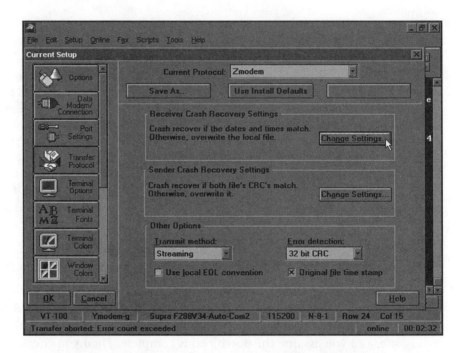

The first outlined area in the Current Setup dialog box is labeled Receiver Crash Recovery Settings. In English, that means "the settings that help recover files from a crash that occurs while downloading." Below that are the Sender Crash Recovery Settings: "the settings for handling crash recovery when you are uploading." Because the options for the two are essentially the same, we'll look only at those for downloading. Click on the **Change Settings** button to swing into a more detailed window (shown in the following figure).

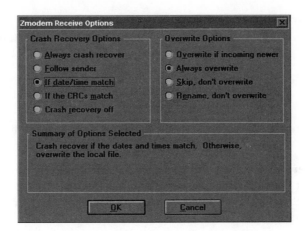

These options determine how Zmodem handles the recovery of interrupted transfers.

The crash recovery options are outlined on the left side of the dialog box. As every sports player ever interviewed says, "We'll take them one option at a time."

➤ **Always crash recover**   If you attempt to download a file whose file name already exists in your download path, Zmodem attempts to continue downloading the remainder of that file. Of course, if the file on your computer is not actually the amputated stub of the file-to-be-downloaded, the result will be a useless mess.

➤ **Follow sender**   Each side of a file transfer has its own settings. In other words, the **sz** command can also be configured with crash-recovery settings (use **man sz** in UNIX to read about that). This option tells ProComm to ignore its own settings and do whatever **sz** tells it to. There's not a compelling reason to do this in most cases, though. It seems more confusing than anything else.

➤ **If date/time match**   When the transfer begins, Zmodem checks certain characteristics of the file to be downloaded and any file of the same name that already exists in your download path. In this case, Zmodem considers the date and time stamp on the two files. If they are the same, Zmodem assumes that an interrupted transfer occurred, and it resumes the transfer from the point of interruption (crash recover). However, if the stamps do not match, Zmodem needs to know what you'd like it to do. That's what the options on the right side of the dialog box are for.

If the date and time stamps on the two files do not match, indicate which of the following procedures you want Zmodem to follow:

Overwrite if incoming is newer   If the file to be downloaded has a more recent stamp, Zmodem copies it over the existing file, erasing the older file that's already on your computer.

Always overwrite   If the stamps do not match, Zmodem overwrites the file on your computer no matter what.

239

Skip, don't overwrite   If the stamps do not match, Zmodem skips the downloading of this file and moves on to the next one (if there is a next one).

Rename, don't overwrite   If the stamps do not match, Zmodem continues downloading the file but names it something else so it doesn't touch the local file in question.

➤ **If the CRCs match**   Don't worry about this option; it is a bit too esoteric for our concerns.

➤ **Crash recovery off**   If Zmodem detects that the file to be downloaded already exists on your computer, it does not attempt to crash recover the file. How Zmodem handles the situation from here depends on your selection in the Overwrite Options section (just described).

It's worth noting that you can use Zmodem's resume capabilities on some files that were not initially transferred using Zmodem. For example, if you use Ymodem-g (for its slight throughput increase), you will find that you cannot crash recover an interrupted transfer using Ymodem-g. However, even if you've downloaded part of the file with Ymodem-g, you can switch to Zmodem and crash recover the remainder.

Reviving FTP?

Now this is a much trickier problem. What about all those happy SLIP/PPP users out there who are proud that they don't have to deal with the hassles of a transfer protocol. These pioneers run FTP clients on their local computer and retrieve goodies directly from anywhere on the Net. Nonetheless, many of the boogeymen I've been talking about (cats, siblings, lightning, and so on) can also interrupt an FTP transfer—especially when it is used over a modem connection.

Unfortunately, this is one case in which TCP/IP types have to admit some degree of defeat to the dumb terminal users. Technically, it is possible for the FTP protocol to support some form of "resumed transfer" or "crash recovery." However, the mere possibility requires that the proper code be implemented in both the FTP server and the FTP client. In some cases, this has been done.

In FTP parlance, this code implementation is known as *reget*. The good news is that a very popular FTP server developed by the University of Washington does support reget requests from a client. The bad news is that very few FTP clients currently are able to send a reget request.

A new version of NcFTP (version 2) is being developed that is mostly for UNIX systems. It will support a limited form of reget, but the how-to of compiling this program on a UNIX platform is not something that I can explain in this book very easily. For those of you who have some UNIX know-how and/or an insatiable, masochistic curiosity, you can find the source code for the aforementioned beast at the FTP site **ftp.cs.unl.edu** in the **/pub/ ncftp** directory.

The Better FTP

NcFTP, which sounds silly however you pronounce it, is an alternative to the standard UNIX FTP client. It reduces much of the repetitive work of using FTP by allowing for automation (auto anonymous login, auto binary mode, remembering last-used paths, and so on). In addition, it supports macros and the capability to remember sites you've used in the past. All in all, if you're stuck in UNIX, NcFTP is the way to go. Unfortunately, you'll need to compile it in your account yourself (which requires some UNIX knowledge), find someone else on your system who already has, or ask your system administrator. Increasingly more systems already have NcFTP installed.

The other, somewhat strange alternative to resuming an interrupted FTP transfer is to use a terminal program and download the remainder of the file by Zmodem. This does work; I have done it on occasions where an FTP died with 2 megs in, and I didn't want to wait all over again. However, it only works if you were ftping the file from your UNIX account, not from a remote Internet site. The catch-22 is that using this approach means you would have retrieved the file to your UNIX account first, before downloading it to your PC, which introduces that middleman step that we were so excited about evading in Chapter 16.

Another downside for users using FTP clients is that the terminal program transfer is not multisession. Therefore, you cannot do any other communications while the transfer is taking place. Clearly, this isn't the greatest solution man ever conceived of. In fact, it's pretty lame. In computerese, we call it a *kludge*: it gets the job done, but in a not-so-elegant way.

The Least You Need to Know

Nothing, er, well, few things are more frustrating than an interrupted transfer. Especially when you start it just before bed and wake up the next morning excitedly expecting a nice big file from the digital Santa—only to find 100KB out of 20 megs downloaded. Ick, I hate that! But there are a few (though I stress the word *few*) things one can do.

➤ Minimize environmental factors that can interrupt a transfer (such as people in the house who might pick up the phone or mischievous mammals who might pull cables for recreation).

➤ Don't transfer files—or use the computer at all—during severe weather.

➤ If you use Zmodem, you can take advantage of its crash recovery feature. Explore the Zmodem configuration settings in your own terminal program to make sure they are properly enabled.

➤ FTP users have few recovery options because the **reget** command has not yet been widely implemented in most clients. Until that beatific day, one can try to complete an interrupted FTP by dialing up a UNIX account and using Zmodem for the remainder of the file transfer.

fsp—The Ignored Protocol

Continuing our exploration of the less-celebrated side of the online universe, we take issue with the rare and widely unknown file transfer protocol with the funny name: *fsp*. Historically, fsp has been the Internet's little well-groomed poodle that trails after the large neighborhood mastiff and hounds him along the way. While most average Net users won't necessarily find a "need" to use fsp, they may find some worthwhile applications for it (especially those types of people who prefer to take the empty side streets to the mall instead of Highway 401).

What Does It Stand For? What Does It Do? Who Can We Trust?

The least enlightening way to explain fsp is to tell you what it stands for. It existed for some time without an official title before "File Service Protocol" was agreed upon. That helps a lot, doesn't it? At its heart, the intention of fsp is the same as that of the more famous FTP: to move a file from one computer to another across a network such as the Internet. What differs is the means and philosophy it uses. And these differences are exactly what make fsp more appealing to some people (it's somewhat like the long-standing Hydrox vs. Oreo debate, but different). While this discussion could easily become technical and boring, it won't. I'll stop before I cross that "glassy-eye" line.

The fsp protocol is based on the same client/server premise as FTP and most of the other protocols discussed in this book. A host machine (usually a UNIX machine) runs an fsp server (techies like to call them *daemons*), to which you connect with an fsp client. In that sense, there's no difference between fsp and FTP. However, fsp does boast a couple of big advantages over FTP:

➤ The fsp host does not suffer under a heavy workload no matter how many fsp clients request data from it. Heavy FTP usage, on the other hand, can weigh a host computer down and prevent it from doing anything very efficiently. This makes fsp an attractive option for sites that may be very busy. And for the client user, it's a major advantage because it all but eliminates the hassle of attempting to retrieve files from an overburdened FTP server.

➤ fsp is more robust, able to withstand unfavorable network conditions. For example, consider the nasty situation that occurs when an FTP transfer is interrupted (we discussed it in Chapter 20). In addition to all of the terrible things people in your home can do to cause an interrupt, the network between your provider and the FTP host can go down, and that, too, will break your transfer. Not so with fsp. If you begin an fsp transfer and leave it unattended, and if 25% of the way through the transfer, the network goes down for three hours, you don't have to start over. The transfer picks right up where it left off when the network comes back up. Even more notably, if your transfer was completely interrupted—say, your computer was shut off—you can go back and retrieve the file via fsp (in a way similar to that of Zmodem), and it resumes from where it was interrupted.

Bearing all these positive points in mind, of course you're wondering why fsp isn't more popular. One of the design features of fsp (in keeping with its "light and healthy" philosophy) is that it achieves slower transfer rates than FTP. And in our workaday world, you can imagine why that's not valued by many rat-racers. The other reason is largely historical: as with all technology, quality does count, but it must be factored with other variables such as publicity, implementation, and so on.

Because fsp is not an overly popular protocol, not many sites have implemented it. This, of course, is a disadvantage that somewhat overshadows its functional advantages.

Naked Who?

Because of the light demands fsp puts on a system and the fact that it's relatively unknown, a number of people have used fsp for, shall we say, "seedier" purposes. Although these practices are not necessarily illegal, by allowing them, fsp gained a reputation for being the way to get pornography on the Net. These same factors led to the use of fsp for the distribution of pirated software. Some hackers find it relatively easy to break into a poorly administered UNIX machine and set up an fsp server.

In some circles, then, fsp has gained something of a tarnished reputation. That's mostly the fault of what some have done with it. Note that there are also plenty of illegal and/or hacked FTP sites by which people share pirated software.

None of the above needs concern you, though, if you're not interested in it. You will find many "legitimate" fsp sites, some of which also host FTP access but are easier to get into during crowded hours via fsp. To do that, the first thing you need is a client.

> **fsp Just Makes It Easy** One of the major reasons why public access sites do not carry adult material is because the market demand—and consequential computing demand—from the public overburdens the host computers. However, with fsp, this is less likely to be the case. Combine that with the fact that fewer people know about fsp to begin with, and you've got the makings for a nice secret-club sort of protocol.

Finding a Client

In an attempt to not be monogamous in this book, I've shifted the focus from UNIX to the PC/Windows platform and even to the Mac on occasion. The same triad scenario exists here.

Originally designed for UNIX by UNIX-y types, the original flavor of fsp is actually a set of about 11 commands that control its various functions. Unfortunately, as with many UNIX programs, you cannot simply retrieve an executable client for your UNIX account. The program must be compiled on your particular system, and that is something far too advanced for this book. So readers who want to run fsp from their UNIX accounts (those using dial-up dumb terminal emulation accounts, for example) have to inquire to the system administrator about the status of fsp, asking whether or not it's already installed, and if they'd be willing to install it if it's not.

Fortunately, the situation is somewhat better for PC and Mac users because there are a few graphical fsp clients available. But before I tell you about what's available for each platform, you need to understand how an fsp site works.

If you're familiar with FTP sites, you know they are referenced in the standard Internet address format *a.b.c.d*, where *a–d* can be either numbers or letters (such as **128.232.10.5** or **mary.poppins.com**). In fsp, you use the same address style, with the addition of a *port*. For example, an fsp address might look like **128.232.10.5 2001** or **mary.poppins.com 2001**. (Note the required space between the standard address and the port.)

If You're Using Windows 95... At the time of this writing, no fsp clients have been written specifically for Windows 95; however, Windows 3.x clients run fine in 95.

When you connect to an fsp site using any of the clients listed in the next few sections, you use this style address. Once connected, you'll find that navigating around the site is almost identical to swimming around an FTP site using a graphical FTP client (such as WS_FTP or Fetch).

fsp for Windows

Two fsp clients are available for Windows. We'll look at just one, WinFSP (version 1.2), which is the better of the two. For availability, see Appendix B. You decompress and install the program like any other. When you start it, you are immediately prompted to enter a site to connect to in the **Site Name** text box of the Connect to dialog box (see the following figure).

When you launch WinFSP, it asks for a site to connect to.

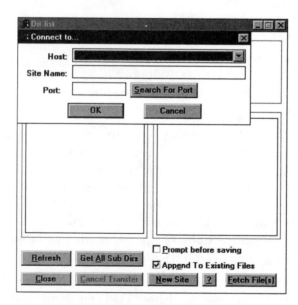

For this example, enter the **doomgate.cs.buffalo.edu 21** site that holds software relating to the kill-'em-all shareware game *Doom*, as well as other games by Id Software. More information on how to obtain sites later in this chapter.... (That'll keep you interested. Learned that from the evening news, I did.) Enter the site information, including the address and the port, in the Connect to dialog box, and click **OK** to start the ball rolling (into the socket, that is, for those who get that bit of geek humor).

WinFSP happily connects, and you see the archetypal window shown in the next figure. The top portion of the window displays some information about what's currently going on. Below that on the left side is a list of the available directories on the remote fsp site. On the right side is a list of the files available in the directory you're currently in (which is named in the Information window).

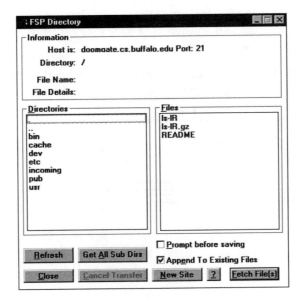

You're connected!

After you connect, fsp works much like FTP, and navigating is relatively intuitive.

➤ To enter another subdirectory, double-click on its name in the list on the left.

➤ To select a file or multiple files for retrieval, click on the file names in the list on the right (hold down the **Ctrl** key to select more than one). When you select a file name, the Information window displays information about the file, such as its size. Use this to judge how long the transfer may take.

➤ To retrieve the highlighted files, click the **Fetch File(s)** button in the lower-right corner. Unfortunately, this version of WinFSP doesn't show such transfer status information as throughput or estimated time.

As you can see, to the end-user (that's you), fsp isn't much different from FTP. It's mostly what goes on behind the scenes that differentiates the two. But don't confuse them. You *cannot* connect to an FTP site using fsp—or vice versa.

Some hosts do run both FTP and fsp servers; in those cases, you can use whichever method you prefer. For example, consider the mega-popular **wuarchive.wustl.edu** site. This site is well known for its FTP offerings, but it also runs an fsp server (**wuarchive.wustl.edu 21**). During daytime hours, it's nearly impossible to get into wuarchive by FTP. However, you can almost always succeed with fsp—and you can laugh at everyone else, if you're the spiteful type.

Macintoo

Even though it's not wildly different, let's take a quick lap around a Macintosh fsp client to prove how similar they are. Shockingly, the Mac take on fsp is called MacFSP. How *do* they come up with these names?

To get started, launch MacFSP and select **File**, **Open Connection** from the menu bar. The window shown in the following figure appears.

Opening a connection with MacFSP.

Enter the same site information you did in the WinFSP box. Then click **OK**. Once you're connected, you see that familiar-style navigation window. Notice how remarkably similar it is in both design and concept not only to WinFSP, but also to the Mac's own Fetch for FTP.

The window on the left side shows the contents of the current directory. In this case, you are currently in the site's root directory, so the list contains a bunch of subdirectories. Double-click on the **pub** directory and look for an interesting file. Oops—this simply brings up more subdirectories. Well then, go with **idgames**; it should have some interesting files.

You're right. There's still not much of interest. But, hey, this is just an example. We'll cope. Get the file called **LAST.7days** and be happy.

The process for getting the file should be relatively obvious by now: click on the file and click the **Get** button. Before you do that, however, you have to choose from the Automatic, Text, and Binary option buttons. The same rules apply here that do in FTP. In this instance, it's fairly clear that this is going to be a text file, so Text or Automatic should work. Stick with **Text** (the honest reason being that Automatic is not yet functional in this version of the program). The following figure shows the screen when you're ready to grab that file with MacFSP.

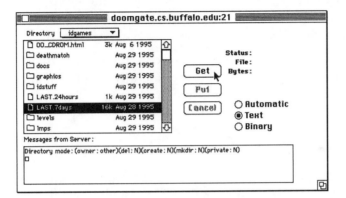

Grab the file of recent uploads.

There you have it! MacFSP offers some brief transfer information, but that's nothing you haven't already seen at least five times in this book. However much difference there is between fsp and FTP in technical design, they work in much the same way, and using them isn't much of a stretch for us brainy humans.

The Tough Part: Finding Sites

Here's where it gets interesting. Ever heard of truffles? Somewhere in the forests in France, old guys go out with dogs at 5 a.m. to hunt for those buried fungi that French people like to eat. In a way, fsp sites are like truffles; in other ways, they're not.

Sites are not abundant, and because the fsping community is small, finding sources for site information can be challenging. As it currently stands, usually one or two people volunteer to organize and maintain a site list. Of course, if they happen to get a new job or find something better to do with their time, there goes the list.

One of the longer-standing fsp site resources is Dan Charrois' list, which is available by both *finger* and the World Wide Web. If you know how to

Wiggly Finger Finger is an Internet resource that you use to find out information about a particular user or to retrieve information that a user might want to make available. In UNIX, you can simply use the command **finger *user@host***. On the PC or Mac, you need a finger client. Some E-mail applications (such as Eudora) include a finger function.

Check This Out...

249

finger someone on the Internet, finger the address **charro@bode.ee.ualberta.ca** to get this list of sites. More reliably, you can access the very same list on the Web at the URL **http://nyquist.ee.ualberta.ca/~charro/fsp**. In addition to Dan Charrois' list, there is another decent list on the Web at the URL **http://www.itunit.cs.rdg.ac.uk/misc/fsp/sitelist/**. These are the two primary fsp site resources. If you want to find others, check the UseNet newsgroup **alt.comp.fsp** and ask around (although they don't appreciate requests for adult or pirate sites).

Depending on the sorts of data you tend to access on the Internet, fsp sites can be a real boon—or they can be completely irrelevant. Explore them for a bit and see what's around. Columbus did it, and look what he got. A day off.

Check This Out...

Not the Net

Even though many of the online services (such as America Online and CompuServe) offer various sorts of access to Internet files via FTP, they do not offer any fsp capabilities. Because those services are restricted to the functions they allow, there is no way to use fsp from non-Internet-based online services.

The Least You Need to Know

Although some people consider fsp a cocktail-trivia protocol, it is useful for some things. It achieves essentially the same goal as the more popular FTP, but it does so in a more flexible and robust way. However, compared to the large number of FTP sites, there are very few fsp sites. C'est la life.

➤ fsp is used to transfer files between a client and a host, just like FTP.

➤ Because it is "lightweight," fsp does not weigh down the host computer even under heavy demand.

➤ fsp can survive various transmission interruptions, including dead networks. In addition, it can resume a transfer where it left off.

➤ fsp site addresses take the form *a.b.c.d port*, as in **128.232.43.65 2001**.

➤ Windows users should get a copy of WinFSP, and Mac users may try MacFSP. Both are available on major FTP sites. Using either one is a snap if you've used FTP.

➤ You can obtain fsp site lists on the World Wide Web at **http://nyquist.ee.ualberta.ca/~charro/fsp**.

## Chapter 22

Packing and Shipping: Creating Your Own File Archives

In This Chapter

➤ Be a good citizen—save rubber

➤ Talkin' compression redundancy blues

➤ ZIP it, Stuff it, **tar** it, Woo!

It may seem odd that this chapter on creating archives is at the end of the book. Considering that you mucked around decompressing and dearchiving a number of chapters ago, you might think this an unusual ordering of events. But a team of world-renowned scientists—ranging from alchemists to zoologists—determined that for an appropriate and final send-off, a how-to on gluing together your own archives would be the way to go. And, really, who am I to question science?

Why Would I Want to Do That?

All those files that are available on the Internet and in some areas of the online services had to get there somewhere. In many cases, the answer is you! (Oh, and only you can prevent forest fires, too.) If you decide to contribute to public file areas—whether FTP sites, UseNet, or online service forums—you have to upload files in the same common archival and compression formats everyone else does. This is one domain where conformity is admirable (although that's arguable elsewhere). So follow the leader....

The best strategy for packaging files for upload is to use whatever format is most common for the intended platform. In most readers' cases, this boils down to either PC or Mac. Users with files intended for the PC will want to use PKZIP, while Mac users can abide by StuffIt.

Some confusion enters, though, when you consider files that are not restricted to a specific platform. Consider, for example, a set of image files in the JPG graphic format or a collection of audio sounds sampled from one television show. In many cases, files like these wouldn't be included in an archive. For one thing, compressing them often doesn't do any good because their file types already include compression. For another, people accessing a site will find it inconvenient to have to download a 1.5 meg archive containing a bunch of pictures just to get one picture that they could have more easily downloaded as a separate file. The same goes for sound files. However, there are some cases where you do want to keep all the files together in one archive because the downloader will want them all.

Platform-Nonspecific?

Some types of files, such as executable programs, work only on the platform they were written for. So a Mac program runs only on a Mac; it's of no use to a UNIX user or a PC person, and vice versa three times.

However, some files that contain data only and no instructions can be used by any platform that has the program needed to handle the data. For example, a JPG-format image file is a set of data representing a picture. Each platform has its own program (a "viewer" for instance) that can handle the JPG data and plop a pretty picture onto the screen. When uploading platform-nonspecific files for public consumption, you don't want to archive them in an unpopular format (such as one limited to your own platform). Make them accessible to everyone because anyone should be able to use them.

Most people fall back on ZIP when they need to create an archive of platform-nonspecific files. There are ZIP'ers and un-ZIP'ers available for Mac and UNIX (and most other platforms) in addition to the PC. Because there are just so darn many PCs weighing down the globe, that platform tends to get the muscle of the masses behind it. While it is possible to un-stuff Mac files on a PC, not many people are prepared to do so, and if you upload platform-nonspecific files in Mac archives, you will annoy more people than you help. You should try to accommodate as many other users as possible.

To Compress or Not to Compress, That Is a Question

Recall that while the two processes tend to be closely linked in practice, there is a difference between compressing and archiving file(s). When a file is compressed, its size is reduced. When a file is archived, it is stored with other files within one larger file. In two of the three walk-throughs you'll digest in this chapter, compression and archiving occur simultaneously. In the final example, each is taken care of separately.

Especially when you're talking about single files (when archiving is not applicable), compression is not always helpful. Those files that include compression in their format, for example, often will not benefit from further compression. Look at the following compression results from a ZIP archive:

```
Length  Method   Size   Ratio   Date     Time    CRC-32    Name ("^" ==> case
------  ------   ----   -----   ----     ----    ------    ----    conversion)
 45393  Deflate  45262    0%   08-27-95  21:08   2eb83f70  00474.jpg
109165  Deflate  74028   32%   08-27-95  21:10   021df43c  Scratchy.WAV
 62594  Deflate  62604    0%   07-10-95  14:44   b98f9cae  bmghalf.gif
 47884  Deflate  34803   27%   08-27-95  21:10   e2acbc9b  luck.wav
192000  Deflate 189513    1%   08-27-95  21:08   372a7456  michael2.gif
```

This archive contains three types of files: one JPG-format graphic image, two GIF-format graphic images, and two WAV-format audio sounds. By looking at the **Ratio** column, you can see how much compression PKZIP achieved with each file. There is a clear pattern: the WAV files compress adequately, and the graphic files do not compress at all. The lesson here is that some files (of which you'll encounter GIFs and JPGs most frequently), don't need to be compressed. So if you are creating an archive that includes such files, you needn't be concerned with it; they'll automatically be included in the archive even if they are decompressable. But if you are just uploading a single such file (one JPG, for instance), there is no need to compress it first. Just upload it directly in its original intact form.

Now, with the theory behind you, it's time to try a little packing. Following the tradition you started early in this book, you can walk-through each typical program you may need to use. After that, it's pizza party time. One out of every 50 copies of this book includes a free pizza in the back cover (though Que is not responsible for freshness—or lack thereof).

ZIP It Up

To make it easy, focus on using WinZip (instead of the command-line MS-DOS based PKZIP) to create an archive. Versions of WinZip are available for both Windows 3.x and Windows 95; the screens shown here are from the 95 version. First things first, when you launch the WinZip application, you see its blank n' ready window (see the following figure).

WinZip is launched, ready for some packin'!

First, you create a wholly new archive from scratch. Start by clicking the **New** button or by selecting **New Archive** from the **File** menu. The New Archive dialog box (shown in the next figure) appears so you can name your new archive.

Enter a file name for the new archive.

Select the directory you want to store the archive in.

Enter a name for the archive.

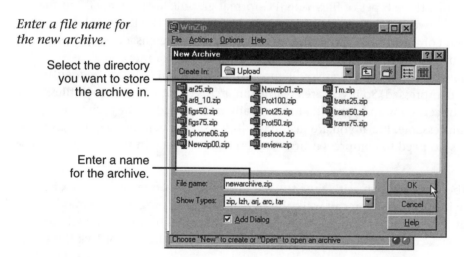

From here, you can navigate into the directory where you'd like the archive to reside once it's created. In this case, select **Upload**. Because the file doesn't already exist, you enter a new file name in the **File name** text box and click **OK**. Note that you don't have to add the .ZIP extension to the file name; if you don't, WinZip adds it automatically. But you can if you like (as I did here). When you click OK, WinZip displays the Add dialog box (as long as you've checked the **Add Dialog** check box). In this dialog box, you select the files you want to include in the archive. The following figure shows the Add dialog box.

The Add dialog box.

Before you select the files for the archive, however, take some time to consider the options this window offers.

First, Consider Your Options...

On the left side of the dialog box near the bottom, open the **Action** drop-down list. Because you're creating a new archive from scratch, make sure **Add** (the default option) is selected. If, on the other hand, you wanted to add to the contents of an existing ZIP archive, you would choose from the following options in the Action drop-down list:

Add (and Replace) Files   Tells WinZip to replace any file already in the archive that has the same name as a file you choose to add. (Any other files you choose to add simply go into the archive, and files already in the archive that don't have conflicting file names are left untouched.)

Freshen Existing Files   Tells WinZip to see if the selected file has a newer modification date stamp than the same file that's already in the archive does. If so, the file in the archive is replaced with the selected one; if not, it is left alone. (Selected files that do not match anything already in the archive are ignored.)

Move Files   This is a tricky option, so beware. This moves selected files and/or directories *from* your current hard drive path *to* the ZIP archive. Once these files are in the archive, they are deleted from their original location. (This one is probably not worth the risk.)

Update (and Add) Files Follows the same idea as Freshen, but any selected files that are not already in the existing archive are added as normal instead of being ignored.

Below Action is the Compression drop-down list. It contains the options None, Fast, Normal, and Maximum. These options regulate how much computing power is put into compressing the files. The more effort that's used, the more they compress—and the longer it takes. In almost all cases, the default **Normal** is perfectly adequate. If you expect people with very fast computers to be using this archive, you may decide on Maximum; in the opposite case (if you expect people with slow computers to patronize the archive), try Fast.

On the right side of the Add dialog box, click on whichever of these three check boxes is appropriate:

Recurse Subdirectories This can be a very useful option. If you enable (check) this box, WinZip archives all subdirectories under any directory that you select for inclusion in an archive. For example, if you decide to add the PIX directory to the archive and you select this check box, WinZip includes all subdirectories within PIX. If you do not check this option, WinZip includes only the files within PIX (not any of its subdirectories).

Save Extra Directory Info Enable this option to store full path information for any directories included in your archive. That is, if you include the PIX directory in your archive and you enable this option, WinZip saves that as C:>GRAPHICS\PIX\ (if that's what the true path is on your system). If you leave this option disabled, WinZip simply stores the name PIX for the directory. You usually only want to enable this option if it's important for users of the archive to maintain the exact same path structures as on your system—which isn't often the case.

What 8.3 Option? Not all versions of WinZip contain this option, but the 32-bit versions do.

Store Filenames In DOS 8.3 Form Some users, especially those with Windows 95, are not restricted by the 8-character file name limit of DOS. Therefore, they may have files with longer names. If those users upload files that break the 8.3 file name rule, DOS users may have problems trying to download and use the files. This option tells WinZip to shorten the file names so DOS users can handle them.

...Then Make Your Move

Now that you know all about your options, you're ready to select several files for inclusion in the new archive. There are two basic ways to do this. The obvious, easy, and most common way is to select them from the dialog box. Hold down the **Ctrl** key and click on the files you want to archive as shown in the next figure.

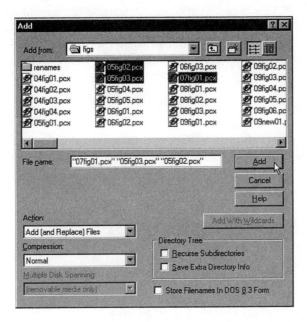

Select the files you want to add to the archive.

Look closely at the File name text box. It contains the name of each file you've selected. Get a close look at that:

> File name: "07fig01.pcx" "05fig03.pcx" "05fig02.pcx"

If you wanted to, you could click in that text box and modify the list. "Yeah, so why would I ever want to do that?" you're thinking. Well, the most common reason is to add more files to the archive using wild cards. For example, suppose you want to add a number of figs named 10fig*something*. Sure, you could highlight them all. But you could accomplish the same goal much more quickly by manually selecting a couple of files, clicking in the **File name** text box, and typing **10fig*.***, which is the wild-card expression for "everything beginning with 10fig." In that case, you would end up with:

> File name: "07fig01.pcx" "05fig03.pcx" "05fig02.pcx" 10fig*.*

When you enter a wild-card expression like that, the Add with Wildcards button becomes available. If you want to add only the files you've selected with your mouse, click the **Add** button. If you want to add the files you selected *and* any files that match the wild-card entry you typed, click the **Add with Wildcards** button. Either way, WinZip begins adding the files to the archive (and automatically compressing them).

257

Slipped My Mind

No need to worry if you forgot to select a file to add to the archive. You can add and/or delete files from any archive anytime you want. If you forgot some files or would like to add more, just choose **Add** from WinZip's **Actions** menu (or select the appropriate icon). Then, you can select the files you want to add to the existing archive. Easy as pie—microwave pie, anyway.

When WinZip finishes archiving the files, it displays the contents of the new archive. As you can see in the following figure, the window looks just like it would if you had just opened an existing archive. Notice that you can see such relevant statistics as the compression ratio for each file.

WinZip displays the contents of your new archive.

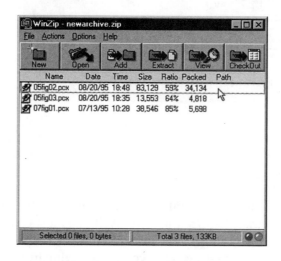

Essentially, that's it. You've created an archive. For safety's sake, open the **File** menu and select **Close Archive** so WinZip will save this baby for good. Now you have a ZIP file that you can upload and that any interested customers can download, dearchive, and use.

All Stuffed Up (Okay, So They're Easy Jokes)

In usage, StuffIt (or StuffIt "Lite" as you'll be using) is very similar to WinZip. Of course, remember that the two create completely different archive types that are not compatible with one another. In general, Mac users can un-stuff archives relatively easily, but users on other platforms will have a more difficult—or impossible—time doing so. So don't use

StuffIt (.SIT) format for archives that are intended for general purpose usage (that is, platform-nonspecific).

Technically, you'll be using StuffIt "Lite" because that is the shareware version available on the Internet. After you install the program (it comes as a self-extracting archive), launch it, and you are greeted with a friendly title screen. To create a new archive, open the **File** menu and select **New**. StuffIt conjures up the dialog box shown in the next figure, in which you enter a name and select a location for the archive you're creating.

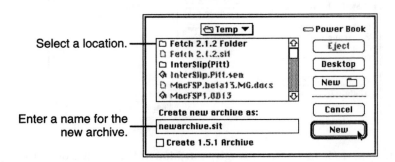

Select a location.

Enter a name for the new archive.

Create a new archive with StuffIt.

Check the **Create 1.5.1 Archive** check box at the bottom of the window if you want your archive saved in a StuffIt format that is compatible with older versions of StuffIt. When you finish in this dialog box, click **New**, and a WinZip-type window displays the contents of the new archive (it's empty right now, of course).

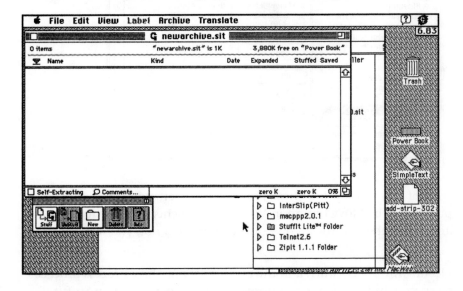

The contents of our new archive: nothing—yet.

To begin adding files to the archive, open the **Archive** menu and select **Stuff**. The window shown in the following figure appears. Here, you select the files on your hard drive that you want to add to the archive.

Choose files to add to your StuffIt archive.

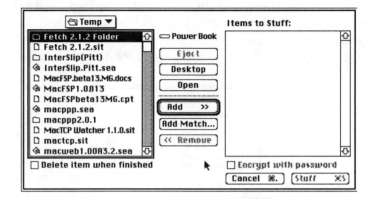

Basically, all you have to do is navigate through your Mac in the left window and select each file you want to add by clicking on it. With the file highlighted, click the **Add >>** button. In the following publicity shot, you can see that five files are selected for inclusion in the new archive.

In this case, you have selected five guests of honor for stuffing.

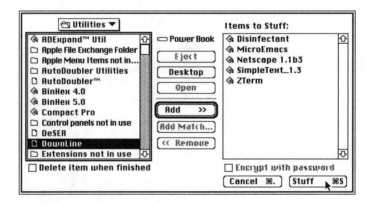

In the lower-left corner of this window is a check box labeled Delete item when finished. It serves the same purpose as the Move option in WinZip: if you check it, StuffIt deletes the original files after adding them to the archive. More often than not, you *won't* want to enable that.

When you finish selecting files, click **Stuff**, and the compression/archive process proceeds forthwith. A stuffing status window keeps you informed of the progress. When StuffIt finishes its stuff, you see a window like the one in the next figure. It shows the files in the archive and fills you in on all the traditional statistics (such as compression ratios). This is just like WinZip.

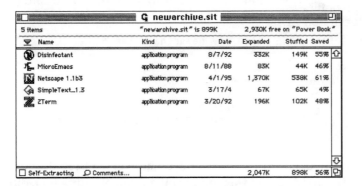

The meal is finally fully baked. Here are the results.

After you create an archive this way, you can add files anytime you want using the Stuff option. For now, select **File**, **Close** to put this baby away. It's ready for upload.

Yabba Dabba tar

Most readers will not need to archive and compress files within UNIX very often. But, who knows, it could come up. (Maybe it will appear as a question on Jeopardy 2000, and you'll need to know it to clinch your five-time champion status.) Regardless, it's not particularly difficult. There are two variations on the concepts you've dealt with so far.

➤ First, **tar** is in fact *only* an archiver, not a compressor. So when you add files to a tar archive, they are not compressed; they're just lumped together in one big file. You'll see how to handle the compression part afterward.

➤ Second, and more obviously, because **tar** is a UNIX command, it's controlled through weird command-line syntax instead of simple point-and-click. But even there, the ideas behind the commands are generally the same.

Begin with the same set of graphic and sound files you used in the ZIP compression illustration earlier. This is what the subdirectory in your UNIX account currently looks like:

```
%ls -l
total 947
-rw-------  1 aaron   user    45393 Aug 27 21:08 00474.jpg
-rw-r--r--  1 aaron   user   109165 Aug 27 21:10 Scratchy.WAV
-rw-r--r--  1 aaron   user    62594 Jul 10 14:44 bmghalf.gif
-rw-r--r--  1 aaron   user    47884 Aug 27 21:10 luck.wav
-rw-------  1 aaron   user   192000 Aug 27 21:08 michael2.gif
```

Check This Out...

Make a List
If you want to include a group of files that can't be "described" using a wild-card expression, you can list their names separated by spaces (as in **tar cfv newarchive.tar filename1 filename2 filename 3**).

Say you want to include all these files in a **tar** archive, which you're going to call **bunchostuff.tar**. To do this, you use the **cfv** parameters, followed by the name of the new archive, followed by the * wild card (which represents all files).

```
%tar cfv newarchive.tar *
00474.jpg
Scratchy.WAV
bmghalf.gif
luck.wav
michael2.gif
tar: tar vol 1, 5 files, 0 bytes read, 471040 bytes
written.
```

The output from **tar** (invoked with the **v** parameter above) isn't too detailed. It lists each file that's added to the archive, and then gives you a total. Nothing incredibly interesting or important.

To view the contents of the fresh **tar** file, replace the **c** parameter with a **t** (for "table of contents" maybe?).

```
%tar tfv newarchive.tar
-rw-------  1 aaron    user        45393 Aug 27 21:08 00474.jpg
-rw-r--r--  1 aaron    user       109165 Aug 27 21:10 Scratchy.WAV
-rw-r--r--  1 aaron    user        62594 Jul 10 14:44 bmghalf.gif
-rw-r--r--  1 aaron    user        47884 Aug 27 21:10 luck.wav
-rw-------  1 aaron    user       192000 Aug 27 21:08 michael2.gif
tar: tar vol 1, 5 files, 471040 bytes read, 0 bytes written.
```

This still is not thrilling stuff. It's not even surprising, really. But that's a **tar** archive, basically.

There Is One Difference...

One caveat worth noting involves adding files to an existing **tar** archive. Unlike with ZIP, you cannot just use the same procedure to add new files to a **tar** archive. Doing so erases the existing archive and overwrites it with a new one—which is not good.

To add files to an existing **tar** archive, use the **r** parameter, like this:

```
%tar rfv newarchive.tar cdlist.txt
tar: Reading archive to position at the end...done.
cdlist.txt
tar: tar vol 1, 6 files, 460800 bytes read, 294400 bytes written.
```

tar adds the file you designated and displays a list of the complete contents of the archive.

```
%tar tfv newarchive.tar
-rw-------  1 aaron    user       45393 Aug 27 21:08 00474.jpg
-rw-r--r--  1 aaron    user      109165 Aug 27 21:10 Scratchy.WAV
-rw-r--r--  1 aaron    user       62594 Jul 10 14:44 bmghalf.gif
-rw-r--r--  1 aaron    user       47884 Aug 27 21:10 luck.wav
-rw-------  1 aaron    user      192000 Aug 27 21:08 michael2.gif
-rw-r--r--  1 aaron    user      207276 Jul 11 15:46 cdlist.txt
tar: tar vol 1, 6 files, 687616 bytes read, 0 bytes written.
```

As you can see, the new file has definitely been added to the archive. Woo-hoo!

Now remember: none of these files has been compressed. The size of this **tar** archive is the sum of the sizes of each component file. There are two possible ways to combine compression with **tar** (something that was automatically done with ZIP and StuffIt).

➤ If the files being **tar**'ed are already compressed (ZIP files, GIFs, or JPGs, for example), there's no problem.

➤ More common in UNIX tradition is the compression of the final **tar** file itself. Notice that this is the reverse of how WinZip and StuffIt work. They compress each individual file and then lump the compressed results into one big file: the archive. In this case, you're going to lump together the individual decompressed files, and then compress the resulting big file. Does it matter? Not really.

To compress the **tar** file, it's traditional to use UNIX compress. (You can use whatever you want, but people tend to expect UNIX compress format and may groan at you if you use something else.)

```
%compress newarchive.tar
%ls -l
total 1322
-rw-------  1 aaron    user      45393 Aug 27 21:08 00474.jpg
-rw-r--r--  1 aaron    user     109165 Aug 27 21:10 Scratchy.WAV
-rw-r--r--  1 aaron    user      62594 Jul 10 14:44 bmghalf.gif
-rw-r--r--  1 aaron    user     207276 Jul 11 15:46 bmglist.txt
-rw-r--r--  1 aaron    user      47884 Aug 27 21:10 luck.wav
-rw-------  1 aaron    user     192000 Aug 27 21:08 michael2.gif
-rw-------  1 aaron    user     633769 Aug 28 16:27 newarchive.tar.Z
```

At the bottom of the directory listing, you can see the compressed **tar** archive, which now has **.Z** appended to the end. The archive is now suitable for transport (such as uploading). And it's pizza time for some of you lucky readers.

tar Tips

You can use a number of options with **tar**, but only a few are relevant in this situation. If you want to learn about others, use the UNIX command **man tar** to see them all. (Some are explained on the Quick Reference tear-out card in this book.) In this chapter, you use the following four options:

c   Creates a new archive

f   Allows you to specify the resulting archive name

v   Operates in verbose mode (i.e., lets you know what's going on)

t   Shows contents of archive ("table of contents?")

The Least You Need to Know

In almost all cases, if you're going to upload anything to the Net or an online service, you have to archive it first. And the archival fairy ain't gonna do it for you. Even for mere mortals, though, it's not too difficult.

➤ Don't archive files that users may want to download separately (usually things such as pictures or sounds).

➤ Keep in mind that some file types (namely JPGs and GIFs) are compressed already, and further compression won't do any good. If they're going into an archive, it doesn't matter. But if you're uploading them singly, don't bother compressing them.

➤ Especially if you're using a minority platform (Mac or UNIX), be careful to use a general-purpose archiver for files meant for general, platform-nonspecific consumption. This usually includes such things as picture or sound files. In those cases, use PKZIP, so everyone has a fair chance at dearchiving them.

➤ In most platform-specific cases, PC/Windows users will want to use ZIP format, which is easiest with WinZip. Mac users lean toward StuffIt.

➤ Within UNIX, the traditional archiver is **tar**, which can wrap a bunch of files into one archive with one command: **tar cfv** *newarchive*.**tar** *filenames*.

➤ Unlike PKZIP and StuffIt, **tar** does not compress. To do so in UNIX, use the **compress** command after creating the .tar file. The command **compress** *newarchive*.**tar** yields the file *newarchive*.**tar.Z**.

Terminal Programs Roundup

Terminal programs are like cars: there are many to choose from, new ones appear every year, and they all perform the same basic function (whether or not they have pinstripes or spoilers or Corinthian leather gas pedal softeners). Likewise, you choose where and how you get your programs just as you can choose where and how you get a car. Some terminal programs are available for free on the Internet; some are available as shareware (meaning that you can use them for free but you should pay for them if you have a conscience); and some are available as big-bucks commercial packages you can buy in software stores and from mail-order houses.

To force this car analogy along, I'm going to tell you to first consider your needs. A light Net user who only checks e-mail on a UNIX account every three days doesn't need much of a terminal program. However, a user who plans to perform any file transfers at all finds that the more minimal terminal programs may not support decent transfer protocols. (Zmodem is often supported only in the slightly more advanced programs.) Other features such as attractive aesthetics, configurable screen characteristics, and even internal programming/scripting languages are all matters of personal preference.

Throughout this book, I've used ProComm Plus for Windows 2.11 for most of my examples. In fact, this program is considered one of the more advanced terminal programs, as it includes many features that are absolutely necessary for an online connection. The focus on that program is not meant to be any sort of particular endorsement—and that's not for legal reasons. The unexciting explanation is that it is a capable and prototypical terminal program and it's installed on my computer. While there are some truly incompetent terminal programs, most programs with any name recognition will do the job for most people (the same way most new cars will get you to the store).

Having said all that, I'll give you a list of some other terminal programs you might look into for comparison shopping purposes.

For the PC

This section outlines some popular terminal programs for Windows and some for DOS.

Qmodem Pro V2.0 for Windows 95

This is the first in what will likely be a series of terminal programs redesigned for the Windows 95 environment. At the time of this writing, only a preview version is available; the final retail version will sell in the $100 range at major computer retailers.

Qmodem for 95 is similar to HyperTerminal in design, behaving in an integrated way with Windows' own modem configurations. Of course, it supports all the standard terminal features, including the full range of terminal emulations and transfer protocols. As is becoming more common among terminal programs, it can also behave as a Telnet client in TCP/IP environments. And, of course, it includes lots of bells and whistles, such as complex scripting and drag-and-drop interfacing.

With its price and feature-richness, Qmodem is clearly attempting to compete at the ProComm Plus level. As such, it's overkill for the casual Net user (especially considering the cost). On the other hand, for people who spend a fair amount of time using a terminal program on BBSs or the Internet, Qmodem provides a flexible and powerful environment. Qmodem is available at software retail outlets.

Contact information:

Mustang Software, Inc.
1-800-663-7512 or 1-805-873-2500
http://www.mustang.com

Telix for Windows 3.1

Available as shareware with a $99 registration fee, Telix is a very comprehensive communications "suite." It offers the important stable of transfer protocols and terminal emulations, in addition to many environment-enhancing comforts. There is even a scripting language for users who are into such things. Not much is missing from Telix, although it seems to lack support for doubling as a TCP/IP client.

Telix is available at WinSite. One word of warning, though: the version currently available on the Net (version 1.00a) does not seem to work under Windows 95. Reportedly, however, a new version (1.10) is available that does work under Windows 95.

You can get the latest Telix information, pick up the shareware program, or place an order at Telix's own Web site (**http://delta.com**) or by calling the deltaComm BBS at (919) 481-9399.

Telemate for DOS

Not everyone has, uses, or even enjoys Windows. For those stalwarts, one available option is the shareware program Telemate. You can find it at major DOS FTP sites, such as Garbo (see the list in "The Site, the Site!" later in this appendix). Telemate supports all the traditional terminal functions, including good Zmodem support and even explicit 16550 FIFO support.

One downside of using any DOS terminal program is that you can't engage in other computing tasks while it downloads. In addition, Telemate does not work particularly well from within a DOS shell in Windows; it's best in a dedicated DOS bootup.

Telemate registration is $50 after 30 days of evaluation (although the program does not cripple itself beyond that period).

Contact information:

White River Software
P.O. Box 73031
Limeridge Mall Postal Outlet
Hamilton, Ont. L9A 5H7
Canada

> *Check This Out...*
>
> Note that as of the time of this writing, there is also a version of Telemate for Windows.

For the Mac

Terminal programs serve the same function on the Mac that they do on the PC. In addition, they operate similarly. The Mac does not have COM ports, as such; instead it has a modem port and a printer port, and a modem can be connected to either one. Aside from those minor labeling differences, Mac terminal programs support the same transfer protocols, terminal emulations, and so forth.

Zterm

This may be the most popular Mac terminal program, partially because it has been around for awhile. Although it hasn't been updated recently, it still does an all-around competent job. The program is shareware and has a $30 registration fee, but no specific time limit is imposed on the evaluation period.

You can find Zterm at any major Mac FTP site, such as Sumex (see the list in "The Site, the Site!" later in this appendix). In addition, a Frequently Asked Questions (FAQ) file for ZTerm is located at **ftp://usit.net/pub/lesjones/zterm-faq.txt**.

Zterm's author is Dave Alverson (**davea@xetron.com**). But don't send him mail asking where to get Zterm; it's widely available. Check the FAQ.

Black Night

Black Night is the newest contender in shareware Mac terminal programs. It is a comprehensive program that's easy for beginners to use, yet it is feature-rich for more advanced users. Definitely worth a look, Black Night is highly competitive with ZTerm: a $30 registration fee and a 28-day evaluation period. It is available at the same sites Zterm is.

Contact Information:

The author is Christopher Swan (**cswan@actrix.gen.nz**).

ProTERM

This package aims more at the retail market than do either of the preceding programs. A demo evaluation version is available online, but many of its features have reduced functionality. In some ways, this program is more advanced than either Zterm or Black Night. ProTERM allows the user more flexibility, such as multithreaded operation (which enables you to use other aspects of the program while it's, say, downloading). It also has strong support for TCP/IP connections, enabling you to use it to open multiple Telnet clients and even FTP. On the other hand, its interface is slightly nontraditional compared to the prototypical terminal program. Thus the user may have a higher learning curve.

ProTERM is undoubtedly a capable package, but you must decide whether its extras are worth the $100 price. It's definitely worth checking out the demo for yourself, though.

Contact information:

InTrec Software, Inc.
(602) 992-1345
http://www.indirect.com/user/proterm

The Site, the Site!

Both the PC and the Mac have a couple of FTP sites that are major collection and distribution points for software. Because these major sites are likely to be swamped with users, many have *mirrors* (other sites that carry the same software). In the best-case scenario, you should use the mirror site closest to you geographically. Some sites host several mirrors, in which cases you may have to go a few directories deep to find the mirror you're looking for. Look in a directory such as /pub/mirrors, /mirrors, or /pub. Many mirror sites display an opening message that tells where the mirrors are located within the site.

These are not exhaustive lists; they simply include the largest and best-maintained sites. You can find software for these platforms at a bunch of different places. Once you start wheeling around the Net, you'll see that it's easy to find more details, such as specific sites.

PC Sites

For MS-DOS, check out **garbo.uwasa.fi**. Garbo contains a massive archive located in Finland. For a closer alternative, you can crawl over to one of these mirrors:

ftp.cdrom.com (California)   **ftp.netnet.net** (Wisconsin)

Users of Windows 3.x and Windows 95 can find hordes at **ftp.winsite.com** or one of its many mirrors.

U.S. WinSite Mirrors

ftp.cdrom.com (California)   **gatekeeper.dec.com** (California)

ftp.dataplex.net (Texas)   **mirrors.aol.com** (Virginia)

archive.orst.edu (Oregon)   **mrcnext.cso.uiuc.edu** (Illinois)

International WinSite Mirrors

ftp.funet.fi (Finland)   **ftp.uni-paderborn.de** (Germany)

info.nic.surfnet.nl (Netherlands) **src.doc.ic.ac.uk** (UK)

ftp.iij.ad.jp (Japan)

For both MS-DOS and Windows, you can find a motherlode of files at Simtel, aka **ftp.Coast.NET**, or one of its mirrors:

oak.oakland.edu (California)   **nic.switch.ch** (Switzerland)

Mac Sites

Mac users needn't fear. Your gold mine of software awaits at Info-Mac. The head site is **sumex-aim.stanford.edu** (California). Mirrors, please:

mirrors.aol.com (Virginia)   **grind.isca.uiowa.edu** (Iowa)

mirror.archive.umich.edu (Michigan)   **ftp.funet.fi** (Finland)

ftp.lth.se (Sweden)   **src.doc.ic.ac.uk** (UK)

nic.switch.ch (Switzerland)   **archie.au** (Australia)

ftp.u-tokyo.ac.jp (Japan)

Another big repository is Mac.Archive, which you find at **mac.archive.umich.edu** (Michigan). This site often responds better to Gopher than to FTP.

Clients Galore

Be it FTP clients, Web browsers, or newsreaders, you have a number of them to choose from, whether you use a PC or a Mac. They range in availability from freeware online to commercial in-store products. (In the case of Net clients, though, the bias tends to be toward Net-availability instead of retail.)

No doubt the best way to survey your options is to ignore the rest of this appendix and download them all for yourself. Give 'em a try. Nobody knows your personal preferences better than you do (unless it's some large well-funded market research team on the top floor of a very tall skyscraper). Note, however, that some clients do achieve more general popularity than others, and sometimes it is actually due to superior quality.

Windows (any version) users can most easily survey their own clients using the World Wide Web. Open a URL to **http://cwsapps.texas.net/**, where you can browse all the available Windows clients with ease. Download any and every file that seems of interest, pop some popcorn, and start evaluatin'. The following sections give you brief list and a description of some of the better-known clients out there. First, we'll consider some clients for the PC, usually available in both Windows 3.x and Windows 95 flavors.

FTP Clients for the PC

WS_FTP

The most popular FTP client for Windows, WS_FTP comes in 16- and 32-bit flavors, depending on what TCP/IP software you use. Users of Trumpet Winsock for Windows 3.x should use the 16-bit version, while users of Windows 95's Dial-Up Networking should grab the 32-bit version. Both are free and available at WinSite, SimTel, or **papa.indstate.edu** in the **winsock-l/ftp/** directory.

CuteFTP

A newer entry to the ranks, CuteFTP is gaining popularity and rivals WS_FTP. Neither is wholly better than the other, and both are free, so try them and compare. You can access all info about CuteFTP at its Web page, URL **http://papa.indstate.edu:8888/CuteFTP/** (that's a smart public relations move if you ask me).

WinQVT

This is actually a suite of clients that includes Telnet and FTP. Because the FTP client in WinQVT is a remake of the standard UNIX FTP client, it is command line operated. Some users, especially those who prefer the command-line environment, might check out WinQVT's FTP client. It also comes in 16- and 32-bit versions, and the same guidelines apply as to who should use which. WinQVT is shareware. It has a $40 registration fee ($20 for students) but no crippling feature or specific evaluation period.

Newsreaders for the PC

WinVN

WinVN is a free newsreader that's very capable and easy to use. It's well-organized and has above-average uudecoding capabilities. The point-and-click interface is simple, but it's somewhat slow to navigate compared to those UNIX newsreaders. WinVN Comes in 16- and 32-bit versions and is available at major PC FTP sites as well as **ftp.ksc.nasa.gov** in the **/pub/win32/winvn** directory.

News Xpress

More modern than WinVN, this client is one of the more popular among Windows users. News Xpress sports quick operation and a lot of news-management capabilities. It's free, and it's available at major PC FTP sites.

Free Agent

The newcomer and current celebrity among Windows-based newsreaders, Free Agent sports every capability the other Windows newsreaders do—and more. Especially nice is its capability to track down parts of a multiple-part posting on its own. Free Agent, which is free, is available from **ftp.forteinc.com** in the **/pub/forte/freeagent/** directory. An even more comprehensive commercial version called Agent sells for $40.

World Wide Web Clients for the PC

Mosaic

Mosaic is the grandpappy of popular graphical Web browsers. While perfectly capable, Mosaic has been criticized for its resouce-hungry nature. It's a very large program that may not be terribly friendly on lower-end PCs. Mosaic has to play catch-up with the extensions to HTML (Web-page capabilities) in which Netscape tends to be a leader. Mosaic is free and is available at **ftp.ncsa.uiuc.edu** in the **Web/Mosaic/Windows** directory.

Netscape

Netscape is easily the single-most popular Web browser in the solar system—and with good reason. Many web pages are designed to take advantage of specific features that only Netscape offers. On the other hand, Netscape can be criticized for attempting to "do everything" (including e-mail and newsreading). Nonetheless, the power of the masses is behind this program, which comes in 16- and 32-bit free and commercial versions. Check out **ftp2.netscape.com** in **netscape/windows**.

WinWeb

A lighter-weight, less feature-dense browser, WinWeb appeals to users with lower-end systems or users who don't care for all the extras. You can find a free evaluation version at **ftp.einet.net** in **einet/pc/winweb/**.

FTP Clients for the Mac

Fetch

This puppy has been around for so long that it has nearly become synonymous with FTP on the Mac. Fetch is certainly a capable client, and it handles standard navigation and retrieval intuitively. Even though Fetch lacks some of the flexibility of command-line browsers (or even the better Windows-based clients), it is an all-around safe bet. And it's available everywhere Mac software is held! More specifically, try the Info-Mac archives at **sumex-aim.stanford.edu** for a start.

Anarchie

A newer contender, this $10 shareware offering has won a number of fans. Its most notable feature is the combination of Archie client and FTP client. This makes it convenient to search for files with Archie and then retrieve them using the same application. In addition, many prefer Anarchie's FTP navigation to Fetch's. A large array of prearranged FTP sites relating to Mac software are included by default in Anarchie's "bookmark" feature. To find Anarchie, check Info-Mac or try **ftp.amug.org** inside **/pub/peterlewis/**.

Newsreaders for the Mac

NewsHopper

The version of NewsHopper available on the Net is only a demo, and with it a user can subscribe to only five newsgroups. Ordering NewsHopper "for real" will run about $60; an order form is included with the archive. What makes NewsHopper notable is that it's designed as an "offline" newsreader, which can really save you money. (Briefly, NewsHopper goes online only to retrieve the necessary files. You then manipulate the files while offline.) NewsHopper is available at Info-Mac.

NewsWatcher

This free newsreader is in fairly wide use, especially at university computer labs. Its only unique feature is that it handles all the necessaries, including auto extraction of binaries from uuencoded posts. But it's free, so give 'er a go and see what happens. NewsWatcher is available at Info-Mac.

Nuntius

That's Latin. A popular freeware newsreader, Nuntius also tends to pop up in university labs. However, Nuntius has the benefit of being under regular development and improvement. It is a competent newsreader worth your evaluation. While you can find it at Info-Mac, Nuntius also sports its own most-up-to-date FTP site at **ftp.ruc.dk** in the **/pub/nuntius/** directory.

World Wide Web Clients for the Mac

There is a striking similarity between the PC and the Mac as far as Web browsers go. In fact, they're all the same. Mosaic and Netscape exist for the Macintosh in equal versions to those in Windows. (Look in the section "World Wide Web Clients for the PC" to read more about these browsers.) The locations for finding them are slightly different though.

Mosaic   FTP to **ftp.ncsa.uiuc.edu** in the **/Web/Mosaic/Mac/** directory.

Netscape   FTP to **ftp2.netscape.com** in the **/netscape/mac/** directory.

Likewise, WinWeb also comes in a Mac flavor, with a slight name alteration: MacWeb. You can find MacWeb at **ftp.einet.net** in the **/einet/mac/macweb/** directory.

Speak Like a Geek: The Complete Scrolls

7-bit   A computer "alphabet" that represents data within the range of 0–127. Most commonly known as ASCII, it represents plain English text well. However, it does not represent complex datasets such as graphics or sounds.

8-bit   The computer "alphabet" known as binary, which supports data from 0–255. Other than plain text, most files are in binary format and must be transferred as such to avoid corruption.

anonymous FTP   Sometimes called "public FTP," this is one way in which you can access files on the Internet. Some sites make files available to the general public. You log into these with the username "anonymous" and enter your e-mail address as the password. Many newer FTP clients take care of this automatically.

Archie   An Internet resource that uses search criteria you provide to hunt for files all over the Net. The search criteria usually includes some portion of a file name, which Archie matches against what's out there.

archive   A file that actually consists of several smaller files. An archive is like a piece of luggage that holds together a number of items to ease transport. Usually paired with compression.

ASCII   American Standard Code for Information Interchange. The semi-English way of referring to the 7-bit alphabet. Refers to text-only files.

AT command   A set of commands that modern modems understand. All begin with the letters "AT" and are followed by other combinations of symbols and characters.

base   The foundation of a numerical system. For example, in everyday life, we use "base 10" because our numbers are all based on a 10-digit system from 0 to 9. Computers prefer binary, which is a base-2 system.

baud rate   The speed at which a modem can transmit data. In consumer usage, it's expressed in kbps or kilobits per second. Modern modems may range anywhere from 2,400kbps (very slow) to 28.8kbps (very fast).

binary   The English word for the 8-bit computer alphabet. Almost every major file you're likely to encounter (GIFs, JPEGs, ZIP, word processor documents, and so on) is binary.

bit   A single on/off unit in binary. ASCII is made up of 7 such units, which can represent base 10 numbers up to 127. Binary contains 8 such units, the maximal equivalent of 255.

browser   Literally, a World Wide Web client. The program used to navigate information and data available on the Web.

carriage return (CR)   An ASCII character that can represent the end of a line of text. Noteworthy when transferring text files between computer platforms.

client   A program that requests data from a remote computer. In almost all cases, when you use the Internet or any online service, you are making use of clients.

COM port   Communications port. A part of the PC hardware architecture that can accept a modem. Various PC programs must be configured to know which COM port your modem is connected to. For most users, this will be COM1 or COM2, but it can be higher.

compression   A mathematical technique used to reduce repeating patterns of data in a file, thus reducing the overall size of the file. A file cannot be used while in a compressed state, but it is quicker to transfer it in that state.

CPS   Characters per second. A common measure of how much data is being transmitted during a transfer. Expect about 1640–1650cps on a 14.4kbps modem, and double that on a 28.8kbps.

crash recovery   The capability of a transfer protocol to resume a transfer that was interrupted in progress. Most famously, Zmodem supports this capability.

CRC   Cyclic Redundancy Check. A way of verifying that data has not been corrupted. If you have configuration problems on your system, file transfers may be subject to CRC errors, which drive sane men mad.

crosspost   A message posted to UseNet news that is directed at multiple newsgroups. Don't do this with binary files.

dearchive   Unpacking the luggage. The process by which an archive is broken down into its component files so that it can be used again. Most files downloaded from online sources are in archived format and, therefore, need to be dearchived before they can be used.

decimal   Our base-10 number system that we learned in nursery school. Computers don't understand decimal.

decompress   The process of returning a compressed file to its original state so it can be used. Dearchiving and decompression often go hand-in-hand and usually occur at the same time by means of the same utility program (such as WinZip).

digital   Any numerical representation. A painting on the wall is not digital, but a painting in a GIF file is because it is represented inside the computer as a series of numbers.

disinfect   To remove a virus. Often when a file has been infected by a virus, the invader can be removed. The file may or may not be useful anymore, but removing the virus prevents it from spreading further infection.

download   The process of transferring a file (or a copy of a file) to your computer.

DTR   Data Terminal Ready. Used as a signaling system between the modem and the terminal program to determine when to hang up the phone line.

dumb terminal   A keyboard and monitor that interact with a CPU located elsewhere. Originally from the olden days of computing; however, when you use a dial-up UNIX shell now, your PC acts as like a dumb terminal.

End-of-Line (EOL)   The convention used to represent the end of a line of text in an ASCII file. Because this varies between platforms, ASCII files need to be handled carefully to avoid strange formatting problems.

error-correction   A technique by which errors in data transmission are detected and retransmissions are requested. Most modern modems can perform this automatically, and some transfer protocols such as Zmodem do it too.

ethernet   A type of networking cable that is run between computers. Although limited in physical scope, it can carry large amounts of data at high speeds (unlike conventional telephone lines).

execute   To run a program. Files known as programs consist of a set of instructions to the computer. The initiation of their instructions is called executing, launching, or running.

extension   The three-character suffix after the decimal point in a file name. (For example, in the file name **dog.gif**, .gif is the extension.) In addition, it often serves as a strong hint of the file type.

extract   Synonymous with dearchiving.

FIFO   First In First Out. The buffer that exists on high-speed PC serial ports (16550 UART) and allows for modem transfers at speeds over 14.4kbps. FIFO must be enabled, though, which takes some fiddling in Windows 3.x but is automatic in Windows 95.

file name   The name given to a particular set of data. We use file names to manipulate and segregate data, moving it between computers and loading it into applications.

file type   A set of data compatible with a particular program. For example, a GIF file type can be read by programs designed to read GIF files, while a WPD file type is meant for WordPerfect. File name extensions often indicate file type.

flow control   A method by which the rate of data flow between computers is regulated. This prevents either computer from "losing track" and missing out on any of the data, which would usually be a major problem. Regulation can occur by software-based means (called Xon/Xoff) or hardware means (RTS/CTS) given a proper modem cable. Hardware is the preferred solution.

fsp   Now known as the File Service Protocol. A little-known and little-used method of transferring files across the Internet. Offers several advantages compared to the more popular FTP, but has very few sites that support it.

FTP   File Transfer Protocol. The de facto means for transferring a file from one computer to another across the Internet.

Gopher   An information-retrieval system based on menu hierarchies. Can also serve files, although that is not its main purpose for existence. Largely eclipsed by the World Wide Web these days.

handshaking   In the context of this book, handshaking is synonymous with flow control. (That is, hardware handshaking is the same as hardware flow control.)

header   Data at the beginning of a file that identifies its type. Whereas file name extensions that identify file type are a convention, headers are a definite way for programs to identify the type of a file. However, headers look messy to humans, so we rely on useful extensions.

HTTP   The HyperText Transport Protocol. Manages data transfer on the World Wide Web.

hypertext   On the World Wide Web, this takes the form of links between certain portions of content and other portions of content, each of which may reside anywhere on the Internet. A user can choose at will whether or not to follow any link towards further content.

import   To open and read a particular file type (usually one that was not designed by the same company as the application itself). For example, Microsoft Word can import a WordPerfect file.

init string   A series of AT commands that you need to issue to your modem before every connection. When necessary, terminal programs allow you to preconfigure these commands so that they are delivered automatically upon startup.

Kermit   An older file transfer protocol that is difficult to configure and often slow.

kilobits per second   Standard measure of modem speed. There are 8 bits in a byte and 1,024 bytes in a kilobyte. With some nifty math, you can determine how many K per second a 28.8kbps modem can push through.

kludge   A not-so-elegant solution to a problem. It gets the job done, though (like packing tape on broken eyeglasses).

LHA   A file compression/archival type commonly used on the Amiga platform and older PC files.

linefeed (LF)   Another ASCII character that can represent the end of a line of text. Depending on which platform you use, text files created elsewhere may appear funny unless you convert them.

local machine   The computer you are using.

mainframe   A big boxy computer that sits in its own room and is controlled via dumb terminals. More common in the older days of computing.

MIME   Multipurpose Internet Mail Extension. A more advanced design of the uuencoding concept. Meant to transport 8-bit data over 7-bit transmission routes such as e-mail or UseNet (although uuencoding is preferred on UseNet).

mirror   A site, usually FTP or World Wide Web, that copies the contents of another site. Reduces the number of people accessing one site.

modem   A device that converts digital impulses into analog sounds that are suitable for transmission over telephone lines (modulation). Also receives such sounds and converts them back to digital data (demodulation). Also a way of life.

multipart post   A binary file that has been uuencoded and broken up into pieces before being posted to UseNet. Must be reassembled and uudecoded before it can be used.

newsreader   Could also be called a UseNet client, although nobody calls it that. The program with which you read the contents of UseNet news.

online service   A privately owned and operated network that maintains centralized regulation of everything that passes through it. Examples include America Online, CompuServe, and The Microsoft Network.

pipe   A UNIX term meaning to shove the data that results from one program into another. In this book, it was used with the newsreader TIN to shove a uuencoded UseNet post into the UNIX program uudecode.

platform   Different combinations of operating systems (software) and hardware comprise a platform. In practice, UNIX is a platform, Windows 95 (PC) is a platform, and System 7.5 (Mac) is a platform.

post   A message appearing in a UseNet newsgroup. That's it.

PPP   Point-to-Point Protocol. A means for communicating in TCP/IP via a modem instead of ethernet.

protocol   Any set of rules, procedures, and expectations that multiple parties agree to follow. Computing contains many protocols, each of which defines some aspect of how the computer should behave. This allows multiple computers to "speak" to one another and exchange information.

reget   An under-implemented FTP command that would support crash recovery in FTP transfers. Very, very few clients now available offer this capability, so we can but dream.

remote machine   Whatever computer your local machine is connected to. It may be 2 feet away or 2,000 miles away.

RTS/CTS   Request to Send/Clear to Send. Synonymous with hardware flow control (which is also synonymous with hardware handshaking). Any program may use any of the three terms or any combination thereof, but they all mean the same thing in this context.

run   See *execute*.

rz   Receive Zmodem. The UNIX program that can receive files by Zmodem. Use this to begin an upload from your local machine to a remote UNIX account.

scan   The act of checking for virus infection. A good habit to get into.

serial port   The hardware port on your computer that accepts the modem cable. For most PC users, this will also be a COM port.

server   A program that doles out data upon request from a client.

service provider   The people you pay for online access.

site   Literally, any computer that is running a server is a site. Thus, an FTP site is a computer connected to the Internet that is running an FTP server. Therefore, it can be reached with an FTP client.

SLIP   Serial Line IP. Another way of communicating with the TCP/IP protocol via a modem.

store and forward   A distribution system in which each node keeps a copy of a given set of data (files) and then sends a copy to another node. This is how UseNet works.

StuffIt   Not only a rude remark, but a popular file archive/compression format on the Macintosh.

sz   Send Zmodem. The UNIX command that sends a file via Zmodem to your local machine's terminal program. Use this command to download from a UNIX account.

tag   In a newsreading context, posted articles chosen for retrieval are said to be "tagged."

TAR   Tape Archiver. A UNIX-based program that creates file archives. Unlike PKZIP and StuffIt, it does not compress.

TCP/IP   Transfer Control Protocol/Internet Protocol. This is the language of the Net. Computers need to be able to transmit data in the means defined by this protocol to communicate on the Internet.

Telnet   Allows a local computer to send commands to a remote computer. Often used for logging into one machine from another.

terminal emulation   Because our modern PCs are not actually dumb terminals, they have to just pretend to be when they're connected to the Net. This game of pretend is called emulation. Among users dialing into UNIX systems, the most common emulations are VT-100 and/or VT-102.

terminal program   The application that you use to dial in and connect to other computers with your modem. Also handles communications between the two, including file transfers.

text editor   A program that creates, saves, and loads ASCII files. Microsoft Word is not a text editor; Windows Notepad is.

throughput   Any measure of speed concerning how much data is pushed through a medium in a given period of time. For modem users, this is usually measured in characters per second (cps).

transfer protocol   A set of rules designed to define file transfer. In this book, the term is used in reference to those supported by terminal programs. The most commonly used these days is Zmodem.

UART   A chip on the PC serial card that contains the FIFO buffer. The model 16550 UART has the FIFO. Also known as Universal Asynchronous Receiver/Transmitter. Neat, huh?

unpack   See *extract* and *dearchive*.

upload   The process of transferring a file (or a copy of a file) from the local computer to a remote one.

URL   Uniform Resource Locator. The syntax for an Internet address accessible from the World Wide Web. For example, **http://some.machine.com/home.html** is a URL.

UseNet   The free-for-all discussion area composed of many thousands of special-interest newsgroups.

uudecode   The process of converting a 7-bit file back into its 8-bit original form.

uuencode   The process of converting an 8-bit binary file into 7-bit ASCII format suitable for transport by e-mail or UseNet.

virus   A piece of executable code designed to replicate itself within and between computer systems. May or may not be malicious or damaging.

VT-100   Popular terminal emulation for connecting with UNIX systems.

Web page   Any document of information on the Web.

wild card   A syntactical pattern representing a set of matching elements. Often used in file names. Different platforms have different wild-card syntaxes. On the PC, the * means "anything." Thus, the file name **bob*.*** refers to any file whose name begins with "bob" and ends with anything else.

World Wide Web   A broad interconnection of computers on the Internet that can share information using several protocols, including the hypertext-supporting HTTP. Supports integration of text, graphics, and audio.

write-protect   To set a disk so that no one can change its contents. You write-protect using those little notches on the floppy disks. Know which position is which, and keep your disks write-protected when using them on a computer whose viral cleanliness is unknown.

Xon/Xoff   Synonym for software flow control. It is preferable to no flow control if you do not have a modem cable that supports hardware flow control. However, the best solution is to buy a modem cable and use hardware flow control.

Ymodem-g   Transfer protocol similar to Zmodem but without the error-checking capability. Achieves slightly higher throughput as a result. Ymodem-g doesn't support crash recovery directly, but you can recover an interrupted Ymodem-g transfer by using Zmodem for the remainder.

ZIP   World's most popular archival/compression format. Especially dominant on the PC.

Zmodem   Best all-around transfer protocol for use with terminal programs.

Index

Symbols

* (asterisk) wild card, 282
16550 UART chip, 135
    FIFO (First In First
    Out), 136
3 1/2-inch floppy disk,
    write-protecting, 51
5 1/4-inch floppy disks,
    write-protecting, 51
7-bit binary alphabet
    (ASCII files), 15, 228, 275
8-bit binary alphabet
    (binary files), 15, 208,
    228, 275

A

accessing
    Archie
        ArchiePlex, 88-90
        Telnet, 91-94
    World Wide Web with
        UNIX accounts, 202
accounts (UNIX)
    accessing Archie, 202
    moving files in, 140
Action option (F-PROT), 55
addresses
    Black Night (Macintosh
        terminal program), 268
    Telemate (DOS terminal
        program), 267
    see also URLs (Uniform
        Resource Locators)

Advanced Port Settings
    dialog box, 115
algorithms, 25
All Disks command
    (Disinfectant menu), 59
America Online, 155-162
    Computing forum, 159
    download log files, 161
    Download Manager,
        160-161
    downloading options,
        160-161
    FTP support, 155-158
    newsreader, 222-224
    software libraries,
        159-160
    uploading files, 162
    World Wide Web
        support, 203-205
Anarchie FTP client
    (Macintosh), 273
anonymous FTP, 275
AOL, see America Online
ARC format, 28
Archie, 275
    accessing
        ArchiePlex, 88-90
        Telnet, 91-94
    finding files, 87-88
ArchiePlex
    accessing Archie, 88-90
    advantages, 90
    search types, 89-90
archived files
archiving, 3, 275
    compression, 36

decompression
    Microsoft Net-
        work, 167
    PKUNZIP, 38-40
    .EXE files, 40
    extensions, 37
    files, 36
        for uploads, 251-252
        location of files, 37
        moving, 255
        replacing, 255
        UNIX, 36-37
        updating, 255
        with StuffIt Lite,
            258-261
        with tar command,
            261-264
        with Winzip, 253-258
    Macintosh
        BixHex 5.0, 41-42
        StuffIt Expander
            program, 40-42
        tar.Z files, 42-43
    StuffIt Lite utility,
        258-261
    UNIX, 36-37
    viewing archives, 38
    Windows, Winzip,
        39-40
ARJ format, 28
ASC files, 19
ASCII files, 14, 275
    7-bit alphabet, 228, 275
    7-bit binary alphabet, 15
    ASC files, 19

289

N

O

X-Z

PLUG YOURSELF INTO...

The Macmillan USA Information SuperLibrary (tm)

See the new SuperLibrary Newsletter

THE MACMILLAN INFORMATION SUPERLIBRARY™

Free information and vast computer resources from the world's leading computer book publisher—online!

FIND THE BOOKS THAT ARE RIGHT FOR YOU!

A complete online catalog, plus sample chapters and tables of contents!

- STAY INFORMED with the latest computer industry news through our online newsletter, press releases, and customized Information SuperLibrary Reports.

- GET FAST ANSWERS to your questions about Macmillan Computer Publishing books.

- VISIT our online bookstore for the latest information and editions!

- COMMUNICATE with our expert authors through e-mail and conferences.

- DOWNLOAD SOFTWARE from the immense Macmillan Computer Publishing library:
  - Source code, shareware, freeware, and demos

- DISCOVER HOT SPOTS on other parts of the Internet.

- WIN BOOKS in ongoing contests and giveaways!

TO PLUG INTO MCP:

WORLD WIDE WEB: **http://www.mcp.com**

FTP: ftp.mcp.com

Complete and Return this Card
for a *FREE* Computer Book Catalog

Thank you for purchasing this book! You have purchased a superior computer book written expressly for your needs. To continue to provide the kind of up-to-date, pertinent coverage you've come to expect from us, we need to hear from you. Please take a minute to complete and return this self-addressed, postage-paid form. In return, we'll send you a free catalog of all our computer books on topics ranging from word processing to programming and the internet.

Mr. ☐   Mrs. ☐   Ms. ☐   Dr. ☐

Name (first) ☐☐☐☐☐☐☐☐☐☐☐☐   (M.I.) ☐   (last) ☐☐☐☐☐☐☐☐☐☐☐☐☐☐☐☐☐

Address ☐☐☐☐☐☐☐☐☐☐☐☐☐☐☐☐☐☐☐☐☐☐☐☐☐☐☐☐☐☐

☐☐☐☐☐☐☐☐☐☐☐☐☐☐☐☐☐☐☐☐☐☐☐☐☐☐☐☐☐☐

City ☐☐☐☐☐☐☐☐☐☐☐☐☐☐☐   State ☐☐   Zip ☐☐☐☐☐ ☐☐☐☐

Phone ☐☐☐ ☐☐☐ ☐☐☐☐   Fax ☐☐☐ ☐☐☐ ☐☐☐☐

Company Name ☐☐☐☐☐☐☐☐☐☐☐☐☐☐☐☐☐☐☐☐☐☐☐☐☐

E-mail address ☐☐☐☐☐☐☐☐☐☐☐☐☐☐☐☐☐☐☐☐☐☐☐☐☐

1. Please check at least (3) influencing factors for purchasing this book.

Front or back cover information on book .... ☐
Special approach to the content .... ☐
Completeness of content .... ☐
Author's reputation .... ☐
Publisher's reputation .... ☐
Book cover design or layout .... ☐
Index or table of contents of book .... ☐
Price of book .... ☐
Special effects, graphics, illustrations .... ☐
Other (Please specify): _____ ☐

2. How did you first learn about this book?

Saw in Macmillan Computer Publishing catalog .... ☐
Recommended by store personnel .... ☐
Saw the book on bookshelf at store .... ☐
Recommended by a friend .... ☐
Received advertisement in the mail .... ☐
Saw an advertisement in: _____ ☐
Read book review in: _____ ☐
Other (Please specify): _____ ☐

3. How many computer books have you purchased in the last six months?

This book only .... ☐   3 to 5 books .... ☐
2 books .... ☐   More than 5 .... ☐

4. Where did you purchase this book?

Bookstore .... ☐
Computer Store .... ☐
Consumer Electronics Store .... ☐
Department Store .... ☐
Office Club .... ☐
Warehouse Club .... ☐
Mail Order .... ☐
Direct from Publisher .... ☐
Internet site .... ☐
Other (Please specify): _____ ☐

5. How long have you been using a computer?

☐ Less than 6 months   ☐ 6 months to a year
☐ 1 to 3 years   ☐ More than 3 years

6. What is your level of experience with personal computers and with the subject of this book?

	With PCs	With subject of book
New	☐	☐
Casual	☐	☐
Accomplished	☐	☐
Expert	☐	☐

Source Code ISBN: 0-7897-0567-2

7. Which of the following best describes your job title?

- Administrative Assistant ☐
- Coordinator ☐
- Manager/Supervisor ☐
- Director ☐
- Vice President ☐
- President/CEO/COO ☐
- Lawyer/Doctor/Medical Professional ☐
- Teacher/Educator/Trainer ☐
- Engineer/Technician ☐
- Consultant ☐
- Not employed/Student/Retired ☐
- Other (Please specify): _____ ☐

8. Which of the following best describes the area of the company your job title falls under?

- Accounting ☐
- Engineering ☐
- Manufacturing ☐
- Operations ☐
- Marketing ☐
- Sales ☐
- Other (Please specify): _____ ☐

9. What is your age?

- Under 20 ☐
- 21-29 ☐
- 30-39 ☐
- 40-49 ☐
- 50-59 ☐
- 60-over ☐

10. Are you:

- Male ☐
- Female ☐

11. Which computer publications do you read regularly? (Please list)

_____
_____
_____
_____
_____
_____
_____
_____
_____
_____

Comments: _____
_____
_____

Fold here and scotch-tape to mail.